THE SUNDOWNERS,
PEGASUS, AND LITTLE BUTCH

THE SUNDOWNERS, PEGASUS, AND LITTLE BUTCH

CARRIER AIR GROUP ELEVEN AND THE WAR IN THE PACIFIC, 1943–1945

BRIAN D. LASLIE

Naval Institute Press
Annapolis, Maryland

Naval Institute Press
291 Wood Road
Annapolis, MD 21402

© 2025 by the U.S. Naval Institute
All rights reserved. No part of this book may be reproduced or utilized in any form or by any means, electronic or mechanical, including photocopying and recording, or by any information storage and retrieval system, without permission in writing from the publisher.

Library of Congress Cataloging-in-Publication Data

Names: Laslie, Brian D. author
Title: The Sundowners, Pegasus, and Little Butch : Carrier Air Group 11 and the War in the Pacific, 1943–1945 / Brian D. Laslie.
Description: Annapolis, Maryland : Naval Institute Press, 2025. | Includes bibliographical references and index.
Identifiers: LCCN 2025000517 (print) | LCCN 2025000518 (ebook) | ISBN 9781682478783 hardback | ISBN 9781682478790 ebook
Subjects: LCSH: United States. Navy. Air Group, 11 | United States. Navy. Fighter Squadron VF-11 | World War, 1939–1945—Pacific Area | World War, 1939–1945—Aerial operations, American | World War, 1939–1945—Naval operations, American | Hornet (Aircraft carrier : CV 12)
Classification: LCC D790.35 11th .L3 2025 (print) | LCC D790.35 11th (ebook)
LC record available at https://lccn.loc.gov/2025000517
LC ebook record available at https://lccn.loc.gov/2025000518

♾ Print editions meet the requirements of ANSI/NISO z39.48–1992 (Permanence of Paper).
Printed in the United States of America.

33 32 31 30 29 28 27 26 25 9 8 7 6 5 4 3 2 1
First printing

For my father, Daniel Clayton Laslie, who introduced me to history, and for my wife, Heather Leigh Laslie, who supports my writing of it.

You who are passing by, a moment halt. These for their country died; they are gone. Ours now to take their torch and hold it high. Consider . . . and pass on.

—In Memoriam, "The Second Combat Tour of Bombing Eleven"

It is for us the living to be hereby dedicated to the great task remaining before us; that from these honored dead take increased devotion for the cause to which they gave the last full measure of devotion.

—Abraham Lincoln, Gettysburg Address

Contents

Maps

PREFACE
Sunset at Taps

The World War II generation is all but gone now. The youngest members of the armed forces who served in World War II, eighteen and nineteen years old at the time, are now at least in their mid to late nineties. Soon, they too will join their comrades in the hereafter, and there will be nothing of their generation left but stories—stories told by books, films, photographs, and countless pieces of ephemera, some of it in museums and archives, some in private collections, and some in the hands of family members, passed down from generation to generation. The ability to gain new perspectives from the original sources themselves will be gone. Their generation will rapidly become as distant from us as the soldiers of the American Civil War or World War I. Historians will continue to comb through archives for many generations to come, and our interpretations of the history of World War II will continue to change, as they have for the last eighty years. However, unless they have been told or written down or in some other way preserved, further first-person accounts are practically gone. As naval historian James D. Hornfischer noted,

"Civilian testimony to their experience may be the last word standing," observing that the "whole World War II generation steamed towards sunset at taps." As a kid growing up in Georgia, I had many family members and friends who served in World War II, and their stories impressed upon me the importance of history. It was these stories and their memories that set me on a lifelong journey of the study of the past.[1]

However, despite the passing of the World War II generation, American readers, historians, and history buffs still clamor for more from that conflict, usually in the form of the heroism of the ground conflicts, but the air wars of World War II also remain a popular field. Hundreds of air units from World War II—air divisions, wings, groups, and squadrons, or individuals in those units—have movies, books, television shows, or podcasts devoted exclusively to them. Some of these books and films now transcend their creation and are considered classics. These include the novel and film *Twelve O'Clock High* and the films *The Battle of Britain, The Great Escape,* and *Memphis Belle.* None of this seems to slake the thirst of historians and history buffs in publishing new books every year on the subject of the war in the air in World War II. This book adds to that literature.

When HBO released the miniseries version of Stephen Ambrose's *Band of Brothers* on September 9, 2001 (at its first showing that evening, the world was less than forty-eight hours away from the events of September 11), fifty-seven years had passed since the events covered in the show occurred. Many members of E Company, 2nd Battalion of the 506th Parachute Infantry Regiment of the 101st Airborne Division were still alive and in their late seventies or early eighties. If you viewed the series, you will remember that each episode either began or ended with the veterans themselves telling their stories. This was, sadly, impossible for the 2024 series *Masters of the Air*, itself the manifestation of a cultural desire for more content from World War II. I do ponder how members of the Bloody Hundredth, including Gale "Buck" Cleven, John "Bucky" Egan, or Robert "Rosie" Rosenthal, might have reacted to having themselves portrayed in the series. I wonder the same for the men in the pages that follow. These real-life men never lived to see themselves portrayed in film or to read the limited amount of literature in which they were memorialized, another bitter reminder that the World War II generation is all but gone now.

It is therefore left to us to determine how we choose to continue to remember World War II. America lost just over 400,000 men and women during the war. Museum curators, filmmakers, documentarians, academics, and popular historical writers continue to shape the collective American memory of the war through various media. In 1984 Studs Terkel published *"The Good War": An Oral History of World War II*, and in 1998 journalist Tom Brokaw published *The Greatest Generation*—and, in doing so, effectively renamed the World War II generation. The cover of Brokaw's book reinforced the gender stereotypes of those who fought in World War II, showing a soldier's feet, duffel bag, and rifle on one side and on the other, the high-heeled shoes of the woman who was being left behind. Both Terkel and Brokaw point toward a proper or correct way to remember that generation. Both focused primarily on the soldiers who fought the war. This raises the question: Is there indeed a precise or accurate way in which to write about a particular unit in this conflict? Does their memory deserve some enigmatic interpretation?[2]

The historiography of the Civil War is rich with literature on the memory of that conflict. American scholars like Drew Gilpin Faust in *This Republic of Suffering* and David W. Blight in *Race and Reunion* delved deeply into how the war fundamentally reshaped the nation. In the same way did World War II reshape not only America, but also the world as a whole. While Faust notes that the American soldiers who died in the Civil War "redefined their nation and their culture," we would be foolhardy not to recognize that our daily lives continue to be shaped by the memory and experiences of the World War II generation. Even in the modern age of social media and memes, the past affects how we live our lives and the assumptions that there are "proper" ways to remember.[3]

Kaylie McCarthy noted in her article "The Ghosts of Past and Present: Analyzing American WWII Memory" that "collective memory, based on social relationships and interactions, informs both individual and group identity, and perspectives of the past and present. The national collective of American WWII memory has been shaped by multiple factors: representation in popular culture formats like film and literature, academic historical interpretation, and curated memory sites that work to reaffirm particular narratives. Ultimately, American memory regarding the events of World War II continues to evolve depending on the dominant narrative that forms due to differences in generational interests, changes within international diplomatic relations, and new academic interpretations."[4]

Thus, this book will attempt to do justice to the memory of individuals, but also to the collective memory of a service (the U.S. Navy), a community (flyers and aircrew), and a generation (those who fought in World War II). As Blight points out, the dominant, if not correct, mode of memory of the Civil War was "reconciliation." Eighty years later, it does not appear that we, as yet, have a correct or dominant "mode of memory" for World War II beyond that of the "last good war." However, I recognize that any published material, be it a film or a book, has the ability to mold and influence our understanding of World War II by how the texts enter into the collective memory. Historian Paul V. Murray pointed out that "the historian searches out new memories indefatigably, writing each one down, not only to get the record straight, but also to acknowledge the responsibility upon the part of the listener to interpret and analyze all memories and, in this way, to assign moral meaning to the past."[5]

In writing what follows, I also struggled to decide who might enjoy this book. I will confess to feeling perturbed about whom this history might appeal to or at least how this book might be interpreted by a larger audience. With the recent release of *Masters of the Air*, I was confronted by numerous articles stating, "Masters of the Air . . . looks like peak Dad TV" and "Tom Hanks' Masters of the Air looks like the Dad TV event of 2024." This reductive and, frankly, insulting caricature of who might enjoy either *Masters of the Air* or what follows in these pages is a destructive perpetuation of the myth that only men—and largely white men—read, watch, or enjoy history. This was not a myth I wanted to continue, add to, or in any way support. Thus, while this work does indeed focus on an all-white, all-male unit, it is important to note the fine work being done by a significantly more diverse group of historians than we have seen in the past. Since the latter part of the twentieth century, many great military historians who happen to be female have influenced my work; included in their ranks are the likes of Barbara W. Tuchman, Tami Davis Biddle, and Carol Reardon. These pioneers have been followed by Hattie Hearn, curator of the American Air Museum in England, Katherine Landdeck, and Sarah Myers, among many others. Even if diversity in academic history has improved, there remains a serious and unnecessary stigma in the wider field of history against women who study military history and war and society.[6]

While this book honors the memory of a particular unit, it places that unit's actions into a greater historical narrative, and I hope that readers will place the actions of the individuals of the unit that follows in these pages into their larger, overall understanding of the war in the Pacific Theater. I hope readers will find meaning in these events: why they matter, why we choose to remember them, and what this means for us as a society.

The primary audience for this work is historians (scholars and history buffs), especially those with an interest in military, aviation, and naval history. It will be of use to faculty and students at both military and civilian colleges and universities, as well as general readers who want to know more about the air war in the Pacific Theater from Guadalcanal forward. The goal is to make the book of interest to both general readers, professionals, and students of military history, particularly those seeking a deeper understanding of tactical change over time and the experiences of naval aviators both on ship and ashore in World War II. Although World War II history is an enormously crowded field, much scholarship remains to be unearthed and studied, and many more stories remain to be told. Therefore, I hope this book appeals to both the serious scholar and the non-professional historian looking for a good tale of men and machines at war. Items important to this work but not covered in detail include amphibious landing operations supported by CVG-11, fleet reconnaissance, naval intelligence, code breaking, and other elements of the war, each of which deserves further study.

The impetus to write this book came from two sources. The first was when members of the Naval Institute Press asked me if I had an interest in writing an airpower book from the perspective of a naval organization during World War II. Having a unique inability to tell the press "no," I heartily agreed, but only if they felt that there was a particular unit or period during the war that had not already received adequate coverage. My editor Padraic Carlin noted he had recently been reading about Carrier Air Group Eleven, and he believed this might fit my desires. I looked at what had already been published on Air Group Eleven, mostly by the great naval historian Barrett Tillman, and decided to explore if there was enough archival material available and to examine whether the story of this air group would fill a hole in the historiography or add to our understanding of World War II.

The decision to write this book became cemented in my mind when I discovered a treasure trove of documentation, including interviews with the participants, the diaries they kept, and materials pulled together from the National Archives and Records Administration, all thanks to the diligent work of George Retelas, a self-described "artist, educator, and historian." George stumbled upon his grandfather's World War II diary and became so enthralled with what he discovered that he decided he needed to make a movie about his grandfather's unit. That unit just happened to be Torpedo Squadron Eleven (VT-11). The diaries George found were filled with "stories of tents in the jungle and storms at sea." George then undertook the type of historical crusade so many have wished they could. He began tracking down members of Air Group Eleven who served with his grandfather. Thus, this book relies heavily on those first-person accounts collected over the last decade as George made *Eleven: The Movie*.[7]

Between George's efforts and the preserved material in the form of after-action reports and war diaries at the National Archives and Records Administration, I knew early in the research process that there would be more than enough material to fill the pages of a book. My second concern was whether the unit did something noteworthy or experienced combat during events not covered in other published accounts; did their story add to our understanding of the war in the Pacific? I soon discovered that the actions of Air Group Eleven "filled the gaps" in between other more well-known engagements. Thus, I decided that this one air group out of hundreds of others might tell us something hitherto unexamined in World War II—namely, operations of great import that contributed to the defeat of the Japanese empire but that were much less well known than the events of the Coral Sea, Midway, the Marianas Turkey Shoot, and others.

In most historical research, historians look for first-person accounts to buttress their research and perhaps add a little color to an otherwise dry narrative, but for the sake of "good historical writing," the historians often eschew the use of large block quotations. However, in the research and writing of this book, I decided early on I was going to allow the participants, as much as possible, to speak for themselves. Thus, this book makes use of substantial and sometimes lengthy quotations from the participants. While in the editing process, I decided to cut these quotes down and minimize overly lengthy paragraphs or page-long quotes, but I wanted their words to echo in these pages. I did this intentionally. Brian H. Mahoney, coauthor of *Reluctant Witness*, his father James' autobiography about flying B-24s in the 8th Air Force, noted that "personal accounts of war, no matter how flawed, have compelling and universal human interest as windows on the best and worst in our nature." I wanted this book to explore those personal accounts as much as possible, to include those of "compelling and universal human interest." In the instances where the remembrances were years or even decades away from the actual events, I cross-checked them with the unit's records. If there was a discrepancy, I used the original source document as the most accurate.[8]

Mahoney also noted that "one can succeed spectacularly in authoring autobiography and in contributing importantly to the historic record, while remaining frustrated in all attempts to forcefully convey *how it felt*" (emphasis in the original). Mahoney's words made me recall Robin Williams' famous soliloquy from the film *Good Will Hunting*,

> If I asked you about art, you'd probably give me the skinny on about every art book ever written. Michelangelo. You know a lot about him. Life's work. Political aspirations. Him and the Pope. Sexual orientation. The whole works, right? But I bet you can't tell me what it smells like in the Sistine Chapel. You've never actually stood there and looked up at that beautiful ceiling. . . . If I ask you about war, you'd probably throw Shakespeare at me, right? "Once more unto the breach, dear friends." But you've never been near one. You've never held your best friend's head in your lap and watch him gasp his last breath, looking to you for help.[9]

It remains impossible to capture certain aspects of the conflict or know exactly what the men of Carrier Air Group Eleven (CVG 11) experienced. No book can make you feel the oppressive humidity on Guadalcanal or experience the malarial bite of the mosquitos. No written word can adequately describe what the ready rooms aboard the USS *Hornet* smelled like or what the matting or teakwood deck felt like beneath the feet of the pilots and crewmembers, but I hope it can, in some ways, allow us to keep those memories alive for future generations.

I would be remiss if I did not mention here that in using the direct quotes of the participants, they frequently use what is considered today extremely racially divisive language. Racial stereotyping occurred in the Pacific Theater more often than it did in the other theaters of war. During the war, American media and film studios more often presented the Japanese people in racial caricature than they did the Germans or the Italians, who typically had their leaders animated and pilloried, as opposed to the entire population. The stereotyping was true not just in the Pacific Theater, but on the home front as well. Furthermore, it is now recognized that while German-Americans' or Italian-Americans' patriotism was rarely questioned, Japanese-Americans found themselves rounded up and sent to internment camps—in no small part due to American perceptions of Japanese duplicity in the wake of the attack on Pearl Harbor.

The Paramount Studios character Popeye was especially virulent in his Japanese bashing. In one cartoon Popeye admits to the audience, "I've never seen a jap that wasn't yellow." This remark was so racially insensitive that some feared it might offend America's Asiatic allies, the Chinese—although how many Chinese were actively watching Popeye cartoons was never discussed. In another Popeye short, a surviving Japanese officer swallows gasoline and a firecracker to "save face" rather than facing the intrepid hero.[10]

Popeye was not alone in his satire and parody of the Japanese people. "Tokio Jokio," a Warner Brothers cartoon, shows all the basest caricatures of the Japanese. Presented as a representation of Japanese news media—Nippon News—the Japanese in this film are portrayed as unintelligent buffoons stumbling their way through the war. Of all the World War II cartoons, "Tokio Jokio" presented the most severe racial caricatures.

Thus, some readers might find the words of the American pilots to be insensitive, but World War II was a war without borders and, especially in the Pacific Theater, a war without mercy. I have attempted to use correct terminology when referring to the forces of the empire of Japan, but I have not changed the direct quotations of the men of Carrier Air Group Eleven or any other quoted contemporary source. I have, however, limited its use and included it only where I felt it absolutely necessary or where the sentence or passage would be irrevocably changed without it.[11]

As previously mentioned, I chose to write about this air group primarily because they missed most of the "big battles." CVG-11 was not part of the Guadalcanal campaign proper, which lasted from August 1942 until February 1943. CVG-11 arrived after U.S. Army Maj. Gen. Alexander Patch, commander of Allied Forces on Guadalcanal, declared the island secured and the campaign over. Nor were they at most of the events for the Battle of Leyte Gulf, arriving late on October 25 and not participating to any great extent in the overall battle. They were not at Coral Sea, Midway, or the Philippine Sea. So why this volume you hold now? I wanted to write about an air unit that participated greatly in the Pacific Theater, but whose actions came in between the landmark battles. So much of television history shows and popular histories follow the U.S. Navy from Pearl Harbor to Coral Sea to Midway to Leyte Gulf, but so many of the smaller engagements and amphibious landing operations occur in between these events. After the securing of Guadalcanal, operations in and around the Solomon Islands and the Solomon Sea continued for many more months. The day-to-day grind of slowly attriting the Japanese forces and of moving island by island toward the Japanese homeland began here, and CVG-11 played its part flying from Guadalcanal up and down "the slot" of the New Georgia Sound. The unit returned for a second tour in the winter of 1944–45. These two tours provided a window into the attacks against Japan that continued daily from 1943 through 1945. In this regard, CVG-11 presented an ideal unit to follow.

Finally, I would be remiss if I did not mention that writing this book affected me in profoundly unexpected ways. This book occurred as I was transitioning from mid-career scholar to seasoned veteran of the classroom and archives. I have reached a point in my career where I can eschew being asked to work on a project by pointing to a younger up-and-coming historian still looking for projects. Depending on how I decide to count my years of education and training, I have been "in the game" for twenty years now. In that time, I have never been affected by something I have written, and I have enjoyed approaching my writing with the detachment of the professional historian. However, there were times in writing this book that I was beset by an overwhelming melancholy and an unexpected solemnity as I combed over after-action reports, diary entries, and the ocean of information and research materials I kept piled on my desk. This work brought me closer to individuals. I was not, on the whole, examining the movement or strategic aims of the U.S. Navy, but following the lives of young men as they did their duty day in and day out. I was following individuals who suddenly disappeared from the narrative; I watched a ninety-four-year-old radioman fly in a TBM Avenger for the first time in seventy-two years. Whether it was the passing of the World War II generation into memory or the more seasoned analytical skills of a man in his middle years interpreting the actions of those in their twenties, I do not know, but I feel that Air Group Eleven and its members will, in some way, guide my interpretation of history going forward, and they have certainly influenced the book you have before you now.

Since this is a work of naval history, I allowed the words of Samuel Eliot Morison to guide my writing. Morison stated in *History as a Literary Art: An Appeal to Young Historians* (1946), "American historians, in their eagerness to present facts and their laudable concern to tell the truth, have neglected the literary aspects of their craft. They have forgotten that there is an art of writing history." What I hope follows is both the science of military history and the art of decent—if not "good"—historical writing. At the end of this journey, I hope for nothing more than to show what the war against Japan looked like through the eyes of one unit, and I hope I have done the men of Air Group Eleven a service in telling their story.

INTRODUCTION

Little is more confusing in the history of aviation than U.S. Navy squadrons, deployments, and air groups of World War II. Even the term air group is now anachronistic. During the war, what are now known as carrier air wings were called carrier air groups (CVGs). During World War II, the U.S. Navy established roughly 150 active fighter squadrons, although at least sixty of these never engaged in combat. Many of those that did see combat in the Pacific Theater had numerous deployments, or cruises, during the war. The fighter squadron (VF) 10 "Grim Reapers" deployed three times during the war: from October 1942 to May 1943 aboard the USS *Enterprise* (CV-6), from January to June 1944, again aboard the *Enterprise*, and finally from February to April 1945 aboard the USS *Intrepid* (CV-11). During those three deployments, the fighter squadron flew three different aircraft—the F4F, F6F, and F4U— and shot down more than two hundred Japanese aircraft. Even so, VF-10 was not the highest scoring fighter squadron. That honor belonged to VF-15, which, during a single deployment aboard the USS *Essex* from May to

November 1944, amassed an amazing 310 confirmed aerial victories. Perhaps the main reason for their superior numbers was that the deployment occurred during some of the major sea and aerial battles of 1944 including the Marianas Turkey Shoot in June, the Formosa strikes of October, and the Battle of Leyte Gulf in October.[1]

At the beginning of the war for America, each carrier air group was typically composed of a fighter squadron, a bomber squadron, a torpedo squadron, and a reconnaissance squadron. The Navy operated hundreds of various squadrons on numerous overlapping cruises in the Pacific Theater of operations—itself subdivided into North, Central, South, and Southwest Pacific operating areas—during World War II.

In December 1941 the primary *Yorktown*-class aircraft carriers and their associated air wings carried a typical complement of roughly seventy-two aircraft, which were divided into four squadrons: fighter, bomber, torpedo, and scouting. Each fighter squadron had eighteen Grumman F4F Wildcats. The bombing squadron (VB) and scouting squadron (VS) each had eighteen Douglas SBD Dauntless dive bombers, so each carrier had twice as many dive bombers as any other type of aircraft. Finally, the torpedo squadron (VT) had eighteen Douglas TBD Devastator or Grumman/General Motors TBF/TBM Avenger torpedo bombers. This composition evolved during the war, and between 1942 and 1943, as American naval power found its footing, the arrangements of the aircraft in the air groups transformed to fit the Navy's needs.

The Navy disestablished the scouting/reconnaissance squadrons in the first part of 1943, after which it began to increase the number of fighter planes assigned to the fighter or fighter/bomber squadrons. With the introduction of the new *Essex*-class carriers in 1943, a typical air group looked very different from the earlier days of the war: thirty-six fighters, thirty-six bombers, and eighteen torpedo planes—doubling the fighter and bomber power of previous ships. By the climactic battles of the Pacific Theater in 1945, the composition of aircraft had changed again, and each *Essex*-class air group now had more than one hundred aircraft. While there was no prescribed aircraft on each carrier, a typical make-up was one to four fighter squadrons of either Grumman F6F

Hellcat or Vought F4U Corsair fighter/bombers; a single squadron of twelve Grumman TBM Avenger torpedo bombers remained.

To keep track of the immense amount of firepower on each aircraft carrier, the U.S. Navy used numerical designations for each of its air groups. Throughout the history of naval airpower, a carrier air group has often been referred to by the acronym CAG; however, the official designation in naval records has always been CVG. In the early years of the war, it was most common for an aircraft carrier's hull number to also be the designation of the fighting air group aboard that ship. For example, the air group attached to and flying from the USS *Enterprise* (CV-6) also carried the 6 designation: Fighting Squadron VF-6, Bombing Squadron VB-6, and so forth. This quickly became untenable with the introduction of ever-increasing amounts of squadrons. As the war progressed and the arsenal of democracy created different classes of aircraft carriers, the designations changed as well: CVBG for the largest *Essex*-class carrier air group, CVG for a medium carrier air group, CVLG for a light carrier air group, and CVEG for an escort carrier air group.[2]

This book is concerned with one air group: CVG-11. The men of CVG-11 were not the highest scoring group of World War II. They did not have the highest number of aerial victories in a single day, nor were they in the top ten for number of aces in a group. Their bombers and torpedo planes did not sink the most Japanese ships. Nothing about this group indicates that they were unique or unusual. The group was in fact just one of the hundred active combat groups in the Pacific Theater, but that is exactly what makes their story worthy of a longer treatment.

This book is also concerned with one aircraft carrier, the USS *Hornet* (CV-12), but the carrier and the air group were not always together. Over the course of the war, three different air wings called the USS *Hornet* home. First, Air Group Two flew from the *Hornet*'s decks from early spring until September 29, 1944. After the first cruise, Air Group Eleven replaced Air Group Two and led attacks through the early months of 1945, including strikes as far reaching as Okinawa, Formosa (Taiwan), the Philippines, French Indochina (with targets struck in what is today Vietnam), and Hong Kong. At this late stage in the war, kamikaze attacks became routine against America's fleets operating in the Pacific, but the flyers also contended with rough weather, including a few typhoons. Finally, Air Group Seventeen replaced Air Group Eleven on the *Hornet* on February 1, 1945.

VF-11 aviators took great pride in the protection given to their shipmates and other squadron members in VB-11 and VT-11. None of the bombers or torpedo planes in CVG-11 fell to enemy fighters. The pilot with the most confirmed aerial victories in the air wing was Charles R. "Skull" Stimpson, who ended the war with sixteen victories serving at both Guadalcanal and on board the *Hornet*. When CVG-11 finished its second tour at the end of January 1945, the pilots and aircrews of Air Group Eleven had a record they were certainly proud of. The totals included 105 enemy planes confirmed shot down, numerous others listed as "probables," and more than 272 strafed, shot up, and destroyed on the ground. The pilots of VB-11 and VT-11 claimed over 100,000 tons of Japanese shipping sunk and another one hundred Japanese ships smashed, broken, and left burning on the surface of the water. The fighter squadron also produced several aces during the war.

But warfare and combat come with a high price tag. In the second cruise alone, CVG-11 lost fifty aircraft and had more than forty men killed, wounded, or listed as missing in action; many of those missing remain listed this way today. The USS *Hornet* continued its wartime efforts after the replacement of CVG-11 by Air Group Seventeen on February 1, 1945. CVG-11 returned to the states, arriving in Alameda, California, on February 24, 1945. For these operations, the entirety of CVG-11 was honored with the presidential unit citation, but the missions flown from the USS *Hornet* were only half the air group's story.

The concept of this book began with an article in the August 2019 issue of *Naval History* titled "The Tale of Eleven," which detailed the exploits of Carrier Air Group Eleven during World War II. This article, in a few short pages, told the story of the three to four squadrons of aircraft—most memorably fighter squadron VF-11, nicknamed the Sundowners for the dual meaning of "downing" Japan's rising sun and the term indicating a hard-working sailor—which composed CVG-11. CVG-11 saw action early in the war at Guadalcanal during its first tour and was later assigned to the USS *Hornet* in

1944 and fought throughout the Central and Southwest Pacific areas including Luzon, Mindanao, Mindoro, French Indochina, and Okinawa. The book also details the exploits of the other two squadrons, illustrious in their own right, VB-11 and VT-11.

● WAR PLAN ORANGE

Well before the outbreak of World War II, the U.S. Army and Navy developed a series of war plans covering confrontations from the possible to the probable in almost every corner of the globe. In 1904 Secretary of War William Howard Taft directed the Joint Army-Navy Planning Board to "agree upon a series of practical problems (taking them in order of their assumed importance) which involve cooperation of the services, and the execution of which in time of emergency the two staffs will be responsible." Thus began creation of what eventually became the "Rainbow" set of plans in which the U.S. military denoted possible enemy countries by a particular color: red for Great Britain, white for France, black for Germany, and orange for the empire of Japan.[3]

In the decades following World War I, the Army-Navy board continually reassessed its plans, adding, deleting, or reassigning colors. Throughout the interwar period, the military war-gamed these plans during annual Army exercises or Navy fleet problems. In 1938 the U.S. Navy exercised War Plan Orange against Japan. This exercise included challenging the defenses of bases from a carrier-based air attack on the American forward basing on the Hawaiian Islands. As the clouds of conflict in Europe billowed on the horizon and the Japanese empire began a war against China and demonstrated its expansionist aims, the United States grouped its individual war plans into the Rainbow war plan system. Naval historian Ronald Spector summarized the five plans:

> Rainbow 1 was a plan for a defensive war to protect the United States and the Western Hemisphere north of ten degrees [south] latitude. In such a war, the United States was assumed to be without major allies. Rainbow 2 was identical to Rainbow 1, except for assuming that the United States would be allied with France and the United Kingdom. Rainbow 3 was a repetition of the Orange plan, with the provision that

> the hemisphere defense would first be secured, as provided in Rainbow 1. Rainbow 4 was based on the same assumptions as Rainbow 1 but extended the American mission to include defense of the entire Western Hemisphere. Rainbow 5, destined to be the basis for American strategy in World War II, assumed that the United States was allied with Britain and France and provided for offensive operations by American forces in Europe, Africa, or both.[4]

Edward S. Miller, a business executive turned historian, wrote the definitive book on the U.S. strategy, *War Plan Orange*. Miller called the plan to defeat Japan "history's most successful war plan."[5] He might be correct in his assertion. It is certainly one of the most complicated plans, having undergone war-gaming and revision for more than four decades before the outbreak of hostilities between the United States and Japan in December 1941. However, contrary to the mythologized "Europe first" plan of battle, the United States executed "a near paradox of an unwavering commitment to a Europe-first strategy and an almost equal expenditure of effort in the Pacific."[6]

● JAPANESE WAR PLANS

The imperial military arms of Japan were no strangers to war planning, either. The strategic aims of the Japanese empire in 1941 were to win the ongoing war in China, maintain control of the peripheral seas and islands adjacent to the empire, secure all strategic approaches to the home islands (including Korea and Taiwan), and acquire the necessary war-making resources from abroad.

The overarching Japanese goal was a "Greater East Asia Co-Prosperity Sphere" stretching from the northernmost islands of Japan east to the island chains of the Marshalls and Gilberts and south to the Solomon Islands and the Netherlands East Indies. Japanese operations in 1941 were thus twofold: first, to secure their southern resource area by taking French Indochina, Burma, Malaya, the Philippine Islands, and other associated areas in the Pacific, and second, to establish a strong defensive perimeter to the east in order to hold any American responses at bay. To do this, Japan needed to destroy or seriously damage the American fleet. An opening came in 1940, when President Franklin D. Roosevelt ordered the Pacific Fleet to move from its home station in the port of San Diego to Pearl Harbor, Hawaii. Just as students at the U.S. Naval War College studied the concept of the "fleet in being," the officers of the Imperial Japanese Navy (IJN) had done the same. The mere existence of the American fleet at Pearl Harbor posed a threat to Japanese security. To accomplish their strategic aims unhindered by American involvement, Japanese forces needed to checkmate the American fleet.[7]

● JAPANESE SHIPS AND AIRCRAFT

In December 1941 the Imperial Japanese Navy counted a total force strength of ten battleships, six heavy aircraft carriers, and six smaller aircraft carriers, with another seven under construction. Despite the surprise attack at Pearl Harbor, the IJN did not recognize the carrier as the principal warfighting ship of the line; that role was reserved for the battleship. The IJN was slow to let go of the concept of a culminating or decisive ship battle throughout the war. The principal leaders of the IJN included Admiral Osami Nagano, the head of the IJN general staff, Admiral Shigetaro Shimada, the minister of the navy, and Admiral Isoroku Yamamoto, commander in chief of the combined fleet, and his chief of staff Rear Admiral Matome Ugaki. The IJN's principal striking arm, the First Air Fleet, was commanded by Vice Admiral Chūichi Nagumo.

Although Japan fielded dozens of different types of aircraft—everything from fighters to reconnaissance to flying boats—five dominated not only this narrative, but also most histories of the war in the Pacific Theater. They were the Mitsubishi A6M2 Model 21 Type Zero fighter that went by the Allied code name "Zeke," the Nakajima B5N2 Type 97 carrier attack aircraft "Kate" (torpedo/bomber), the Aichi D3A1 Type 99 carrier bomber "Val," the Mitsubishi G3M2 Model 22 "Nell" medium land-based bomber, and the Mitsubishi G4M1 Model 11 "Betty" medium land-based bomber.[8]

The Japanese used a quad alphanumeric designation system. For example, the Zeke was the A6M2: *A* was the type symbol for carrier fighter (just as the U.S. designator *F* indicated fighter), *6* the type number, *M* for manufacturer (in this case, Mitsubishi), and the 2 the model number; as newer updated versions entered service this number went up. At Pearl Harbor, Japan used

A6M2s. In 1943 during the Solomon campaigns, there was the A6M3 and so on throughout the war. Americans used a similar system.[9]

● OUTBREAK OF HOSTILITIES THROUGH GUADALCANAL

The political and military leaders of Japan made the decision to go to war in spring 1941. The attack on Pearl Harbor and surrounding bases was meant to destroy or neutralize the U.S. Pacific Fleet, although it is well recognized now that missing the American aircraft carriers and not destroying the drydocks and fuel farms allowed for a more rapid American response. On November 26, 1941, six Japanese carriers sortied for Pearl Harbor under strict radio silence. In certain circles, conspiracy theorists spilled much ink about what President Roosevelt knew and when he knew it. The truth is that most leaders at the senior levels of the U.S. military and the administration knew the likelihood of an attack was becoming more probable, but where the first strike might fall continued to be debated. Most believed the Japanese would first move against the Philippines and then move toward a decisive battle with the U.S. fleet when it sortied to respond.

Unknown to the American Navy, the IJN sortied all six of their aircraft carriers toward Hawaii for a devastating surprise attack. Participating in the raid were the *Akagi*, *Kaga*, *Soryu*, *Hiryu*, *Shokaku*, and *Zuikaku*. The surprise attack began at 0748 Hawaiian time on December 7. Three hundred fifty-three carrier-launched aircraft attacked in two waves. Sitting side by side on Battleship Row, all eight of the U.S. Navy battleships received significant or fatal damage. Four of them sank where they sat. With the U.S. fleet at Pearl Harbor seemingly neutralized, the combined strength of the United Kingdom, New Zealand, Australia, the Netherlands, and the United States Forces in the Far East were left to hold the line. This included forty-six Army divisions, thirty-one fighter and thirty-six bomber squadrons, and a total of fifty ships.

The attack on Pearl Harbor was the opening salvo, and the Japanese moved quickly to secure the southern resource area and establish a defensive perimeter that would hold what remained of the U.S. Pacific Fleet and its allies at bay. Japanese expansion planned after December 7 would cut the U.S. lines of communication to the Philippines. The Japanese began a massive assault by seizing the approaches and islands in rapid succession: Malaya, Luzon, and Borneo. First to fall was Malaya, attacked only fifty minutes after the strikes at Pearl Harbor began. Lieutenant General Tomoyuki Yamashita's forces launched an amphibious assault on the Malay Peninsula, trapping British Lieutenant General Arthur Ernest Percival's army there. Japanese forces continually outflanked British forces, forcing them back toward the city of Singapore, which surrendered on February 7, 1942.

The invasion of the Philippines began on December 8. Launching from the stronghold at Formosa, Japanese forces landed at Batan Island and two days later on the main island of Luzon. A major attack came on December 22, when the IJN successfully put 43,110 soldiers ashore at three points along the east coast of the island. On Christmas Eve, the United States invoked War Plan Orange 3, consisting of five delaying positions while forces withdrew into Batan; the withdrawal was completed on January 6. American forces fought a valiant but largely ineffective defensive campaign, eventually retreating to Corregidor, which also surrendered on May 8, 1942.

The Japanese onslaught continued into Borneo and the Netherlands East Indies. Sumatra, Dutch Borneo, and the Netherlands New Guinea all fell. Historian Mark R. Peattie noted, "For the next two months Japanese naval aircraft raced out in front of Japanese landings in Malaya, the Philippines, and the Netherlands East Indies, blasting Allied military and naval facilities, crippling Allied naval units, and shooting up the remnants of Allied air defenses." Peattie also noted, "Through the early spring of 1942, therefore, Japanese naval airpower, like a sword of finely tempered steel, had slashed away everything that stood in its way." However, that finely tempered steel was about to be blunted when it slammed against a wall of American technological prowess, daring, and just old-fashioned good luck.[10]

On April 18, 1942, the United States finally responded with the Doolittle raid: Sixteen B-25B Mitchell medium bombers, commanded by Lt. Col. James "Jimmy" Doolittle, launched from the USS *Hornet*. The results of the raid were not spectacular and for the Americans did little more than boost morale. However, the strategic importance of the raid cannot be overstated. Rather than allowing the Japanese to build a veritably impenetrable barrier in the

Pacific, the United States had not only breached this wall, but also struck at Japan's homeland.

In May 1942 the Japanese moved to phase two of their southern plan and pushed into the South Pacific to cut off Australia by taking Port Moresby and Tulagi. However, the United States and Australia learned of the Japanese offensive and moved to intercept with Rear Adm. Frank Jack Fletcher's Task Force 15 and the carrier task group 17.5, which included the USS *Yorktown* (CV-5) and its CVG-3. With CVG-3 was VF-3 led by Lt. Cdr. John S. Thach. The Japanese took Tulagi on May 3–4 but were caught completely by surprise by the arrival of U.S. carrier airstrikes. The Japanese fleet turned its attention to finding the carriers, and the result was the Battle of the Coral Sea (May 6–8), where each side lost a carrier sunk and one damaged. Tactically, the Battle of the Coral Sea was a draw. Strategically, it was a massive victory for the Allies. It stopped Japanese expansion short of its goal of cutting off Australia.

The Doolittle raid and the Battle of the Coral Sea convinced Japanese leaders to push their defensive perimeter out farther and prevent further U.S. interference. Their goal became the island of Midway. The IJN hoped that by first seizing Midway, the U.S. Navy would be forced to come out and fight. However, what the Japanese did not plan for was the United States cracking their communications code, learning of their plans, and setting up a trap off Midway. At the Battle of Midway (June 3–6), U.S. forces sank four Japanese carriers (between Midway and Coral Sea, four of the six carriers used at Pearl Harbor were now on the bottom of the Pacific Ocean). The Japanese offensive was over; the United States and its allies were soon to begin theirs.

The Allied and American advances began in August 1942. On August 7 Allied forces, predominantly from the U.S. Marine Corps, made landings on the islands of Guadalcanal, Florida, and Tulagi. The Japanese made another attempt at expansion. Beginning on August 25, Japanese forces landed at Milne Bay in the territory of Papua hoping to capture the airfields there and push on to Port Moresby in the Gulf of Papua, directly across the Coral Sea from Australia. The defeat at Coral Sea denied the Japanese their first attempt at capturing Port Moresby, and they would be defeated a second time with their landings at Milne Bay. After the initial landings and a push inland, Australian forces forced a Japanese withdrawal after two weeks of hard fighting. Port

Moresby was saved for a second time. American forces now moved to the offensive, but to continue what was going to be a prolonged, multi-year fight against Japan, the U.S. Navy was going to need more pilots, more aircraft, and more squadrons.

CHAPTER 1

THE FORMING OF AIR GROUP ELEVEN

The story of Air Group Eleven began on a relatively mild October day in 1942 at North Island. The island sat in the San Diego Bay on the northernmost point of the Coronado peninsula and directly above the city of Coronado itself. The air station had a long history with the development of airpower dating back to the earliest naval aviators in 1911, and aviation pioneers operated a flying school on the barren sand flats until World War I. Congress officially appropriated the island in 1917, and it became home to both U.S. Navy and U.S. Army assets until the Army's departure in 1937 left the airfields in the hands of naval aviation. During World War II, North Island was a major installation for ships, aircraft, and personnel departing for operations in the Pacific.

On October 10, a perfect California fall day with temperatures in the mid-70s, CVG-11 came into existence as Replacement Air Group Eleven. In the years to come, the unit recorded its fair share of significant firsts and eventually attained a rightful place as one of the Navy's top fighting organizations, but for now that all lay in a distant and unknown future. The Navy's newest air group included VF-11, VT-11, VB-11, and VS-11—fighter, torpedo, dive bomber, and scouting/reconnaissance squadrons. Each squadron also flew an aircraft unique to its particular mission: TBF Avengers (flown by VT-11), SBD Dauntless (VB-11 and VS-11), and F4F Wildcats (VF-11). Unlike their opponents in the Japanese navy, these aircraft changed throughout the war.[1]

Air Group Eleven would be under the command of Cdr. Paul H. Ramsey, a native of Springfield, Ohio, and a graduate of the United States Naval Academy (USNA, class of 1927). Ramsey had already commanded VF-2 aboard the USS *Lexington* and had participated in the Battle of the Coral Sea, where his squadron of F4F Wildcats provided cover for the Douglas TBD Devastators of VT-2 as they engaged and sank the Japanese light aircraft carrier *Shōhō*. This action earned him the Navy Cross:

> In spite of numerical superiority in favor the enemy, Lieutenant Commander Ramsey attacked and destroyed three and damaged two enemy fighter aircraft. His timely initiative and capable leadership were responsible for the high combat efficiency of his squadron to destroy twelve and damage eight enemy aircraft.[2]

At the same ceremony where Ramsey took command of CVG-11, Lt. Cdr. Weldon L. Hamilton took command of VB-11, Lt. Cdr. Charles R. Fenton of VF-11, Lt. Cdr. Hoyt D. Mann of VS-11, and Lt. Cdr. Frederick L. Ashworth of VT-11. In addition, Commander Ramsey presented Lt. (jg) George H. Gay a Navy Cross for his actions at Midway.[3]

● VF-11 SUNDOWNERS

The VF-11 Sundowners came into being in August 1942 at North Island Naval Air Station, although at their activation ceremony, they had no name or identity, just their number. Commanding officer Lt. Cdr. Charles R. Fenton was a native of Annapolis, Maryland, and a 1929 graduate of the United States Naval Academy, where he had participated in basketball, swimming, and tennis. Fenton, like Ramsey, already had extensive combat experience, having served as the executive officer and later commander of VF-42. During the Battle of the Coral Sea, Fenton also earned the Navy Cross. His citation read:

> For extraordinary heroism and conspicuous devotion to duty as Commanding Officer of a Fighting Squadron in action against enemy Japanese forces during the period May 4–8, 1942, Lieutenant Commander Fenton led his squadron in skillfully maneuvered and timely interference against enemy Japanese aircraft attempting to break up attacks on Tuglagie [*sic*] by our carrier-based bombing and torpedo planes on May 4, and on enemy carriers in the Coral Sea on May 7 and 8. . . . The squadron [under his leadership] shot down a total of twenty-two enemy planes . . . [and assisted] in the sinking of one enemy Japanese carrier and the sinking or damaging of a second carrier and eight other enemy vessels.[4]

Clearly, the new air group was being led by combat veterans ready to impart their knowledge to the newer pilots.

Fenton's new job, like those of the other air group and squadron commanders, was primarily administrative: to organize the new fighter squadron and ready it for operations against the Japanese. To aid him in this task, three other combat veterans joined the ranks of the new fighter squadron: Lt. William N. Leonard (USNA 1938), Lt. Frank B. Quady (USNA 1938), and Lt. (jg) Walter J. Hiebert. Three other senior pilots who joined the squadron did not yet have any combat experience to speak of: Lt. Clarence M. White Jr. (VF-11 executive officer, USNA 1933), Lt. Raymond W. "Sully" Vogel (operations officer, USNA 1936), and Lt. Gordon D. Cady (head of tactics and gunnery and a graduate of the University of Florida). Of the six senior pilots forming the squadron, four of them were Annapolis graduates: Fenton, Leonard, Quady, and White. Historian Barrett Tillman noted that "this depth of leadership was unusual," but the fact that so many of them were Naval Academy graduates was not unusual for the time. The Naval History and Heritage Command points out, "While only 5 percent of the total number of serving naval officers in the war were academy graduates, the school produced the professional core around which the Navy's unprecedented expansion from 119,088 uniformed personnel in 1938 to 3,405,525 in 1945 could occur. Nearly all of the war's key naval leaders—including William Halsey, Class of 1904; Ernest King, '01; Chester Nimitz, '05; and Raymond Spruance, '06—were graduates." Also, many of the Navy's regular officers joining before the start of the war were graduates and were planning to make the U.S. Navy a career. However, a core of pilots formed the nucleus of VF-11 during both of the unit's wartime cruises; two in particular, Charlie Stimpson and Jim Swope, were both aces by war's end. Stimpson was the Sundowners' top ace with sixteen victories, receiving the Navy Cross and three Distinguished Flying Crosses.[5]

After the squadron left California for Hawaii and before its deployment to the Central Pacific, the unit adopted its distinctive "Sundowners" name and emblem. The patch and name both referenced the fighter squadron's primary mission of shooting down the aircraft of the rising sun of Japan, but it also represented the idea of a sailor willing to work long, hard hours until the sun was well below the horizon. Tillman notes that the term "originated in the days of sail when grog was customarily served on ships, but a strict captain might withhold the ration until dark while others relented when the sun sank below the main yardarm." Regardless of the term's origins, it proved to be a self-fulfilling prophecy on both definitions for the unit's future operations.[6]

The aircraft VF-11 pilots were going to use to fight the Japanese was, from a certain point of view, obsolete. By no measures of performance was the Grumman F4F Wildcat superior to the Mitsubishi A6M Zero. The Zeke, as the Allies named it, was faster, had a tighter turning circle, and could climb and dive better than the Wildcat. By the time VF-11 reached its destination in the Pacific, many other American units operated the Vought F4U Corsair. This was the hand dealt to the men of VF-11. As Tillman noted, "For better or worse, the Wildcat was the U.S. naval fighter during the year after Pearl Harbor. . . . F4F squadrons were forced to devise superior tactics in order to survive."[7]

The F4F Wildcat and F4U Corsair show the similarities to the naming conventions used by the Japanese. In the case of American aircraft, an aircraft's name denoted the mission, design number, production company, and a modification number. So the F4F was a fighter (*F*) of design number *four* built by Grumman (*F*). As newer models rolled off assembly lines, the modification number changed to denote the newer aircraft: F4F-1, F4F-2, and so forth.[8]

● TORPEDO SQUADRON 11

Torpedo Squadron Eleven (VT-11) was established at Naval Air Station San Diego along with the other squadrons on October 10, 1942. The squadron initially received Grumman TBF-1 Avengers, the newest carrier aircraft.

Previously, torpedo squadrons were equipped with the obsolete Douglas TBD-1 Devastators, which the Japanese ravaged at the Battle of Midway. The new TBMs were larger, faster, and more heavily armored and had longer range than the older Douglas TBD-1 Devastators. Over the next five years, the squadron upgraded through several models of TBF and TBM Avengers. A crew of three operated each aircraft: pilot, turret gunner, and radioman, also called the "bilge man." No one on the aircraft was busier than the bilge man, whose duties included operating the radio, radar, and plane intercommunications, and having responsibility for the bombsight. The bilge man also was responsible for setting the intervals and rack selection for dropping bombs or a torpedo.[9]

The Avengers typically carried the U.S. Navy's Mark 13 torpedo, which was a few inches over thirteen feet long, weighed over 2,200 pounds, and contained 600 pounds of high-explosive "Torpex," which was 1.5 times the explosive power of TNT. With a speed of thirty-three knots, it proved to be the most versatile of the Navy's torpedoes in World War II, as well as the most widely produced. The TBFs were heavily armed: a .30-caliber machine gun that fired down and behind the plane, a .30-caliber machine gun that fired through the propeller, and a heavier .50-caliber gun that covered the sky from the sides and overhead rearward of the plane. The pilot had armor plating under his feet, under his seat, and behind him. The gunner had armor plating under his seat and up his back. The bilge man only had a piece of armor plate to sit on.

The squadron's first commanding officer, Lt. Cdr. Frederick. L. Ashworth, was born in Beverly, Massachusetts. Ashworth added to the squadron's complement of Naval Academy graduates, having received his diploma in the class of 1933. He had initially entered Dartmouth College, but during his first year decided to follow his brother's example and join the ranks of the Naval Academy. He obtained a recommendation from his congressional representative, but after testing, he was informed that although he passed the exam, he did not get one of the two appointments allotted to his congressman and was now listed as first alternate. Ashworth thought Annapolis was out, so he took a summer job in a construction company in Vermont, believing he was headed back to Dartmouth. Fortunately for Ashworth, one of the other nominees was medically disqualified, so he entered the academy that fall.[10]

After taking command of the squadron, Ashworth later recalled, "TBFs were certainly rugged. The first time you get into it, it seems like a colossal plane, but when you got familiar with it, it was very comfortable to fly." An old joke associated with the TBF was that the Grumman engineers built the first aircraft of concrete and then made the future models even heavier.[11]

Ashworth knew his job was preparing the squadron for combat, and he implemented a training regimen to do just that. He received orders to the Advanced Carrier Training Group at Naval Air Station North Island in June 1942, four months prior to his squadron's activation. His job was to organize and train his pilots for combat operations in the Pacific Theater, ostensibly for combat flying from aircraft carriers. Ashworth, an inexperienced commander, remembered, "I was certainly in this category, for, as you know, I had not had any combat experience. Shortly after I arrived there, I was surprised to learn that I was to train the new pilots for duty in torpedo squadrons. Well, I didn't know anything about torpedo plane tactics, but I assumed that since I had just completed a postgraduate course in aviation ordnance, I was supposed to know something about torpedoes, at least."[12]

Ashworth and the commanders of other torpedo squadrons formed at the same time were well aware of the devastating losses those squadrons had suffered at the Coral Sea and at Midway. Ashworth remembered, "I resolved that these lads would not go to war to drop their first torpedo in a combat situation attacking a Japanese carrier. . . . We worked up procedures for attacks against single ships using destroyers as targets out in the local sea training areas, and coordinated attacks with aircraft attacking from both bows, with each pilot releasing a torpedo in the dummy attack. We would have as many as twelve torpedoes in the water at one time."[13] Ashworth also recognized there was a possibility that the torpedo squadron could be required to perform operations at night: "Since I was sure that there would be a lot of night operations out of Henderson Field on Guadalcanal, we turned the squadron into a night-flying squadron and did nothing but night-flight operations for the next month or two. This was worth its weight in gold, for we all were very well qualified for these operations when we arrived on the island. As it turned out we did better than half of our operations up the 'Slot' at night."[14]

VT-11 was the first squadron in the air group to come up with an official emblem. Not long after the establishment of the squadron, some of the members reached out to Walt Disney Studios. The artists at Disney already had a reputation for designing squadron and other unit insignia for American units all over the globe, and Walt Disney himself established a separate five-person organization within his animation department whose full-time job was to design and produce custom drawings for American units free of charge. After Pearl Harbor until the end of the war, Disney animators turned out over 1,300 emblems. Disney historian John Baxter said each insignia was a "stand-alone masterpiece." Animators at the Disney studios designed the patch for Torpedo Squadron Eleven sometime in late 1942. Early in 1943 Ashworth received a letter "c/o Fleet Post Office, San Francisco, California, at the request of Lt. Commander F. J. Frank, Jr. (U.S. Navy, Fleet Schools, Destroyer Base, San Diego, CA)." In the response on November 4, 1942, studio chief of public relations Vern Caldwell specifically noted: "Walt Disney is happy to present this insigne to SQUADRON NO. [ELEVEN]." The official description of the insignia was a "caricature of a cupid with helmet and goggles on head, flying through space and hurling torpedo through air." The patch designed for VT-11 by the Disney team consisted of a black torpedo with a skull and crossbones on it and a winged cherub wearing a green helmet nicknamed "Little Butch." Since the squadron was composed mainly of personnel who had no combat experience, the "baby" hurling a torpedo was considered the appropriate design.[15]

● VB-11 WINGED PEGASUS

The men of VB-11 flew in the Dauntless SBD (which stood for scout, bomber, Douglas Aircraft). A tale, perhaps apocryphal, says the men who flew in it said SBD actually stood for "slow, but deadly." The SBDs carried the same Norden Mark IV Mod bombsite that could be found on the Army Air Forces B-17s and B-24s. The SBDs also had a primitive radio direction finder for use in returning to base after night raids or over water. Even at this relatively early stage in the war, the Dauntless was already famous for its actions at the Battle of Midway when the men of VB-3 and VB-6 dropped out of the sky to decimate the Japanese aircraft carriers *Kaga*, *Akagi*, and *Sōryū* in a matter of minutes.[16]

Bombing Squadron 11 (VB-11) was fortunate to have a wealth of experience in its ranks at its formation. Five veterans of VB-2, displaced from the lost USS *Lexington*, formed the core of the squadron from which the other pilots would learn. They were Lt. Cdr. Weldon Hamilton, Lt. Ralph Cousins, Lt. Paul J. Knapp, Lt. (jg) Joe Riley, and Lt. (jg) Herb Shonk. Hamilton, a native of Darlington, South Carolina, and a year behind air group commander Paul Ramsey at the Naval Academy, was no academic star. His senior yearbook noted, "He starts each term by going unsat [unsatisfactory] in at least two subjects. At the end of the term he is sure to come around with that big sigh of relief saying, 'Well, the Academic Department almost knocked me off this time.'" Sports were more to Hamilton's liking, and he spent all four years at the academy on the track team, serving as its captain his senior year. Lt. Cdr. Raymond B. Jacoby joined Hamilton as his executive officer.[17]

Hamilton—called "Ham" or "Hammy" by his friends—was a living legend to the newer pilots, having already received the Navy Cross, not once, but twice. In April 1942 Hamilton "led his squadron 125 miles over uncharted mountains and jungles, to press home in the face of heavy anti-aircraft fire, a vigorous and determined dive bombing attack on enemy ships, sinking or crippling three of them." Less than a month later, during the Coral Sea battles, "he led his squadron in a dive bombing attack against an enemy disposition. In this attack, made in the face of heavy anti-aircraft fire and opposed by enemy fighters, he dropped his 1,000-pound bomb on the deck of an enemy carrier. The success of the attack by his squadron attested to the high state of combat efficiency developed under his leadership and inspiring example."[18]

Hamilton decided to bring the Pegasus, the insignia of the now-defunct VB-2, with him when he became commander of the new VB-11. The official history of the squadron's first tour noted, "The original origin is vague but supposedly Pegasus was chosen because it had been the first, according to Greek mythology, to make use of the dive in combat." Thus, the squadron's motto was "First to Attack."[19]

Another member of VB-11 went into more detail on the origins of the squadron's patch. Edwin M. Wilson recalled many years later that if one studied Greek mythology, the Gorgon Medusa—she of the many snakes for hair—was in fact mortal and capable of being slain. The task fell to Perseus, who decapitated her but in doing so gave birth to Pegasus, the winged horse of the Muses. The Corinthian hero Bellerophon, a son of Poseidon, tamed Pegasus with the aid of a golden bridle given to him by Athena, the goddess of wisdom. The hero now became the world's first dive-bomber. Wilson picked up the story and recalled how Pegasus gained the notoriety and appreciation by the men of VB-11:

> Riding on Pegasus, Bellerophon plunged down on the monster Chimaera from a great height and killed it, thus becoming the first dive-bomber and recording the first "hit" by a dive-bomber. Chimaera was a troublesome monster, with a fire-breathing goat's head, the forequarters of a lion, and hind part of a dragon. Certainly a worthy target for the first dive-bombing attack. Pegasus was also in the service of Zeus as a carrier of thunder and lightning (how's that for a lethal payload!). Pegasus was also the favorite mount of Apollo and the Muses. Later, when Bellerophon tried to ride Pegasus to heaven, the winged horse was stung by a gadfly sent by Zeus, and threw Bellerophon to his death. Pegasus continued the ascent alone, becoming the constellation of the same name. So, Pegasus was not only the first dive bomber, but still holds the all-time altitude record.[20]

● VS-11

The saga of VS-11 proves a bit more difficult to trace, since the Navy disestablished the scouting/reconnaissance squadrons in the first part of 1943 just as VS-11 was starting operations on Guadalcanal. Thus, CVG-11's scouting and reconnaissance arm was initially established as Scout Squadron Eleven on October 10, 1942, but was redesignated Bombing Squadron Twenty-one (VB-21) on March 1, 1943, and eventually disestablished completely on September 25, 1943. Lt. Cdr. Hoyt D. Mann of Roanoke, Alabama, USNA 1936, was the junior commanding officer of the air group. Mann was also a veteran of previous battles. As a pilot for Scouting Squadron Two on board the USS *Lexington* (CV-2), Mann survived the ship's sinking during the Battle of the Coral Sea in May 1942 and received a Distinguished Flying Cross for his efforts in the fray. His VS-11 also had SBDs, usually flying the same missions as the bombing squadron.

There was one significant difference between VF-11 and the other squadrons in the air group. Unlike the fighter pilots of VF-11, the torpedo and bomber squadrons each had enlisted aircrew that flew on the Dauntless and Avenger aircraft. They were not pilots, but it was impossible to do the job without them. In VB-11, enlisted men served as the rear gunner and faced the rear of the aircraft. This meant any forces that acted on the pilot, such as G forces in a dive, were reversed for the gunner. The radioman sat in the interior of the aircraft and had it worse than the rear-facing gunners, having a limited view outside and having to hold on to whatever was available while the aircraft maneuvered.

CARRIER AIR GROUP ELEVEN

After their activation and between October 11 and 22, the air group engaged in "routine training" in the lead-up to a deployment to the Pacific. As VT-11 commander Ashworth noted, training was necessary to prepare the new men for combat operations and to ensure that when combat came, the men's actions were second nature to them. Fear would be present, but the training ensured that when it was needed, training would overtake the fear. Training included carrier landings and dive bombing, gunnery, navigation, and field carrier landings. Finally, on October 24, 1942, the entire air group headed for Hawaii under "secret orders." Three days later, their destination, the USS *Hornet*, was sunk at the Battle of the Santa Cruz Islands—leaving the air group without a home when it reached Hawaii on October 31. The months of November and December saw more routine training at the bases surrounding the Navy base at Pearl Harbor. VB-11, VS-11, and VT-11 flew out of the newly constructed Naval Air Station (NAS) Barbers Point on Oahu. VF-11 landed and flew from NAS Maui.[21]

While at Maui, the pilots of Air Group Eleven trained, but they also enjoyed the hospitality of the von Tempsky ranch. The matron of the ranch was Countess Alexa von Tempsky Zabriskie, "a gracious, affable, very nice looking woman at age 52." Some 20,000 aviators visited Erehwon—"nowhere" spelled backward—Ranch during the war. Erehwon was one of dozens of Hawaiian cattle ranches where local "paniolo," Hawaiian cowboys, lived and worked. When World War II brought a significant increase in the number of flyers passing through the island, Alexa von Tempsky Zabriskie continued her prewar practice of opening the grounds of her estate to naval aviation personnel assigned to the air station on Maui. Here, flyers could enjoy "horseback rides and hunting . . . picnics at the beach and barbecues up the mountain." Every person passing through the ranch signed either a large pine wall or a separate guest book. Names adorning the wall or guest book included "many dignitaries and well-known pilots: Fleet Admiral Chester Nimitz, 'Butch' O'Hare, John Thach, 'Dusty' Rhodes, Jimmy Flatley's VF-10, the 'Grim Reapers.'" Her hospitality became legendary for the thousands of aviators who passed through the Hawaiian Islands during the war. Boyd, Maria, and Alexa von Tempsky made sure CVG-11 and dozens of other groups and squadrons had a place to relax when they were not training.[22]

That being said, Alexa had a very strict set of rules for the aviators enjoying her hospitality. One visitor recalled that prior to arriving at the ranch, all the men were told that the rules were inviolable, and violation meant never being invited again. Classified information was not to be discussed, nor any security protocols breached. There were to be no last names, no rank, and no discussion of what squadron a man was in, what job he held in his unit, or where he thought he or his unit might be going in the future. All conversations were to center around non-work-related issues, including one's hometown, favorite baseball team, and other banal topics—nothing that could lead to any information slippage. Upon arrival at the home, each guest entered the vestibule to be greeted by Alexa, who had two cigar boxes placed on a small oak table beside her. One box was for rank insignia, and wings, which were removed and placed in the red Roi-Tan cigar box. The second box, a yellow Dutch Masters box, was for neckties. Officers were to remove their neckties and place them in the box. The color of the ties indicated the officers' service: black, Navy; olive-green, Marines; khaki, Army.

If any of these rules were broken, Alexa could "be in deep trouble with the top brass! She has many high-level friends in [commander in chief, Pacific], Honolulu. They are willing to let her have these morale-raising inter-service get-togethers" as long as the rules continued to be observed. One frequent visitor recalled, "If a guest refuses to take off his tie, even an admiral, or general, Alexa, with a smile, will pick up the large shears from the table, and cut his goddamn tie off, right below the knot, and throw it in the fucking yellow box!" Alexa had no trouble getting visitors to comply with these requests.[23]

December continued what many of the pilots now regarded as a monotonous routine of training, broken up only by a "joint Army-Navy interception and firing exercise" held on December 10. During this training event, VF-11 was "attacked" by U.S. Army P-40s (one P-40 was determined to have been "shot down"). VB-11 struck targets at Pearl Harbor, while VT-11 hit targets in the harbor of Honolulu. Exercises and training events continued throughout December and into January.[24]

On February 8, a series of promotions and job assignments shuffled up CVG-11 and VB-11. Group commander Ramsey moved to Washington, DC, where he became a director of flight tests at Anacostia Naval Air Station. VB-11 commander Hamilton took command of the group, and his executive officer, R. B. Jacoby, took command of VB-11, but he is conspicuously absent from future operations. Apparently, shortly after arriving on Guadalcanal, Jacoby took a falling coconut to the head; his injuries were serious enough that he did not participate in operations for the entire tour at Guadalcanal. He was briefly succeeded by Lt. C. A. Skinner before Lt. Cdr. Lloyd A. Smith (USNA 1935) assumed command.[25]

The monotony of training continued until February 17, 1943, when the group began loading onto the USS *Altamaha*. On February 18, "18 SBD-3s of VB-11, 18 SBD-3s of VS-11, 12 TBF-1s of VT-11, and 16 F4F-4s of VF-11 were loaded aboard." The USS *Altamaha*—named for a river in the state of Georgia—was an escort carrier used primarily to move units into the Pacific Theater throughout the war. The next day, the entire group—minus eighty-three men of VF-11—departed Pearl Harbor and headed for Nadi, Viti Levu, Fiji. The men of VF-11 boarded the USS *Long Island*. The air group reached Fiji on February 28. From there it was off to Espiritu Santo, and CVG-11 continued to train and fly simulated combat missions. The USS *Altamaha* unloaded the men, and the aircraft catapulted into the sky. After this, the *Altamaha* returned directly to Pearl Harbor.[26]

While at Espiritu Santo, the maintenance officer for VS-11, Harry A. Fredrickson, went in search of a Navy cook famed for his ability to make delicious meals out of the much-maligned Spam. In his search, he ran across an old acquaintance who was heavily bandaged and his head wrapped in gauze. Fredrickson asked his friend just what had happened. In a humorous and macabre story, his friend related that while sitting at the base movie theater, "A sailor had found a 100-pound bomb to sit on since seats were coconut logs or what else you could find. The bomb was fused and the sailor didn't realize what he was doing by spinning the fuse. He armed the bomb and it exploded. Everyone thought they were under attack and ran everywhere."[27]

On March 16 an F4F of VF-11 crashed during a training exercise, killing the pilot, Ens. Robert Wayne Baumgartner. This loss was followed by more on March 25, when Lt. (jg) Herbert Bronson Shonk and his radioman Francis F. Brown died after a mid-air collision with a Royal New Zealand Air Force P-40. Losses in training—as well as in combat—were expected, even commonplace, but it did nothing for the morale of the squadrons to know they were already losing men before they even had a chance to engage the enemy. Training and preparation for combat continued. On the last day of March 1943, and just weeks ahead of their planned departure for the theater and combat, VF-11 commanding officer Lieutenant Commander Fenton received orders to report for duty in Washington, DC. Fenton, a Navy Cross recipient and veteran of the Coral Sea, had been the commander of the squadron since its inception, but VF-11 was going to have to prove their combat worth without him. Lt. Cdr. Clarence M. White, the squadron executive officer, took over as commanding officer.[28]

CHAPTER 2

GUADALCANAL

Early Operations

Guadalcanal sat at the southeastern end of the Solomon Islands. To its southeast sat the slightly larger San Cristobal, and closer to the northeast was Malaita. Between Malaita and Guadalcanal were the Florida Islands (Nggela Islands), Savo Island, and Iron Bottom Sound, where more than three dozen Japanese and Allied ships now eternally rested. Flying northwest "up the slot" from Guadalcanal were the New Georgia Islands and the beginnings of Japanese resistance. Japan continued to operate out of seven different bases including Buin-Faisi, Kahili, and Ballale, and all the way north to Rabaul, Japan's main base on New Britain. These were just a few of the dozens of Japanese outposts in the region, but this was more than enough for continual operations.

The Japanese began their final withdrawal from Guadalcanal on February 1–2, 1943, as part of Operation Ke. There was confusion in the Allied ranks. Coast watchers along the slot picked up a number of Japanese destroyers coming from the direction of Rabaul toward Guadalcanal. Samuel Eliot Morison noted, "The constant shuttle of evacuation barges between Guadalcanal and

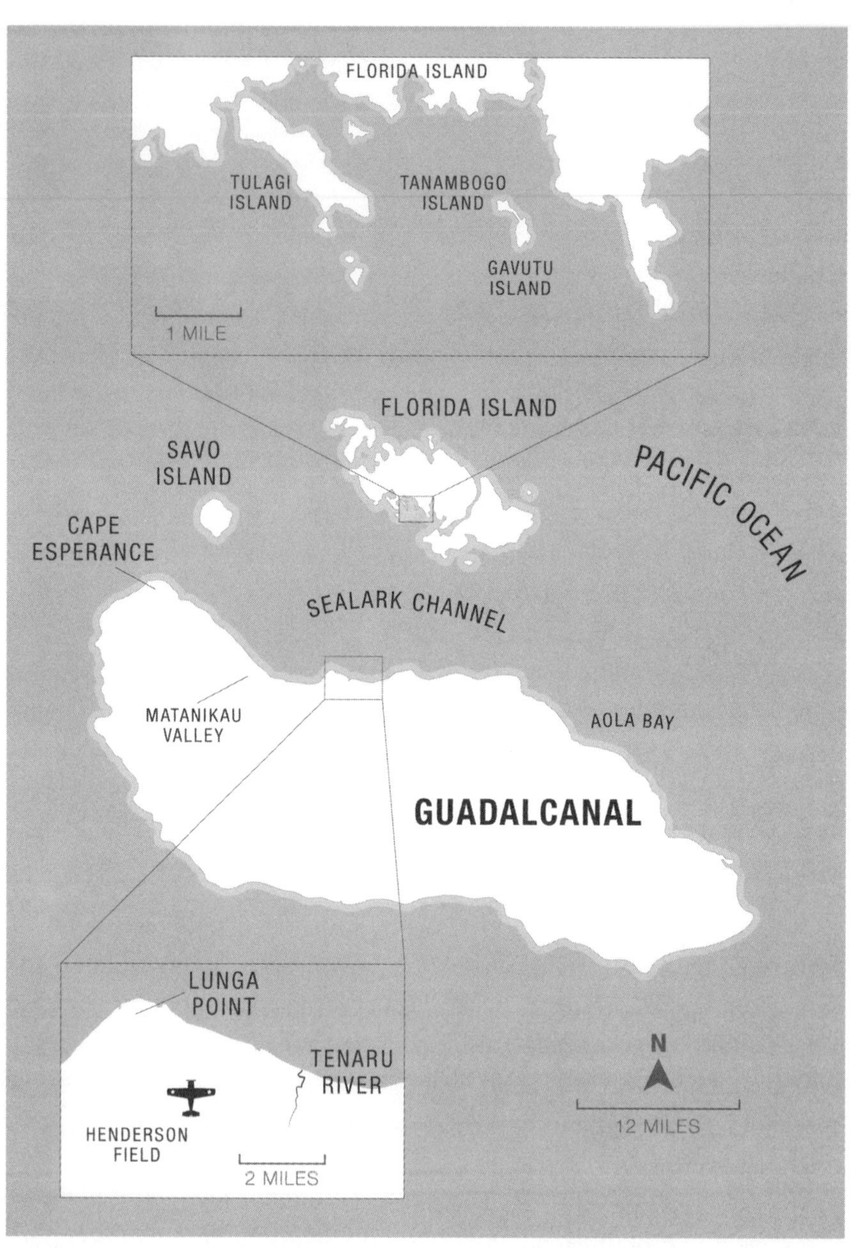

Map 1. CVG-11 Operating Area

the Russells looked like a southbound reinforcement and not a northbound evacuation."[1]

In response, Adm. William "Bull" Halsey moved American carriers—there were only two in theater, the *Saratoga* and the *Enterprise*—toward Guadalcanal as reinforcement to Vice Adm. Marc "Pete" Mitscher's aircraft parked there. The Tokyo Express, moving personnel, supplies, and equipment to Japanese forces operating in and around New Guinea and the Solomon Islands, successfully evacuated 11,706 men from Guadalcanal. However, one coast watcher stated that three thousand of those men pulled out "were set ashore . . . and told to fend for themselves." On February 9, Gen. Alexander Patch informed Admiral Halsey, "Total and complete defeat of Japanese forces on Guadalcanal effected 1625 today."[2]

The Guadalcanal campaign, which lasted from August 1942 until February 1943, cost over 7,000 American lives and another 7,700 wounded. The Japanese fared far worse, having lost nearly 20,000 men during the campaign. Calculating material losses during the campaign is more difficult, but here the numbers of aircraft, ships, and other supplies were significantly closer. Guadalcanal is often, justifiably, cited as one of the turning points of the war. Although the Guadalcanal campaign was over, operations from the island continued as Allied forces began the slow, inexorable march toward Japan. The Japanese forces had been checked at the Coral Sea and defeated at Midway and Guadalcanal, and Allied operations toward Japan now began in earnest. While many history books have been written about these major battles, fewer works cover the time in between the major battles. The men of Air Group Eleven were about to begin where most history books ended.

Admiral Halsey dispatched Vice Admiral Mitscher to the island as the commander, Air Forces, Solomons (ComAirSols). Mitscher, an early proponent and leader of the development of naval carrier aviation, was the right man for the job, having already spent decades developing naval airpower. Mitscher had also commanded the USS *Hornet*, CVG-11's initial home prior to its sinking, and was captain of the ship during the Doolittle raid. At Guadalcanal, Mitscher commanded all airpower in the region including Army Air Forces, Navy, Marine, and New Zealand aircraft. Halsey later commented, "I knew we'd probably catch hell from the Jap[anese] in the air. That's why I sent Pete

Mitscher up there. Pete was a fighting fool and I knew it."[3] As if to underscore the situation, on the day Mitscher landed on the island, an aerial dogfight occurred over the airfield as he exited his transport, as if the Japanese fighters were there to welcome him.[4]

Mitscher biographer Theodore Taylor noted that Mitscher's forces included "a conglomeration of Corsairs, Avengers, Wildcats, Army P-38s, Catalinas, Army bombers, New Zealand [Royal Air Force] planes—anything with wings." Historian Thomas Hughes noted that "the Air Solomons' unusual amalgam might have been a recipe for the ambiguous employment of airpower, especially from separate service perspectives. Although it was inconsistent with prewar doctrine, the command was nonetheless well fitted to the air tasks at hand in the South Pacific." The predecessor organization to the Air Solomons Command was nicknamed the "Cactus Air Force," after the Allied code name for the island, and now nearly thirty different air units operated from the congested air base on the island. The name "cactus," although officially replaced by Air Solomons, was appropriate. Somehow, under the austere conditions found on the island, the varied air forces found ways to not only survive, but thrive.[5]

American servicemembers on Guadalcanal still had to contend with Japanese aircraft coming south to attack them. Between the end of the Guadalcanal campaign and the opening of Operation Cartwheel to neutralize Rabaul, "Japan chose to wage attrition battles throughout the war, but it did so most effectively on the approaches to Rabaul, in jungle grapplings, combats aloft by day and in narrow straits by night."[6]

However, Japan made "a strategic oversight of major consequences" by not establishing a "single full-service air station south of the one at Rabaul." This put major pressure on Japanese flights from the Rabaul bastion. They now had to fly between 200 miles (to Bougainville) to 565 miles (to Guadalcanal). The Japanese air arm in early to mid-1943 now fought a war of attrition at long range—one they could not hope to win.[7]

The Battle of the Bismarck Sea took place March 2–4, 1943. As the Americans and other Allied nations were now routinely reading the Japanese communiques, codebreakers discovered that the Japanese were going to attempt to move a large force of reinforcements from Rabaul to the Lae Harbor on the eastern side of Papua New Guinea. Naval aviation had little role in the operation, and forces of the U.S. Fifth Air Force and the Royal Australian Air Force launched their attacks against the convoy. In the end, it proved to be a disastrous loss for the Japanese. Allied forces sank eight of the troop transports and four of the escorting destroyers. Of the seven thousand reinforcements sent to Lae in the convoy, few more than one thousand arrived unharmed. After the battle, chief of staff of Japan's combined fleet, Rear Admiral Matome Ugaki, noted that "there will be no hope of future success in this area."[8]

However, a more personal loss soon befell the Japanese forces and the people of Japan. On April 18, shortly before the men of CVG-11 arrived at Guadalcanal, U.S. Army Air Forces carried out Operation Vengeance, intercepting an aircraft bearing Isoroku Yamamoto. Naval intelligence, reading Japanese transmissions, learned of his itinerary and set the trap. Yamamoto's aircraft was shot down, and the admiral was killed. On April 25, Admiral Mineichi Koga, the new commander of the Japanese combined fleet, departed Tokyo and arrived at his new flagship. This was the strategic situation CVG-11 faced as it arrived in theater.[9]

● ELEVEN ARRIVES

CVG-11's first "cruise" was spent flying from the Cactus airfield. Although arriving after the Guadalcanal campaign ended, the unit still saw plenty of action, and the men of VF-11 downed at least fifty-five enemy aircraft in the coming months, as well as the shipping and facilities destroyed by VT-11 and VB-11. By the time CVG-11 arrived in the Pacific combat zone, only two aircraft carriers were operational. This meant the entire air group would be land-based at Guadalcanal, and they would conduct their strikes in a small, localized area; not flying from a carrier prevented freedom of movement for the air group, and they were forced into strikes against the same locations repeatedly. At least the squadron pilots knew where they would be landing.

On April 25, 1943, Easter Sunday, the fighters from the Sundowners arrived at Guadalcanal. The pilots of VF-11 found themselves at Lunga Point, about five hundred yards away from the rest of the air group at Henderson Field. The runway for the fighters was constructed in late 1942 as an addition to the existing Henderson field. Thirty-six F4Fs of VF-11 arrived in three separate groups of twelve on April 25–26. Flight leads for each of the three groups were the new commanding officer Lt. Cdr. Clarence M. White, the executive officer Lt. Raymond "Sully" Vogel, and Lt. Cdr. Gordon Cady. VB-11 departed Nadi, Fiji, on April 27 and arrived at their new home island on April 28. By the end of the month, the entire air group plus enlisted personnel were on the island.[10]

Regardless of arrival date, the squadrons set about turning their small piece of Guadalcanal into a livable space. Enlisted sailor George Retelas wrote in his diary, "We put up our tent 200 feet from the beach near the Lunga River. Dug our foxholes, received a beer card." Retelas, nicknamed "the Greek" or "Rattle-Ass," looked every bit the ideal U.S. Navy sailor from World War II. In a squadron photo taken on Guadalcanal, Retelas stands, hands on hips, shirt unbuttoned below the chest, and hat cocked far back on his head. His skin was so bronzed that he stood out in every photo and was instantly recognizable.[11]

Day-to-day operations began in earnest. The pilots of VF-11, having trained for several months for escort missions providing cover for the bombing and torpedo squadrons, set up a squadron headquarters tent and operations center. Across the runway, VB-11 and VT-11 did much the same. The Sundowners were keen and ready to search for and destroy any Japanese aircraft operating in the region, but their thirst for aerial combat would not be slaked for some time. Shortly after their arrival to Guadalcanal, changes in the U.S. Navy at large caught up with scouting squadron VS-11, which was redesignated as bombing squadron VB-21. Therefore, as the men readied for operations, the air group had a complement of three "attack" squadrons, VB-11, VB-21, and VT-11, capable of conducting patrol, search, spotting, strike, and night mine-laying operations.[12]

Dick Miralles, an eighteen-year-old radioman and gunner in one of the SBD-4s of VB-11, harbored dreams of soft beds, warm sheets, and a cool pillow in a room on an aircraft carrier. Instead, "when the *Hornet* got sunk, in this battle of Santa Cruz, they didn't have an aircraft carrier to put us on, so they put us down and put us under MacArthur's air force." He remembered his arrival to the island this way: "When I got to Guadalcanal I looked around and said what am I doing here? It was not a very delightful lookin' place."[13]

● OPERATIONS PLANNING

Shortly before arrival on Guadalcanal, the units received and reviewed three of roughly a dozen briefing sheets from Naval Air Combat Intelligence,

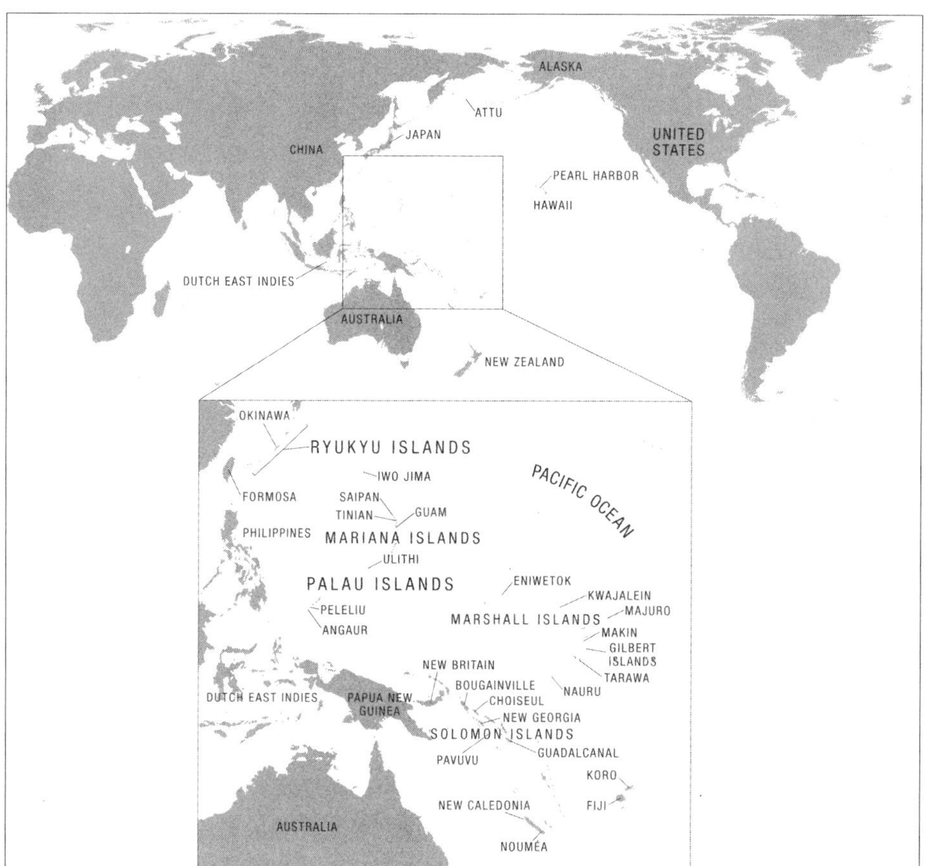

Map 2. Guadalcanal

commander, South Pacific, relating to Japanese positions in the area. These included Munda Point, "in excellent position for offense or defense—offensively to bomb our positions on Guadalcanal or to provide air coverage for surface forces," Vila Plantation (Kolombangara Island), and Rekata Island. Each report included a general overview of the target, approaching landmarks, and notes on the target area.[14]

For example, around Munda Point were at least five other islands that were "oblong," "narrow," "U-shaped," and "shaped like a boomerang." Although the pilots might not have thought of it at the time, it would soon become critical to know these islands, what forces might be on them, and what routes they could take back to Guadalcanal should a pilot or aircrew have to bail out over them. CVG-11 joined the other U.S. Army Air Forces, Navy, and Marine Corps units on Guadalcanal in attacking Japanese bases up and down the slot—bases with names—Segi, Munda, Kolombangara, Bougainville, Kahili, and Bonis—that would soon be as familiar to them as the streets they grew up on.[15]

LIFE ON GUADALCANAL

Guadalcanal was no island paradise. The men lived in pyramidal tents, with wooden decks, pierced plank, and Marston matting floors. Before the group's aircraft and pilots arrived, some of the ground officers attempted to make Guadalcanal feel like home: "By a process of theft, tearful pleading and vague threats, the ground officers had collected cots, mosquito nets, transportation, mail, ready tents, parking space, and incidentally, done a little skillful propagandizing as to the general excellence of the Squadron." Kermit Enander, a VF-11 ground crew member, remembered, "There was no fun in Guadalcanal. Zero. It was from the sack, to the line, to the chow hall, to the sack again. That was it." Charlie Stimpson, a VF-11 fighter pilot, decided he did not like Enander's first name and asked, "Would you mind if I called you Tim?" The name stuck. Kermit was called Tim Enander for the rest of his life. Enander had enlisted in the Navy on the advice of his father, a veteran of the Great War. Navy life seemed preferable to Army life on the ground. His thoughts were also of ships with beds: "What happens to me, I'm in Guadalcanal in a tent city by the Marines, sleeping on a cot and eating chow at a Marine mess hall."[16] Assistant Secretary of the Navy Artemus Gates commented that the living conditions were worse than those of "sharecropper's establishments in the less enlightened parts of the deep South." During the duration of Eleven's stay on Guadalcanal, conditions improved as U.S. Navy Seabees crushed coral for roads and walking paths and added new construction to include an improved kitchen and shower areas. The latter was a vast improvement over water hand-pumped out of barrels.[17]

On the other side of the world, a member of the fledgling 8th Air Force compared his living conditions to those in the Pacific: "Somewhere out there a war was going on, and it seemed worse than ours. . . . We would read Stars and

Stripes, put pins in our wall map showing where our Pacific and North African forces were digging foxholes and eating K rations. We got shot at, same as they did, but after we landed, we could go to a pub . . . and talk to young English girls." The frontline view of the war depended largely on time and theater.[18]

WASHING MACHINE CHARLIE

Washing Machine Charlie was a crude and rudimentary Japanese attempt to disrupt American sleep schedules: by flying a twin-engine bomber aircraft that had its engines out of sync and thus sounded like a washing machine. This was not a nightly occurrence, but it occurred often enough to cause discomfort to the men trying to catch some much-needed sleep:

> The more or less frequent alarms in the night with the melancholy moan of the siren and the reel rockets crashing in on the peaceful slumber of weary men became a fixture in the routine of life at Guadalcanal. Once, twice, three and sometimes four times a night (and, of course, often not at all) there would be the sleepy fumbling for shoes and pants, the groggy groping for the outside, the fruitless peering up through the coconut trees to the sky where sometimes the searchlights would play and the excitement of the moment when they would catch in their shafts the small outline of a twin-engine bomber.[19]

Dick Miralles noted that "Washing Machine Charlie was a nuisance raid. It was pulled every night by the Japanese. And during the air raids we went to our personal foxholes that we had dug. So that's where we went during the air raids. You never knew if they was just gonna make a noise or drop a bomb. So you had to be ready to go to the foxhole."[20]

The men of the outfit developed a difference of opinions about whether to seek shelter in a foxhole or simply remain in the sack, giving over to providence their chances of survival. The two sides to the same coin developed into something of a religious holy war according to intelligence officer Lt. Don Meyer: "The adherents to the religion of the foxhole were led by 'Chief Easterling,' long a proponent of the foxhole religion became a veritable high priest of the cult. Others became sincere and devout believers. As time went by, some of the more youthful converts began to back slide a bit in their devotion to the foxhole, but their stalwart elders . . . continued to keep the faith." Many others became "devout practitioners."[21]

During one bombing raid, Miralles made a decision he would almost come to regret: "One night I'm not gonna get up, so I stayed in bed. Pretty soon one of the guys in the [foxhole] hollered, 'Dick, you better get out of there.' So I jumped up and was just in the entrance, the final entrance into the shelter, and a bomb went off, a 100-pound bomb, and it through [*sic*] me bodily right through the air about eight feet and I landed on three guys sittin' across the thing. So from that time on, I got out of bed and went to the shelter."[22]

In reality, there were many "Charlies," as the nuisance aircraft pilot was known, but one in particular had apparently been employed as a San Francisco cab driver prior to the war and spoke reasonably good English. During his raids, he often contacted the airfield operators at Henderson Field. According to George Gay, "There were loudspeakers all over the area and these chats were aired for everybody's benefit." What Charlie relayed to the men on Guadalcanal is lost to history.[23]

"Religious" preferences aside, the bombings were not always inaccurate or merely a nuisance. Don Meyer wrote in his diary, "On May 19 came a grisly affirmation of the wisdom of taking cover when enemy planes were overhead. Eight men were killed in their bunks when 'daisy-cutters' fell in the Lunga Point area." After that, the devotion to the religion of the foxhole increased with a fervor.[24]

● OPERATIONS FROM GUADALCANAL

CVG-11 went ashore, operating under ComAirSols. The command was a true combined and coalition organization headquartered in the Solomon Islands. The "cactus air force" of Allied airpower that operated on Guadalcanal during the height of that campaign was absorbed into the larger ComAirSols with members including the U.S. Navy, Marine Corps, Army Air Forces, and the Royal New Zealand Air Force.

John W. Fike, a member of VT-11, described in his memoir *The Deadly Green* Carrier Wing Eleven's operating area:

> The emerald jewels of the Solomon Islands stretch in a split band from New Ireland and New Britain in the northwest chain to San Cristobal

> in the southeast end of the chain. In the middle of the chain there are two major islands: Bougainville—nearest the northwest end—and Guadalcanal—nearest the southeast end. The space in between the two chains was called "the Slot," due to its open run from Bougainville to Guadalcanal. As one flies over these waters, various shades of green are encountered. The water itself turns into various shades of green, from the dark blue-green of the deep water—shadowed by passing clouds—to the yellow-green of the water washing up on the white sands of virginal beaches bathed in bright, unpolluted sunlight. The foliage of the islands is a dark, forest green.[25]

Opposing CVG-11 and the other members of AirSols was the Japanese 11th Air Fleet at sea under the command of Vice Admiral Jinichi Kusaka and the Fourth Air Army under Lieutenant General Kumaichi Teramoto headquartered at Rabaul. The Japanese reinforced their air bases at Munda and at nearby Vila on Kolombangara. VT-11 pilot Edwin M. Hughes noted that now that Guadalcanal was secure, "The campaign was on against the Russell Islands, which was 50 miles north, and up the slot, defending islands like, Kolombangara, Munda, Choiseul, and right up the slot, right up to the base on Bougainville. Our main duty was to contain the Japanese fleet, from reinforcing Guadalcanal, or reinforcing Russell Island. And to neutralize the bases in Bougainville." Many of the daytime operations sent the torpedo and bomb squadrons to the airfield and the bivouac areas on Munda Island about 150 miles north of Guadalcanal in preparation for a future amphibious invasion.[26]

Munda had an operational airfield and a nearby area where roughly six thousand to seven thousand Japanese troops were billeted. The squadron commander of VT-11 noted that the operations to Munda became a "milk run," and since the Japanese had no fighters at the airfield, the members of VF-11 did not tag along

● APRIL

The air group's first combat mission was flown from Henderson Field and Fighter One as part of CVG-11 on April 29 in a strike against Munda Airfield and Kolombangara. The strike consisted of six TBFs of VT-11, six SBDs of

VB-21, two other SBDs of strike command (acting as identification aircraft for the strike), four Marine F4Us, and sixteen fighters from VF-11. The mix of aircraft and squadrons suggests the difficulty in knowing how many aircraft were in a particular strike or even what unit they were from. On this first mission, the TBFs carried four five-hundred-pound bombs and not torpedoes. One of the fighter squadron's histories noted that during the first strike, the pilots viewed "for the first time the subtle malevolence of [anti-aircraft] intended and directed with unkind intentions."[27]

The attack on the morning of April 29 was the first taste of battle for most of the members of the squadron, and for Lt. William "Bill" Strahan, it was almost his last. He released a bomb from his SBD at three thousand feet and started his pull-out from the bombing run. A well-placed Japanese anti-aircraft shell burst near his plane, and the inexperienced Strahan yanked so hard on his control stick that he momentarily blacked out from the G forces. The uncontrolled aircraft rolled over and began plummeting toward the ground. Luckily for Strahan, gunner George Molloy started shouting for all he was worth, "Pull out, Mr. Strahan! Pull out!" This was enough for Strahan to instinctively pull back. As his greyed-out vision started to return, he realized how close to the ground he was as his view was filled with palm trees. It was a narrow escape for the bomber pilot, and he credited George Molloy with saving his life.[28]

Other than Strahan's close call, "the attack was carried out as ordered." The two planes from strike command marked the target and the SBDs rolled in first from 9,500 feet, dropped their bombs, and executed the necessary pull-up maneuvers. Next, the TBFs flew in column and dropped their bombs from a height of two thousand feet. The fighters then strafed the target area. The first strike report was as mundane as a combat mission report could be: "Mission: Bomb Village . . . believed to be site of enemy installations. Load: 4 x 500 lb. bombs. Take-Off: 0600–0613. Landed: 1027–1031 . . . and all planes returned safely."[29]

This began a routine of near-daily operations for the next three months ending on July 17. For VF-11, this included having "eight planes on alert at 0530" and another set of fighters prepared for a prearranged mission. Mission types included "knucklehead patrol," "local patrol," "dumbo escort," and "ship cover," but they were not seeking out and engaging Japanese fighters. VF-11 members started to chafe at what they viewed as a collar holding them back.[30]

One new member of VT-11 was George H. Gay Jr., whose exploits at Midway were, even at this time, well known (his actions later featured prominently in the 1975 and 2019 films *Midway*). Gay had joined the torpedo squadron at its formation in Alameda in October 1942, where he received his Navy Cross at the squadron's commissioning. The citation noted,

> Grimly aware of the hazardous consequences of flying without fighter protection, and with insufficient fuel to return to his carrier, Ensign Gay, resolutely, and with no thought of his own life, delivered an effective torpedo attack against violent assaults of enemy Japanese aircraft and against an almost solid barrage of anti-aircraft fire. His courageous action, carried out with a gallant spirit of self-sacrifice and a conscientious devotion to the fulfillment of his mission, was a determining factor in the defeat of the enemy forces and was in keeping with the highest traditions of the United States Naval Service.[31]

Gay was now an "old hand" and combat veteran at the age of twenty-six. He provided a calming presence and reassurance to those untested in VT-11: "Another question I was asked quite often was, 'Aren't you worried about all those bullets with your name on them?' My reply was, 'I figure those were used up at Midway. The ones I worry about are marked "Miscellaneous" or "To whom it may concern." Those things have no conscience at all.' " Gay's participation in various raids with VT-11 is indicative of operations at that time. Between April 26 and July 17, Gay flew twenty-one combat missions, including attacks against runways, shipping in the Kahili Harbor, support to landing operations at Rendova, nighttime mine-laying operations, and daytime shipping strikes.[32]

The TBFs had an early radar as well as the range needed to reach the end of the slot and the targets in the New Georgia Islands. As opposed to similar aircraft used by the Japanese, the American aircraft were rugged. VT-11 squadron commander Fred Ashworth recounted that on a raid made up toward Japanese shipping at anchor at Bougainville Island, one of the TBFs received a significant hit during the glide-bombing attack: "One of my planes came back with one side of his horizontal tail surface gone right up to the fuselage and with a big hole in his rudder. He pulled out of that and flew back to Henderson Field and landed with no trouble." To add insult to the anti-aircraft artillery hit, the same pilot, Bill Hirsch, was jumped by two Japanese Zekes and also received a significant number of bullet holes in the airframe, causing Ashworth to note that "the plane was a pretty sturdy machine."[33]

Ashworth's aircraft received damage on the same raid. After landing and unstrapping, his plane captain and maintenance officer climbed up on the wing and informed Ashworth he had received some major damage. Ashworth had not noticed anything amiss during the mission but climbed out to see a hole in the engine cowling. Further examination showed that the bullet had passed between a "couple of rocker boxes and struck one of the major joints in the engine mount where several of the members are welded together." The joint was destroyed, and the round deflected and passed out through the side of the fuselage and then through the wing, leaving a traceable route back through the aircraft. Ashworth thought it had been a 20-millimeter round that had passed through the engine, siding, and wing but had not exploded during its trajectory. Ashworth said, "If you were to trace its path until it hit the engine mount, it was headed right for my head. And I didn't even know it." Perhaps Ashworth summed up the feelings of every man in VT-11 when he recalled decades later, "I'll buy a Grumman airplane any time."[34]

Missions for VB-11 and VT-11 seemed promising, but the flyers of VF-11 felt left out, believing "that all of the Japanese forces had been disposed of before we arrived, that we would go through our tour without ever seeing one." On May 12, a large collection of "bogeys" was sighted, but instead of VF-11, ComAirSols sent the Marines and their F4U Corsairs out to engage the Japanese. Don Meyer noted, "There were cries of 'favoritism' and dark innuendo that all was not kosher with the Marine-run Fighter Command." The fighter pilots began to doubt the possibility of seeing combat and their own abilities.[35]

VB-11 started their combat operations on April 30 with a strike against Vila airfield. A wide assortment of munitions could be loaded underneath the aircraft depending on the mission: a one-thousand-pound bomb in the centerline, four five-hundred-pound bombs, or twelve one-hundred-pound bombs. A unit history noted two strikes on May 4 and one on May 5, continuing from there against the targets at Vila airfield, Vanga Vanga, and Ringi Cove and against ships in the Blackett Strait. The tactics VB-11 used never wavered: "Using the six-plane division composed of three two plane sections. Attacks were made from 12,000 feet, high speed approach pushing over at 10,000 feet, interval between planes was approximately six seconds." VB-11's tactics also remained the same whether the target was on land or at sea.[36]

Ensign Edwin Hughes was a torpedo pilot but remembered the bombers would "shove over at about 12,000 feet, and would dive in column, dropping a 2,000 pound." On one of the first raids, the members of VB-11 and VT-11 experimented with a two-thousand-pound "daisy cutter," as the aircrews called it (not to be confused with the larger, more modern bomb of the same name). The bomb had a delayed fuse that exploded about two seconds after it contacted the earth—as opposed to most other bombs, which had fuses set for hundredths of a second. This allowed the daisy cutter to penetrate the ground before it exploded, creating an enormous crater and leveling everything above ground.[37]

While the early hunting was good for VT-11 and VB-11, the same was not holding true for the fighters of VF-11. VB-11, VB-21, and VT-11 were able to settle into a relatively good routine and carried out missions for which they had spent the many previous months training. Meyer noted, "The belief was now prevalent that VF-11 would never meet the Jap in combat, that even if they did come over, the Marines with their F4U's would get the nod. A persecution complex slowly but surely made its first small appearance among some of the pilots. The burden of the complex was that VF-11 was earmarked for the drudgery, the labor battalion of the air, so to speak, while the marine glamor boys got all the gravy."[38]

MAY

The existing after-action reports—actually "U.S. Aircraft—Action with Enemy"—for VB-11 detailed bombing missions for May 3, 4, 6, 8, 10, 11, 12, 17, and 25. VT-11 and VF-11 posted similar dates. This indicated the ongoing back-and-forth effort between the United States and Japan as they attempted to exert dominance in the South Pacific. The Guadalcanal campaign was over, but action over and around the island and islands to the north certainly was not. May also marked the first losses for CVG-11. George Retelas noted that on May 5, VT-11 returned all of its planes to the island with no losses, but damage to the aircraft had started to mount: "T-14 tail shot off, T-8 bilge shot up, T-5 Bullet holes in wing . . . gunner and radioman wounded." One of the interesting aspects of operations around Guadalcanal was that being shot down or forced to land was not necessarily a death sentence. Many members of CVG-11 who crashed, bailed out, or landed in the water or on one of the islands successfully made their way back to Guadalcanal. In the coming months, many members of the air group bailed out or ditched their aircraft and began arduous journeys back to their base.[39]

● THE SAGA OF LT. (JG) ROBERT MAXWELL

On the afternoon of May 2, VF-11 experienced its first loss. Sixteen F4F Wildcats of VF-11 rumbled down the airstrip on Fighter One and departed Guadalcanal. While headed toward the target at Munda near East Island, the F4F Wildcat piloted by Lt. (jg) William Robert "Maxie" Maxwell collided with the F4F piloted by Lt. Cdr. Raymond "Sully" Vogel, the squadron's executive officer. The aircraft were "stepped down" and separated by approximately ten feet, with Maxwell on Vogel's left wing. Suddenly, one of Vogel's wing tanks ran dry and his aircraft dipped, losing altitude; in the process, he dropped out of Maxwell's sight. Losing sight of aircraft is extremely dangerous but even more so in close formation flying. With Vogel somewhere below him, Maxwell flew straight and level, waiting for Vogel to pop back up into the formation. When Vogel failed to reappear, Maxwell motioned to the plane on his left to slide farther out so Maxwell could slip left and look for Vogel. As soon as he started to move to the left, he felt a jarring collision as Vogel's aircraft below him slipped up into his underbelly. Maxwell recalled,

> My plane went out of control and I threw back the hood at once, the plane nosed up in a half loop and it was on its back. I loosened my safety belt. By the time I had it loose the plane had fallen off, right side up, in a flat leaf-like spin. I climbed up on the seat, put my right foot on the cockpit side and tried to jump out, but was held back by my oxygen mask and radio

> gear. I gave another lunge and everything broke free—the mask came off and the headphone cord broke loose from the box—and in a fraction of a second I had found and pulled the ripcord. The opening of the chute snapped me up short and I was able to look around and see my plane falling in two pieces—the tail section and about 6 feet of fuselage was drifting crazily downward and the fore part fluttering down like a leaf.[40]

The collision occurred at an altitude of fourteen thousand feet and at about 1600 in the afternoon, meaning that evening and darkness were not far off. It was later determined that when Maxwell began his move to the left above Vogel, the propeller of Vogel's plane severed the tail of Maxwell's aircraft, causing Maxwell to immediately lose control and forcing his bailout. Vogel made it safely back to the airfield at Fighter One, landing around 1730. An inspection revealed "a bent propeller, crushed cockpit canopy, twisted gun sight, and rubber marks, apparently from Maxwell's tail wheel, across the right wing."

An incoming storm delayed Vogel's landing upon his return to base and thus delayed the reporting of Maxwell's bailout; this same storm would soon cause considerable problems for Maxwell. CVG-11 members immediately dispatched reports from their headquarters at Fighter One and Henderson Field to other units in the area and to the coast watcher stations up and down the slot: "Bob Maxwell plane downed in aircraft collision with flight lead" and "Pilot Maxwell down at 1540 today. He was later seen in rubber boat near East Island west of Vangu." Due to the weather and the approaching gloom of evening, no aircraft departed to search for Maxwell; he was on his own for the time being.

The other members of VF-11 continued on their mission to attack Munda. About an hour later, they were returning to the base when they spotted Maxwell paddling his rescue raft. At about 1700 Maxwell was somewhere between Vangunu, Nggatokae, Rendova, and Tetepare Islands in the Blanche Channel.[41]

After jumping from his aircraft, Maxwell serenely floated toward the emerald and blue waters below. He landed in the water, disengaged himself from his parachute, and grabbed his raft from the contents of his survival equipment. He had lost his pump and had to inflate his raft orally. Having done this successfully, he climbed aboard and took stock of his situation. In his possession he had the following items:

- two railroad hand flares
- one fifty-four-inch-square sail
- six Army type "O" rations
- one jackknife
- one container with three fish hooks, three pork rinds, two lead sinkers, two wire leaders, and about fifty feet of line
- one waterproof match case with compass on top
- one headset
- one twenty-seven-ounce canteen
- one sheath and knife and a .45 caliber pistol.

Maxwell also had two additional kits of gear. The first was a first aid kit, which was supposed to contain

- one small can of zinc oxide (an ointment to treat minor cuts and burns)
- one small can of petroleum jelly
- one small can of sulfathiazole pills (used to treat infections and an anti-microbial)
- one small can of quinine pills (anti-malarial)
- two bandages
- one bottle of iodine
- three packages of sulfanilamide powder (anti-bacterial)
- one sling cloth
- three morphine syrettes
- One roll of gauze
- six safety pins
- one set of instructions for use of sulphathiazole, sulfanilamide, and quinine
- one roll of adhesive tape (Maxwell believed this was "omitted accidentally from my kit").

Finally, and probably most importantly given his current situation, Maxwell had his survival raft containing glove-type paddles, rubber plugs, a dye sea marker, patching equipment, and one twelve-ounce can of water.[42]

Bob Maxwell now floated alone in the Pacific Ocean. Taking stock of his situation, he realized his injuries were relatively minor: one gash to his chin and another to his right shin. He applied sulfanilamide powder and placed one of the compress bandages on his ankle (it was here he noticed the absence of adhesive tape to keep the bandage in place). An hour or so after floating in the water, the members of VF-11 passed him on their way home. Maxwell signed with his mirror and received a welcome "wing rock" in return. At least VF-11 knew he was alive and roughly where he was. While this was good news, the approaching black cumulus clouds were not. Maxwell spent the night in the throes of a torrential storm, bailing water as best he could and huddling low under his sail for protection.

Maxwell spent the next day (May 3) paddling for land and praying he was not blown out to sea. The storm had ruined any chance that a rescue plane might return to the location where his squadron mates had spotted him the day before. "By four in the afternoon my forearms were raw and chafed from the friction with the sides of the raft as I rowed. Only two or three times during the day I had stopped paddling momentarily to eat a bite of chocolate and take a swallow of water." Overhead, aircraft from both the U.S. and Japanese forces moved back and forth to their intended targets. The rest of May 3 and all the next day, Maxwell continued to paddle in hopes of reaching the island of Tetepare on the southern side of the Solomon Islands. After that, there was nothing but open water to his south. Steady winds and high seas kept him moored in place and hindered him from making any progress until the morning of May 5, when the winds finally gave him a chance of making landfall. By that evening, he was finally in a position to make it to shore.

Despite being at sea for three days, the most dangerous part of Maxwell's journey was still in front of him. Around 1800 by his estimation and as the tide moved him toward shore, he observed towering waves capable of capsizing a good-sized boat and certain to destroy his meager life raft. Maxwell recalled the "waves were at least fifty feet high, the biggest surf I've ever seen." Too late to turn back, Maxwell held on for the ride, completely powerless to turn away or escape. Riding the first wave in, Maxwell felt as if he was well above the island. As that wave broke, Maxwell was on its backside, ahead of the crash. He was not so lucky for the following wave: "I could see in front of me was the jagged coral of the beach. I tried to beat the next one in but it caught me just after it broke and tossed me end over kettle into the coral. Fortunately, I missed hitting the sharpest coral and received only a few cuts on my hands. My boat landed about 50 feet away in sort of a channel leading into the beach."[43]

Soaking wet, Maxwell made it to shore, pulled his raft and sail over him, and fell into a fitful sleep. May 6 dawned to find the VF-11 fighter pilot turned into Robinson Crusoe: "I had my usual 'breakfast' of a chocolate bar, laid out my things to dry, cleaned my knife and gun as best I could, and rested some more." May 7: "Packed all my gear in my backpack, rolled up my life raft and set out to walk along the coast to the west end of the island." May 8: "Most of the time I walked in the water up to my knees and soon the coral ledge ended and I had to strike inland because I couldn't get through the immense surf that was washing against the high rock and coral of the shore. I would go inland a little way, parallel the coast clambering up and down the ridges, and then go back to the shore to see if I could make my way along it." May 9: "I was always hopeful that I would be able to make my way along the coast, but this was impossible. During the day I ate some fern leaves and the remainder of my last chocolate bar." May 10: "I was near the end of the island and could see Rendova about 2 or 3 miles across the channel. In the shallow water I found two small crabs and about eight mussels. I ate the crabs raw and putting the mussels in my pocket headed for a small bay. It was a fine afternoon and built a lean-to of sticks and palm fronds and blew up my raft."[44]

On May 12 Bob Maxwell prepared to strike out for the island of Rendova to the west and contact the Australian coast watchers there: "I washed my clothes and set about making some oars. I found a couple of small pieces of lumber with a few nails and a screw in them and using the nails and a screw I attached two sticks to the pieces of lumber and had a serviceable pair of oars." He spent the rest of the day preparing the raft and his equipment for his return to sea; at least this time his destination was a close one of only a little over a mile away. Maxwell had now spent ten days completely alone, cut off entirely from his squadron, the war, and the rest of the world.[45]

The next morning, Maxwell struck out again: "With the meat of two coconuts and my canteen of water as provisions, I set out early in the morning on my voyage to Rendova." By noon he was ashore, enduring the same rough surf close to the beach, but this time when he surfaced, "I heard someone shouting and was overjoyed to see two natives in a canoe about 50 yards off shore waving to me." Although "rescued," Maxwell's journey was still far from over. The natives rowed him around the island, where they finally arrived at a village near Buruka about halfway up the east coast of Rendova. Maxwell emerged from his rescuers' canoe and was greeted by "Chief Pendoro," who asked him in good English if he wanted to send a message to a nearby coast watcher station. Maxwell penned a short note, which the chief handed to one of Maxwell's rescuers, and off the local man went through the island's interior. While waiting, Maxwell feasted on pineapple and taro and was given a place to sleep in a corner of a low platform along with a clean bamboo mat, a soft pillow, and a blanket. After resting, Maxwell spoke with villagers and with the chief's son, Abraham, who had been to the mission school at Munda and was quite interested in hearing Maxwell's stories and of his life in America. After dark it was back to sleep in the company of the chief, his sons, daughter, and several other small children in the hut.[46]

Bob Maxwell spent two more days with this group of natives and finally received a note from a local coast watcher on May 15: "Dear Maxwell, Very glad to hear you are O.K. My radio is out of action or I would have heard about you and sent for you, as it is, I am sending food and cigarettes and a constable to take you to the next place where you can be taken back to Cactus. Hope you have a good trip. Yours sincerely, Horton." Finally on May 16, after a fifteen-day journey, Lt. (jg) Bob Maxwell clambered aboard a PBY and returned to Cactus 1.[47]

A month later his story was featured in the Wausau, Wisconsin, *Daily Record Herald*, under the headline " 'Bob' Maxwell: Survivor of Grim Gamble with Death":

> It is felt that Lt. Maxwell's ultimate return to the squadron was due in large part of his own resourcefulness and intelligent utilization of the equipment which he had with him. The fact that he knew where he was and where he was most apt to find assistance enabled him to pursue a definite objective and save himself much futile and aimless wandering and mental distress. He knew that if he could make contact with the natives he would be all right. His first goal was to reach land, then to make his way to where he knew there were friendly natives. If such an

experience can ever be called fortunate, it was perhaps opportune that Lt.(jg) Maxwell was the person to have it inasmuch as he is the Squadron Parachute Officer and was thoroughly familiar with the 'chute, backpack, rubber boat, and other gear. Appended hereto is an inventory of the equipment which he had with him when he bailed out, along with his comments and recommendations with respect to the various items.[48]

● A "TYPICAL MISSION"

The day after Maxwell began his sojourn, VB-11, VT-11, and VF-11 all hit targets on Rekata Point on Saint Isabel Island. This strike was probably fairly typical of operations from Guadalcanal as far as force composition was concerned: fourteen SBDs, twelve TBFs, and sixteen F4Fs, all from CVG-11. Along for the strike were U.S. Army Air Forces P-38s, P-40s, and one B-24 as well as twelve Marine F4Us—seventy-one aircraft in all. That day's mission was providing fighter support for an attack force composed of twelve TBFs from VT-11, and fourteen VB-11 and VB-21 bombers. Marine F4Us strafed Japanese anti-aircraft positions, allowing VT-11 and VB-11 to drop their bombs relatively free of interference. Each member of VB-11 carried a one-thousand-pound daisy cutter. The VB-11 aircrews nosed over from ten thousand feet in their seventy-degree dive, full flaps out. Bomb release occurred at 2,000 to 2,500 feet, followed by the G-inducing pullout at one thousand feet. Following the bombing, the F4Us strafed the area.[49]

A VT-11 after-action report from that mission noted, "After crossing the southern coast of Isabel Island, the force took interval, with the strafing F4Us going in first to neutralize the reported A/A positions, the SBDs following and dive-bombing the heavy A/A positions at the tip of the peninsula and on Papatura Point, and the TBFs going into a wide S-turn to delay and permit the SBDs to complete their attack. The TBFs then attacked in column from seven o'clock and the axis of the road bisecting the peninsula."[50]

VF-11's first casualty came on Thursday, May 6 (since Maxwell had been spotted the day of his loss floating in his raft, he was not considered a casualty or even missing in action) when Ens. Leroy W. "Winnie" Childs' aircraft fell out of formation over Munda. No radio communications or indications of trouble came from Childs. His Wildcat just slowly descended, started to leak smoke, and disappeared. The same natives who would later rescue Maxwell saw the aircraft hit the water but also reported seeing a parachute. They rowed out to the location, but found no sign of Childs. Squadron mates remembered Childs as "intelligent, amiable, and well-liked."[51]

E. Howard Hunt joined the group on May 18 and flew with Lt. George Gay on a mine-laying operation up the slot. Hunt—already the author of *East of Farewell*, a 1942 book about the convoys across the North Atlantic based loosely on his own experiences on the destroyer USS *Mayo*—now turned his attention to the war in the Pacific and later authored the book *Limit of Darkness* about his experiences with VT-11 on Guadalcanal. The book, released in 1944 and dedicated to "the men who flew from Henderson," followed the lives of five—fictional—members of the squadron through the twenty-four hours leading up to a strike up the slot that, predictably, some would not return from. Although the characters in the book are not meant to represent anyone "living or dead," the characters are clearly connected to the men whom Hunt observed and flew with at Guadalcanal. For example, Lt. (jg) Ben Lambert, "survivor of the battle of Midway," is clearly Gay, while the commanding officer and executive officer in the book—both Naval Academy graduates—are stand-ins for Ashworth and Turner. As the book was one of the first published during the war relating to the events in the faraway Pacific, it was a hit. The *New York Times* called it "one of the few superior works of fiction about Americans in Combat."[52]

On May 23 two Japanese ships made a run from Bougainville to New Georgia under cover of darkness and an overhead storm. This mini-convoy did not go unnoticed. The men of VT-11 were awakened at 0200 and were in their TBF Avengers ready to launch by 0345. That early morning the men of VT-11 remembered, "The rain was coming down as nowhere else on earth. It was a cold rain and made all of us shiver." A few hours later, they were on their way to the strike. They pushed over into a sixty-five-degree angle at about 6,500 feet. Inside one of the Avengers, bilge man John Fike remembered hearing a very loud popping noise as if his gun had misfired. He cleared the chamber, and an unused round dropped out. This indicated the noise had not come from his weapon, so he began looking around the compartment for its source. As Fike scoured his area, the plane pulled out of the steep glide and settled into straight and level flight at five thousand feet. Fike recalled hearing the pilot shouting something over the intercom, but his attention was internal to his compartment and not on listening to the pilot. Just then, the other crewmember, the Avenger's gunner, came down out of the turret, hit Fike on the shoulder, and pointed to the port wing. Next to the folding joint, in the thick, stubby "root" of the wing, Fike saw a "ragged hole about a foot in diameter, two feet from the trailing edge, spitting bluish-white fire." The aluminum wing was clearly in the process of melting, and pieces of it broke away toward the tail surface and the horizontal stabilizers. This caused a piece of the tail to catch fire and melt its leading edge. Fike then heard the pilot's voice come over the intercom: "Jump, boys, jump! It may blow—JUMP!"[53]

Fike began unhooking himself from his equipment and reached for the handle that would release a hatch to the world outside. The hatch refused to open. The tail gunner joined Fike in pulling on the handle, but to no effect. In desperation, Fike put his shoulder into the hatch and shoved with all his might while the tail gunner placed his boots against Fike and pushed. The hatch gave way, and Fike hurtled into the air above the Japanese-held base at Munda. Exiting the aircraft proved to be the easy part of the ordeal that was unfolding around him: "There I was alone, looking down on the Japanese airfield at Munda, heavy grey clouds around me, anti-aircraft bursts going off over the field, and smoke from several huge fires beginning to billow."[54]

Immediately after landing in the water, Fike came under fire from Japanese soldiers on the shore of New Georgia, and he wisely decided to swim away from the airfield. Unlike Maxwell, Fike had not departed his aircraft with any survival gear, and he thought ruefully after he landed that he now had no protection from either the Japanese or the jungle. Fike fought against the massive swells and valleys of the surf around New Georgia. Surviving the surf rapidly took second place when "I felt something rubbing against my left leg, and then, I realized it was a shark. A large shark. A very large shark. We had been taught in Hawaii, during a one-hour survival lecture that a shark was like a little puppy-dog. All you had to do was clap your hands under water and scream and yell, and the shark would go away." In Fike's case, this worked, and he returned his concentration to making landfall as far away from Munda as possible. Fike was saved from sharks and surf by five natives in two canoes, who pulled alongside and hoisted him into one of the boats: "Imagine the thoughts of a southern young man, 12,000 miles from Alabama, being saved by five black men."[55]

Fike's plane had been shot up. He had parachuted out but did not see his comrades, had been shot at by the Japanese, had two encounters with sharks, was picked up by locals, escaped a Japanese patrol, and finally arrived at a coast watcher's house only to be told,

> The pilot acknowledged that he told you to jump, and was very sorry that he had to stay with the plane when the gunner couldn't get out, but then the fire went out, and the gunner, not being able to hear because his intercom line was disconnected, almost jumped anyway when the pilot dived the plane down to the surface of the water to put out any fire that might be in the wing. Both got back all right, and the fire was hydraulic fluid and not gasoline. He further says he is tremendously relieved that you're all right, and the gunner and he both are waiting for you to get back. They send their best.[56]

During the time spent making the trek back to Henderson Field, Fike had contracted a disease and was running a fever. Medical personnel evacuated him to a hospital, and he missed his opportunity to go on R&R with his squadron on June 8. This would prove to be a blessing in disguise for Fike.

The raids for CVG-11 continued unabated through the rest of May. VT-11 pilots conducted the first daylight raids on Bougainville in the Solomon Islands. They flew patrol, search, spotting, strike, and night mine-laying missions. Their official unit history noted strikes against Vila airfield, Kahili Harbor, and other shipping targets. On May 19 TBF Avengers from VT-11 and from Marine Scout Bomber Squadron 143 damaged *Houn Maru* and forced the ship to run aground off southern Bougainville. Also in May, VT-11 began night operations, and this was also when the torpedo squadron had its first casualties of the war. During night mine laying operations on May 19, James Loring Sweetser, Nelson Lee Whitehead, and Lloyd George Cramer were declared missing in action. Two nights later, another crew went missing in action: Harry Thomas Brown, Joe Lewis Harper, and James Walter Tinsley.[57]

CHAPTER 3

OPERATION CARTWHEEL AND BOUGAINVILLE

June proved to be a month of major operations, not just for CVG-11, but also across the Pacific Theater. Operation Cartwheel, Gen. Douglas MacArthur's advance toward Rabaul, began late in the month. Forces from two separate areas, MacArthur's Southwest Pacific Area and Admiral Halsey's South Pacific Area, both had operations scheduled to begin this month. Under MacArthur, Operation Chronicle looked to begin operations with invasions of Woodlark Island and the Kiriwina Islands. Operation Toenails, better remembered as the New Georgia Campaign, began on June 21 with the first landings at Segi Point, New Georgia. A week later, forces went ashore at Vangunu on June 30 and again on the northern side of New Georgia July 3–5. As Marines and Soldiers waded ashore (Chronicle and Southwest Pacific Area were Army operations; Toenails and New Georgia were Marine Corps operations), VB-11 stood ready to knock out any enemy strongpoints giving the troops on the ground considerable trouble. This included a strike against heavy gun positions at Viru Harbor on July 1. These operations continued until CVG-11 departed the combat area in July. Shortly after CVG-11 left, across the globe in Quebec City, Franklin

Roosevelt and Winston Churchill were making the decision to bypass Rabaul rather than conduct another invasion. MacArthur objected, of course, but he need not have. As the Allies marched up the Solomons and around Rabaul, they destroyed Japanese airpower and severed the Japanese lines of communications in the process. Rabaul was left to wither on the vine.[1]

The first half of June found the entire air group flying numerous missions in anticipation and preparation for the New Georgia campaign. The island, slated for invasion in late June, sat just northwest of Guadalcanal. On June 5 eighteen TBFs of Torpedo Squadron 11 launched a daylight strike against Japanese shipping around Shortland Island (just south of Bougainville) as part of an attack that included SBDs of VB-21. This was to be the first daylight strike against targets in and around Bougainville. To give the VB-21 SBDs the required flying time and enough gas for their trip to the target and back to base, the mechanics of CVG-11 took wing tanks intended for the F4Fs and rigged them to the SBDs. The extra wing tank and fuel cut down on the number of bombs used for the strike. The increase in fuel necessitated a decrease in tonnage. So, each SBD was load-limited to a single five-hundred-pound bomb. Again, the combined and multi-national command of AirSols saw this mission launch with an additional twenty-four Army Air Forces (AAF) P-40s. Fighters from the Royal New Zealand Air Force led the way and made a sweep of Kahili in front of VT-11 and VB-21. The bombers and torpedo planes also found themselves escorted by the Marine F4Us.[2]

The mission was beset with problems from the time the aircraft started lifting off Guadalcanal. Eleven of the thirty-two F4Us turned back, which limited their effectiveness. The Corsairs meant to escort and suppress enemy anti-aircraft artillery instead opened the bombers and torpedo planes to an increased attack from the Japanese. The strike from CVG-11 lasted only ten minutes, and while results were promising, losses were high. Two SBDs of VB-21 did not return to base. The first, piloted by Lt. (jg) C. T. Larsen with gunner Aviation Machinist's Mate Third Class Ose Veesey in aircraft number B-15, crash-landed in the Russell Islands. The second aircraft, flown by Lt. (jg) David Allen Beck with his gunner Aviation Machinist's Mate Third Class Kaini Robert Henderson in S-10, disappeared, although some members of the squadron claimed to have seen the aircraft crash. One VT-11 TBF also went down, and all three crewmembers were declared missing in action. The VT-11 aircraft flown by Lt. (jg) Robert Jefferson Snell crashed with Aviation Radioman Second Class Reginald Leon Drake and Aviation Ordnanceman Second Class Wayne Lowell Wood.

Ose Veesey picks up the story during the attack:

> And so Larsen and I were last. And when we came out of the dive, there were several Zeros waiting for us. The Zeros made pass after pass, and you believe it or not, that Dauntless could move. Old C. T. kept it floorboarded, losing all the Zeros but one. As we went through the trees on Santa Isabel, they got the best of us. They filled us full of holes. Canopy, the pilot's canopy and then the radio direction finder canopy and then my canopy and then the tail. Larsen called me and said, "Ose, we're gonna have to ditch."

Larsen and Veesey ditched the aircraft, got into their raft, rowed for shore, and made contact with a coast watcher almost immediately. Two days later, "we bummed a ride in a canoe loaded with bananas and we started towards Guadalcanal. And during that time we could hear the PBY coming. C. T. got the Very Pistol and started shooting in the air so that they could see the flares. That's how we notified the PBY that we were friends and we were lookin' for a ride, I guess."[3]

The day also began inauspiciously for radioman Dick Miralles. His aircraft caught fire after engine start-up, so his pilot Ensign Hogue and Miralles headed for a spare. However, Miralles was unaware the machine guns in this aircraft were not fully locked into their mounting attachment. In their first dive over Bougainville, the machine gun came loose, and Miralles was ripped from his seat. The SBD was in a nearly vertical dive with Miralles "hanging on with my toes." As Hogue pulled out of the dive, another SBD Dauntless from the squadron went roaring by in a vertical dive with no flaps. It plowed directly into the sea. The crew of Beck and Henderson died on impact.[4]

Pulling out of the dive, Hogue and Miralles knew Japanese anti-aircraft fire had damaged their aircraft by the amount of oil flying around inside the aircraft. Hogue decided to try and make a friendly airfield in the Russell Islands. On their way, two Japanese Zeros attacked them. Miralles recalled that "both [ammunition] belts were all jammed up, so they wouldn't fit through the [machine] gun. I had to do something. I was sittin' there and these guys were comin' in at, so I pulled out radio coils and I was throwin' radio coils at 'em. And I threw the Aldis lamp at 'em, which is a signal lamp. Anything I could get that I could throw, I threw at 'em. I don't know why, but I thought maybe I'd get lucky and hit the pilot or somethin'."[5] For whatever reason, perhaps out of sheer surprise at the American literally throwing pieces of his aircraft at them, the attacking Japanese did not bring the SBD down.[6]

Among the fighters, one American P-40 pilot and two Japanese pilots were killed. With the early June transports to Vila in progress, there was considerable shipping in the area, including four destroyers, but the only loss the Japanese suffered was the 780-ton *Shintoku Maru* and the large barge it was towing. On the positive side, the improvised drop tanks worked, bringing targets at Kahili and Bougainville Island within range of the SBDs. Although this limited the amount of bombs each member of VB-11 or VB-21 carried that far north, it still greatly improved the air group's ability to strike into more distant Japanese territory.[7]

● MINE LAYING

Mine-laying operations were another mission the men of VT-11 conducted. The operation, conducted May 18 and 20, called for the closing of a Japanese anchor spot on the south end of the island of Bougainville. VT-11 laid mines

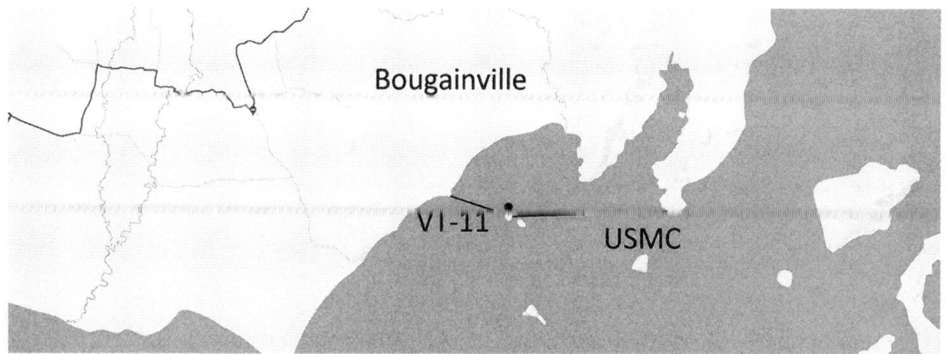

Map 3. Bougainville Mine Laying

from Bougainville to the nearby island of Erventa, and Marine Corps planes dropped mines from Erventa to an area known as "East Point" on Bougainville, thus closing off the harbor. In order to act unhindered by Japanese resistance, the mining operations occurred at night, but only if the moon was a half-moon or greater to allow for visibility. Mine laying was an extraordinarily dangerous operation. Each TBF could carry only one mine; each of the mines had to be dropped at sixty knots from no higher than one hundred feet. In order to seal off the harbor, VT-11 dropped a total of fifty-four Mark XII mines. An initial wave of eighteen planes dropped the first set of mines, followed by two more consecutive nights of two eighteen-ship formations. The first night's operations occurred without prohibitive interference from the Japanese, but the men of VT-11 knew the Japanese would be waiting on subsequent nights. The first night, two aircraft failed to return to Guadalcanal. They belonged to Lt. (jg) John P. Ayres (T-120) and Lt. (jg) James Loring Sweetser (T-111). With Sweetser was Aviation Ordnanceman Third Class Lloyd George Cramer and Aviation Metalsmith First Class Nelson Lee Whitehead. Although the after-action report clearly indicated Ayres did not return, the aircraft and aircrew eventually turned up at Guadalcanal sometime later, and their status was removed from the missing in action lists.[8]

Squadron commander Ashworth noted that "the only navigation we could work out required each pilot to locate visually a point on the shore, take departure from there, fly on the selected course for a calculated number of seconds at the 60-knot required speed, and let the mine go. If done correctly, this would place the mines at the desired interval and fairly accurately in the area required. We also knew full well that the small caliber anti-aircraft guns would very quickly be fully alerted and fire at us." Since the mines had to be dropped at different intervals, each TBF pilot had a different number of seconds on his "leg" to the position where he released his mine, which settled gently into the ocean under a parachute. Ashworth, as the commander, took the longest leg on each operation, one minute and thirty seconds of flying straight and level, at the miserably slow speed of sixty knots and flying at one hundred feet: "This was to be the longest 90 seconds that I had ever known."[9]

Before the second night of mine laying, Ashworth went to see the commanding officer of the strike and search patrol commands of AirSols, Brig.

Gen. Christian Schilt. He asked Schilt to send an AAF B-25 unit based on Guadalcanal ahead of the TBFs to "bomb along the shoreline to suppress the small-caliber fire we were sure to get while we would be planting the mines," since the Japanese were now alerted to the ongoing mining operation. Schilt concurred. Ashworth handed off details of the mission, including timing and the flight profiles, to the B-25 unit. Two nights later, VT-11 departed Guadalcanal and headed for their target on Bougainville. There, they waited for the B-25s to appear and start their bombing run.[10]

On Shortland Island, twenty miles south of the main island of Bougainville, Japanese forces installed a highly effective heavy anti-aircraft battery under the command of a Japanese officer whom someone had nicknamed "the Little Professor." On the second night of mine-laying operations, Fred Ashworth, circling above waiting for the AAF to begin their suppression efforts, noticed the battery on Shortland Island light up with gunfire in his peripheral vision. The squadron scattered in a prearranged dispersing tactic, and no aircraft received any damage. In short order, the B-24s arrived in the company of some additional AAF B-17s, which delivered the requested diversionary attack with good results.

One of the problems with the mining operations was that they occurred under cover of darkness. As losses and deaths mounted in the air group, new replacements arrived to fill the shoes of the lost men, including Lieutenant Sweetser. However, having the replacements fly night operations was dangerous. Even Ashworth admitted to finding himself with his altimeter at zero during these missions. He later recalled, "You can't say, 'Look, Boss, these six pilots do not have adequate training.' 'Why don't they?' 'They just arrived as replacements and were not trained, and we haven't had them long enough to train them.' 'This is war. Do it.' Two or three didn't come back from one of those operations due to weather and darkness. They weren't trained for night flying. They just disappeared. There were two weather fronts to fly through. The old hands had no problem, we were trained for it. I guess that is what commanders are paid for."[11]

As if to buttress the squadron commander's thoughts, shortly after midnight on the last night of mining operations, a small section of four TBFs took off to conduct skip bombing operations near Kahili. Shortly after takeoff, all four aircraft ran into a strong storm front and were separated from each other. The lead element of Lt. (jg) Edwin M. Hughes and Lt. (jg) Raymond B. Cook decided to turn back for Guadalcanal, and despite having been separated, both successfully landed at the airbase at 0207 and 0338, respectively. Meanwhile, Lt. (jg) Martin J. Stack and Lt. (jg) Harry T. Brown continued north before also deciding to turn back. Brown's aircraft was receiving transmissions but could not transmit. Somewhere in the clouds, the two aircraft became separated, and Brown's aircraft simply disappeared. Stack landed at 0722, but Brown "failed to return." No trace of the aircraft or aircrew was ever found, and Brown's name along with those of his crew, Aviation Radioman Second Class Joe Lewis Harper and Aviation Machinist's Mate Third Class James Walter Tinsley Jr., were added to the growing roster of missing in action. In less than a month of action, CVG-11 already had seven losses, with six of those coming from the torpedo squadron.

Actions on June 5 saw another six losses, all reported as missing in action. Eighty-three aircraft, another mix of the squadrons and outside support, launched to attack shipping in the Kahili Island area. Most of the men lost that day never returned, including Lt. (jg) Robert Jefferson Snell, Aviation Radioman Second Class Howard Ely Crain, Aviation Ordnanceman Second Class Wayne Lowell Wood, and Aviation Radioman Second Class Reginald Leon Drake. Members of VT-11 saw Snell's aircraft jumped by four Zekes, but no one saw his plane go down—thus the missing in action status. June 5 also saw the first loss for VS-11/VB-21: Lt. (jg) David Allen Beck and his gunner Radioman Second Class Kaini Robert Henderson.[12]

The men of the air group expected combat losses, but losing comrades in more unexpected ways was always a shock. In the case of VT-11, these losses almost completely destroyed the squadron.

● THE CRASH OF VT-11 R&R PLANE

On June 8, 1943, the air group suffered a tremendous loss in an unusual way. Although in combat for just over a month at this point, air group leaders started to rotate the men to the rear for rest and relaxation (R&R). The men of VT-11 received leave to Australia, and sixteen men from VT-11 clambered aboard a Douglas R4D-5 (the U.S. Navy's variant of the DC-3). Taking off from Guadalcanal, they flew first to the island of New Caledonia, roughly 750 miles east of the Australian continent. While leaving New Caledonia, one of the three transport planes crashed, killing all twenty-four men on board. Included in the casualties were air group commander Weldon L. Hamilton and fifteen pilots and aircrew from VT-11, five full TBF Avenger crews. In one accident, VT-11 lost its commander, 25 percent of its officers, and 10 percent of its enlisted force. A later history noted that the aviators of Eleven considered Hamilton "a man among men and a very fine skipper. He loved the Navy and had an ardent dislike of the Japanese. We can only hope we did enough damage the second tour to satisfy even him."[13]

George Gay was supposed to be on the flight. He had even boarded the plane. Just before the door closed, a jeep roared up, and out hopped Hamilton. He told Gay something had come up and he needed Gay's spot to go on a flight that night. Disappointed, Gay got off and waited twenty-four hours for the next R&R flight. He arrived in Sydney only to learn that the previous night's flight had crashed. Gay's name had not been replaced by Hamilton's on the manifest, and so Gay was presumed dead with the rest of the flight.

The plane had climbed out of Tontouta, New Caledonia, before losing an engine. The pilot, no doubt remaining calm, turned the airplane back toward the field. Flying on board the aircraft in addition to the sixteen members of CVG-11 was Marine Corps Col. Pat Moret, sitting next to the commander of Air Group Eleven. Those killed included Virgil Edmund Flynn, John Clifford Livezey, Paul Edward Babel, Donald Randall Burke, William Robert Weiss, Sidney William Quick, Robert Haywood Barnes, Carl Lee Cobb, Alley Burton Conrad, William Thomas Owens, Bernard Gordon Robinson, Ellwin Albert Teal, Jack Foster Young, and Ordien Fenmore Herr. This was a major tragedy for one squadron to suffer.[14]

Squadron commander Frederick Ashworth remembered hearing the devastating news. Losing pilots and aircrew in combat was expected and part of the job, but losing such a large contingent of his squadron, the men under his command he was responsible for, in this way must have been especially hard on the thirty-one-year-old Ashworth:

> I was in Sydney when I was told about it. That was the plane that I was supposed to go on with my division of pilots and crews. I am not sure

> what I was looking for, but when I learned about it, I found a cathedral, went in to pray, and I suppose, mostly just to think. The resident pastor found me there, and we talked for quite a while. I think that had this taken place in a combat operational situation, the trauma would not have been quite as bad. These things happen and you lose people. But the way this accident happened, it is very hard to rationalize the loss of so many fine people.[15]

A final poignant story bears telling and that is of the group commander Lieutenant Colonel Hamilton. Sometime before the R&R trips to Sydney, the senior leaders of the air group had come into possession of some so-called medicinal whiskey. The whiskey had apparently been confiscated in the United States—from whom and for what purpose remain unknown—and was shipped to units serving in the Pacific. Hamilton ended up with a gallon jug of Old Rocking Chair bourbon whiskey. He had also recently received a letter from his wife saying that his Naval Academy class would soon be eligible for promotion to the rank of commander. Knowing that he might not be able to get a cap with the proper "scrambled eggs" braid, she sent one out to him. The other senior leaders in Hamilton's tent, including Fred Ashworth, agreed that they would not touch the gallon of whiskey until Hamilton received official notification of his promotion, at which time he would put on his new hat and everyone would raise a toast to the new commander. The tentmates placed the jug with Hamilton's new hat on top of a table in the middle of their tent. Ashworth later recalled, "Well, you now know the rest of the story. Ham was never able to put on his new Commander's hat. One night shortly after the accident, we opened the jug of whiskey and made a toast to his memory, toasted the new hat which he never got to wear, and the next day we wrapped it up and had it sent back to his wife."[16]

VT-11 returned to normal operations on June 21 in a strike against Munda Airfield. Replacement pilots and enlisted personnel arrived. The war continued.[17]

● VF-11'S FOUR VERSUS TWENTY-FOUR

On the morning of June 7, Lt. Cdr. Gordon Cady's division of aircraft was flying west at twelve thousand feet roughly ten miles south of the Segi Point at the southern tip of New Georgia. Cady, VF-11's gunnery officer, was considered a great pilot and also a good tactician. Cady took the famous "Thach weave" maneuver and improvised his own version of it, which the pilots of VF-11 called the "Cady weave." As originally designed and executed by Lieutenant Commander Thach, a division of four fighters would break into two pairs and fly in mutual support, constantly turning their aircraft into each other and "weaving" back and forth. The basic principle was that if an enemy got the tail or six o'clock position of one pair of fighters, the second pair would come in behind the first pair. This tactical maneuver eliminated some of the Japanese Zero's advantages. After Thach inadvertently proved the maneuver's viability at the Battle of Midway, it became standard practice throughout the U.S. Navy. After Midway, Thach returned to the states as an instructor—another advantage the United States had over Japan—and taught new and replacement pilots the art of air combat. Cady simply took the division of four aircraft performing the tactic in elements of two and broke it down further into two aircraft weaving individually.[18]

Cady, his wingman Lt. (jg) Terry Holberton, and a second element composed of Lt. (jg) Edward "Smiley" Johnson and Ens. Dan Hubler had broken away from other members of VF-11 on an escort mission. The four F4F Wildcats were over Vangunu Island and south of Segi harbor on the morning of June 7 when twenty-four Japanese Zeros spotted them, and the lopsided fight was on. There were six Japanese fighters for each Wildcat. The four-aircraft division broke into two elements, and then the two into singles. Cady dove into the clouds, but the Japanese tore into the other three Wildcats. Johnson looked back over his shoulder for Hubler and could see his plane "stagger as a stream of tracers went into him." Hubler's aircraft arched out wide of Johnson at that time, and as he passed behind Johnson's Wildcat, Johnson lost sight of him. Turning his attention forward, Johnson saw that at least three planes were firing at Holberton, and another was firing on Cady from above. Johnson's situation was this: He had just observed his wingman disappear behind him with Japanese aircraft pouring bullets into him. To his front, three aircraft were attacking Holberton and another was chasing Cady into the clouds. His aircraft was also taking fire; he saw tracers shooting past his nose, and he heard other bullets impacting his wings and fuselage. It was a testament to the Grumman builders that his F4F remained airworthy long enough for

Johnson to dive into a cloud bank. Although the aircraft was severely damaged and his engine cut off and on intermittently, he remained in the sky. Johnson shot through the cloud cover and was immediately jumped on the other side by two or three Zeros before he could turn into another cloud. The cockpit began to get exceedingly hot, and Johnson now recognized his plane was on fire. With oil streaming out of his wing and a partially functioning engine, he knew he was in real trouble. Johnson "heard violent explosions, which could have been cylinder heads blowing off, or exploding 20 m.m. cannon shells." He continued to weave in and out of the clouds, but every time he emerged from a cloud, he was subjected to withering fire from the enemy fighters: "They seemed to be everywhere, flying around like a swarm of bees."[19]

Within minutes, Hubler, Johnson, and Holberton had all been shot down. Cady's aircraft dove in and out of the low cloud banks in an attempt to break away from the Japanese and make his way back toward Guadalcanal. Twice Cady's F4F emerged from a cloud bank to find a Zero directly in front of him, and twice he made a head-on pass, destroying both Zeros. Although the Japanese certainly got the better end of the engagement with three victories to two losses, VF-11 had scored a victory against the still formidable Japanese Zeros.[20]

Holberton, Hubler, and Johnson had each safely escaped their stricken aircraft. Holberton ended up in the water in his life raft and was able to make it ashore at New Georgia, where he intercepted some natives and trekked south to Segi Harbor, where he was rescued by a J2F Duck. Grumman built the Duck, a single-engine amphibious biplane, and it looked like a fighter with additional pontoons and wings. Despite its appearance, it served throughout the Pacific as an air-sea rescue platform. Meanwhile, Hubler was picked up by natives in a canoe and returned to base the next day.[21]

The same could not be said of Smiley Johnson, who had parachuted onto Vangunu but erroneously believed he was on New Georgia. Johnson now joined Maxwell as one of CVG-11's "Robinson Crusoes." He was actually dangerously close to Wickham Anchorage and an outpost held by the Japanese. He was also hindered by a nasty gash in the back of his right leg suffered during the fall from his aircraft. Thanks to his emergency medical kit, he was able to put sulfanilamide into the wound, wrap it, and take two sulfathiazole tablets (for possible infection). Johnson set out heading east: "The terrain was very rough with little ridges and valleys, and the jungle growth itself was practically impassable in some places. There were many fallen logs, vines, and broad-leafed plants with hooked thorns up and down their edges. These latter made every move a plan to be figured out in advance." Smiley reached the beach and started walking toward what he figured was Segi, but he was on Vangunu and not New Georgia. As evening turned to night, Johnson pushed a little inland, found a palm tree to sleep under, had some chocolate from his kit, and dozed off.[22]

Johnson awoke early the following morning and began an eight-day ordeal of trekking through jungles, up and down rivers, along beaches, and across rivers and muddy fields, all the while avoiding small units of Japanese soldiers. Johnson made good time while he traveled along the coast and could maneuver along the beach, but he soon discovered that this was the exception rather than the rule. He experienced tough traveling when he arrived at a small cove, which went far back into the jungle, slowing down his progress. Johnson later highlighted his ordeal in a memoir: "If I had kept my life raft or life jacket, at this point I could have gone right on across from one point to the other, but it was too late to bemoan this loss, so I started around through the brush." He encountered knee-deep mud, vines, and thick thorny bushes, which proved to be impenetrable. He felt discouraged at his slow progress and noted, "It took me an hour to work all the way around this cove, thereby gaining one hundred and fifty yards on my way up the coast."[23]

On June 10 he found a well-defined trail that was cut away through the jungle, but he knew this meant someone else, possibly Japanese soldiers, had created this route. Johnson started down this trail with his .45 pistol in hand, although he thought the weapon might be of little use since it had been exposed to copious amounts of salt water. Johnson had stripped and cleaned the weapon after making landfall and oiled it with Vaseline from his medical kit, but he was wary of betting his life on the weapon functioning. He continued to move slowly down the trail. After going no more than 150 yards, he stumbled upon a soft, muddy spot in which there were several definite boot tracks, which he did not recognize as coming from American shoes. This was enough for the intrepid aviator, and he hastily retraced his steps and got off the trail.[24]

Johnson's adventures continued the next several days, and he often came close to detection by Japanese forces, including one soldier who was "the biggest SOB I ever saw in my life." He finally came across natives and an Australian coast watcher, was transported to New Georgia, and was picked up by a PBY Catalina.[25]

After being shot down on June 7, Johnson finally returned to Henderson Field on June 17. The ordeal of being shot down, trekking through the jungle, and making contact with natives and coast watchers before arriving back to Guadalcanal was becoming something of a CVG-11 tradition: Maxwell, Fike, Hubler, Holberton, and now Johnson had all survived and found their way home again. In the meantime, VF-11 continued hunting Japanese aircraft and on June 12, their luck improved significantly. The Sundowners were about to truly earn their name.

● JUNE 12

Vengeance for the "four versus twenty-four" arrived five days later on June 12. At 0715 that morning, sixteen F4F Wildcats—four divisions of four under the lead of Lt. Bill Leonard, Lt. (jg) Les Wall, Lt. Ken Viall, and Lt. (jg) Charley Wesley—were escorting a group of PBYs when they received a request for assistance from Marine Corps F4U Corsairs engaged with a large formation of enemy aircraft. The leads turned their sections toward their engaged comrades. Ground control vectored the Wildcats into a large group of Zeros, and soon the fight was on. The sixteen F4F Wildcats were stacked from 23,000 to 26,000 feet but were still sandwiched between the enemy formations above and below them. By the time they arrived, the Marine F4Us and AAF P-40s were already engaged in an aerial melee. Leonard was an experienced flight lead and already had four aerial victories to his name. Knowing his division was low on fuel, he called for a single slashing attack and a sprint back to Guadalcanal without becoming embroiled in an extended turning dogfight.[26]

One of the hallmarks of any fighter pilot, but perhaps more so in American fighter pilots, is aggressiveness—some might say recklessness—and eagerness to engage in combat. VF-11 pilot Vernon Graham noted, "I looked at my gas gauge. My tanks were low and I doubted I'd have enough fuel left to climb to 25,000 feet and still get home. Two of the four division leaders quickly checked their gas supply and reported back that it would be impossible for them to intercept. I looked across at Lieutenant William Leonard, leader of the other division, and got his nod. That meant he was going up, gas or no gas. I checked my gauge again and nodded back."[27]

Leonard, despite his low fuel situation, was not going to allow the Japanese to escape without a challenge, and he was not going to leave the outnumbered Marine and AAF pilots alone against thirty-five Japanese. The lives of the pilots and the honor of the U.S. Navy were on the line. Two groups of Wildcats, eight strong, headed up. This now put the ratio at roughly twelve to thirty-five, "a figure that has come to be considered more or less equal, in view of current air battles." The after-action report noted that the engagement was a "duel between fighter planes. For it was an action of individual combat, fighter against fighter with no distractions of bombers or torpedo planes to interfere with the primary purpose of kill or be killed."[28]

Graham, flying F4F-4 number 12119, was on the left wing of Claude Ivie, and Graham's wingman Lt. (jg) Bob Gilbert was left of him when they rolled into the engagement and split into two elements. They immediately took hits from one of the Zeros, "but nothing happened to the Wildcat. It was absorbing his lead like a sponge." This was an important point learned early by the American flyers in the Pacific. Their aircraft could withstand damage better than the enemy's could. Pilot Lt. (jg) Bob "Cactus" Flath noted, "The thing about the Wildcat is that it could take so much punishment, whereas the Zero, hell you [put] one bullet in it and it would explode." The same Zero that had just made an attack on Graham rolled above him, turned, and made a head-on pass. Vernon Graham let him have it: "The Zero seemed to shudder a little as it swept by and when I looked back it had nosed down into a dive. A moment later it was spinning dizzily with flame and smoke pouring from it."[29]

The overall engagement rapidly "devolved into a free-for-all with our planes tangling with Zeroes in quick passes as they lost altitude." Meanwhile, William Leonard had splashed two more Zekes, bringing his victory total to six and making him an ace. The Sundowners were finally earning their name in grand fashion. Bob Gilbert claimed three; Viall nailed one. Les Wall drew a bead on one Zeke, only to have his wingman Teddy Hull shoot it down first, for a total of seven victories for VF-11.[30]

VF-11 pilots noted that the coloring and size of the P-40s made them difficult to discern from the Japanese Zeros. Gilbert opened up on an enemy but released the trigger, thinking it might be a friendly P-40: "As he pulled in a climbing left turn to the left I saw the red balls on each wing. I said to myself, 'Thank Goodness!' and let him have it until he caught fire." Marine F4Us and AAF P-40s teamed up with VF-11 F4Fs, making for an odd assortment of wingmen; pilots fought alone and in groups of mismatched aircraft. The blue-gray Wildcats, the sea-blue Corsairs, and the olive-drab Warhawks fought the green-over-grey Zeros. More than fifty aircraft turned, swirled, and dove across each other.[31]

After Graham's first kill, he quickly found himself making another head-on pass against an enemy. The Zero had lined up on Graham at five hundred yards and rolled onto its belly, planning to make an attack and dive away: "I fired a short burst into that exposed belly. The plane never completely righted itself again. It flashed by below me and kept right on going down, down, down. That familiar trail of smoke marked its plunge seaward." In mere seconds, Graham had two kills.[32]

The aerial combat continued, and Graham noted, "It was fairly raining Zeroes." Graham's attention was now drawn to a third Zero making a head-on attack. Graham opened fire and "his ship simply went all to pieces. One wing exploded and I flew through a shower of plane splinters and parts. An object which could have been the Zero's motor lurched past me. A moment later I saw the other wing and part of the fuselage whirling crazily toward the water. That was No. 3." Graham earned three kills in as many minutes.[33]

As Graham emerged from the remnants of the exploding aircraft with his third victory of the day, he looked ahead and over to his starboard and port sides for more enemy aircraft, but he was clear for the moment. Finally, he noted another Zeke going "after one of my boys." This turned out to be Lieutenant Gilbert, who had already claimed a Zeke in the day's fighting. While Gilbert had been busy disposing of his Zeke, he failed to see another drop in behind him and open fire. Graham banked his Wildcat and made a side run on the Japanese fighter. As Gilbert focused on his kill and the enemy aircraft focused on Gilbert, the latter likewise failed to see Graham making his own run. Graham opened fire and "that Zero burst into flames that completely enveloped him. He dropped like a blazing torch."[34]

Graham made one more quick pass, opening up on an enemy trailing a friendly Wildcat, but he did not have time to observe the results. His engine started sputtering. He was out of gas. At 25,000 feet he pushed over and headed down, hoping to be able to glide back to the landing strip in the Russell Islands; he had no chance of making it back to Guadalcanal. As soon as he started down, two Japanese Zeros set upon him. Graham could not turn to defend himself without bleeding off energy and speed, but he was saved by the timely arrival of two of the F4Us, who engaged and chased the Zeros away. Graham and the remaining Wildcats headed for the landing strip with not enough gas left to "fill a cigar lighter." Graham coasted in, dropped his landing gear, and settled onto the runway, only to have his landing gear fail. The front wheel strut compressed like an aluminum can. The Wildcat rolled forward, flipping over, and Graham was knocked unconscious. Lieutenant Leonard landed with eight gallons of fuel left (only a few minutes of flying time). Gilbert landed with three gallons of fuel left.

Lt. Vernon E. Graham awoke sometime later in the hospital with a fractured skull and broken collar bone but was otherwise unhurt. Later in the day, a Marine Corps Captain Ford approached Graham. Ford had been in the F4U under attack by a Zero when Graham made his last-ditch firing pass and ran out of gas. The captain informed Graham he had brought that Zero down with his pass. In a few moments of combat, Graham had shot down five Japanese aircraft and become the Navy's very first "land-based ace in a day." The after-action report said, "This remarkable record of five enemy fighters in single combat is one of the most outstanding feats of [the] present phase of the war in this area and, so far as is known, is without parallel in Naval Aviation."[35]

While Graham was busy with his engagements above, Ken Viall's and Les Wall's groups of four were at a lower altitude and were jumped by a number of the Zeros. Viall shot down one. Wall took a piece of shrapnel in his knee and was forced to ditch off the Russell Islands to the northwest of Guadalcanal. Wall's enemy did not get far, though, as he was shot down by Lt. Teddy "Peanut" Hull immediately after Wall was hit.

The total of the engagement came to fourteen enemy aircraft destroyed and only four Wildcats lost. Lieutenant Ivie set his plane down in the water, and Lt. (jg) Charles Wesley parachuted into the sea. However, all of the downed pilots survived and returned to Guadalcanal and to the fight. Graham downed five, Gilbert three, and Leonard and Hull both bagged two, while Viall and Ivie had a kill each: fourteen Zeros. It was a great day for the Sundowners of VF-11, and "ace in a day" Vernon Graham earned the Navy Cross for his actions, but this was just one engagement, and the war was heating up for the Sundowners.

● A DESPERATE GAMBLE

The morning of June 16 dawned like all the rest on Guadalcanal, with tropical humidity and an unrelenting heat at Henderson Field and across the Solomons. North at Rabaul and other bases, the Japanese launched an armada of aircraft and flew south to attack the shipping anchoring off Guadalcanal and Tulagi in a last desperate effort to hinder Allied operations. More than seventy Zeros escorted a strike force of twenty-four Val dive bombers and additional aircraft. Coast watchers called ahead and radar picked up the incoming strike force. In response, the Americans of AirSols at Guadalcanal launched more than one hundred fighter planes. The mixed bag of American fighters—P-40s, F4Fs, and F4Us—savaged the attacking Japanese, but it was VF-11 that truly reaped the benefits of the engagement. In a matter of minutes, fighter pilots knocked down nineteen of the twenty-four Vals and another fifteen Zeros. The remaining Zeros turned and escaped north. Author and historian Mark Stille noted that "this debacle marked the end of daylight Japanese raids over Guadalcanal and showcased the growing impotence of Japanese airpower in the Solomons."[36] Aviation Mechanic's Mate Second Class Elio Bertolini, a member of VS-11 and VB-21, remembered, "On June 16, 1943, the Japanese decided to give it one last shot, and they threw everything they had at Guadalcanal. Well, they didn't fare too well. I guess the fighter pilots really had a ball that day."[37]

Down on Guadalcanal, VB-11 member Harry Fredrickson stepped from the group's headquarters and ready tent and turned his attention to the sky overhead: "The enemy group had eluded the protective barrier of Marine, Air Force, and New Zealand squadrons that were vectored to the wrong place. At the time, I was in the ready tent on Henderson Field. I saw the large formation of enemy planes headed our way and thought that we were really in for a bad time. Fortunately, they were only interested in shipping and turned before they got to us. VF-11 was on [combat air patrol] and had a field day shooting down enemy planes (thirty-one kills that day)."[38]

The engagement on June 16, 1943, pitted between 94 and 120 Japanese planes against twenty-eight pilots of VF-11 and a group of Marine Corps Corsairs and AAF P-38s and P-40s that closed in to engage after their erroneous vectoring. It was a dogfight greater than any film could ever duplicate. Hundreds of aircraft engaged in a whirling, swirling dogfight ranging from 20,000 feet down to sea level. VF-11 first set upon the Japanese Vals and hit them in their dive but before they could release their bombs. Shooting down more than a dozen in a few minutes, the rest of the dive bombers broke off their attack and scattered, becoming prey for the F4Fs. The escorting Japanese fighters were, of course, there to protect their own dive bombers, but they were unable to engage VF-11. At the same moment that VF-11 dove into the Vals, a group of AAF P-38s tore into the Zeros. What followed was a "general melee."[39]

Charlie Stimpson and Jim Swope accounted for seven of the downed Vals: four for Stimpson and three for Swope, the first victories for either officer. Stimpson, born in Salt Lake City, Utah, on August 24, 1919, grew up in Santa Barbara, California, and graduated from Pomona College. He completed Navy flight training in June 1942 and was assigned to the newly established VF-11 Sundowners at San Diego. He traveled with them to Guadalcanal, but thus far in the first tour, Stimpson had been relatively quiet, his greatest contribution being to coin the nickname "Tim" for the young enlisted man Kermit Enander. Stimpson was tall and rail-thin, and had a cadaverous look about him; fellow VF-11 pilots nicknamed him "Skull." On the morning of June 16, Stimpson flew in a four-ship as the second section lead with Swope. They first attacked the Japanese dive bombers with abandon. After that, the two men performed the Cady weave, intertwining each other's paths, taking deflection shots at any Japanese brave enough to enter their path. That day "Skull" earned a second nickname for his downing of four of the Japanese aircraft: "Trigger Mortis."[40]

VF-11 brought down a total of thirty-one Japanese planes that day. Only four Wildcats fell from the sky, but none to enemy fire; collision was the suspected culprit. Barrett Tillman noted, "Collision was the often unavoidable result of so many planes crowded into such a limited space." Lt. (jg) John Pressler ditched and was pulled out of the water by air-sea rescue, but Lt. (jg) Teddy Hull collided with an Army P-40 and died in the accident. Also killed in this engagement were Lt. (jg) George Ricker and Lt. (jg) Chandler Boswell. Since no one saw parachutes or witnessed their aircraft strike the sea, all three were listed as missing in action. The Japanese suffered a debilitating and humiliating defeat. The majority of the Japanese attacking force of Zeros and Vals did not return to their base. As many as 107 of the 120 possible attackers fell from the sky, and VF-11 played a major role in the victory.

Meanwhile, down below, in a foxhole on an island high point stood Vice Admiral Mitscher, having told his staff, "Let's go watch the fun." Mitscher remained on the hill, arms crossed, watching the aerial melee overhead until a Henderson Field pilot flew over his position and launched into the traditional aerial victory roll. Mitscher smiled and told his attendants, "That's about the end of it." Mitscher sent two cases of whiskey to VF-11 for its major role in the mission. The VF-11 history called it the "greatest aerial victory of the war in the Southwest Pacific."[41]

● JULY

Strikes continued throughout July. On July 18, 34 TBF Avengers from VT-11 and VT-21, 36 SBDs, 114 fighters of VF-11, and AAF B-24s participated in a shipping strike against southern Bougainville. Other operations included more mine laying and more skip bombing. While sitting on Henderson Field, a machine gun on one of VT-11's TBF Avengers misfired and sent a bullet through a propeller. An aircraft engine and propeller can be delicate things, and although the bullet hole did not ground the aircraft, it did make it difficult to fly. The pilot continued to request a new prop, but to no avail. A ground crew member took the aircraft's machine gun, aligned the propeller blades, and neatly shot a hole through each of the remaining blades. This act balanced out the propeller, although now the aircraft made a heinous whistling noise.[42]

Meanwhile, VB-11 innovated by adding wing tanks to their SBDs, or at least following the example set by the mechanics of VB-21 earlier in June. Two maintenance crewmembers worked out that the wing tanks being used by the F4F fighters could be fitted to the SBDs, and this "paved the way for increased range of the SBD both land based and carrier base." This innovation also allowed for an extended and devastating attack on July 17 in which thirty-six SBDs of VB-11 and another one hundred aircraft including TBFs, F4Fs, and F4Us attacked Kahili Harbor where the Japanese had six destroyers, one light cruiser, and one oiler. AAF B-24s attacked in the ten minutes prior to the arrival of VB-11 and alerted the Japanese forces, which began moving the destroyers. The bombing raid caught the Japanese forces completely by surprise; even the pre-raid by the AAF did not give the Japanese navy enough time to move its forces into open water before VB-11 struck.[43]

When the attack was over, the Japanese cruiser was aflame, and three of the six destroyers were seriously damaged. On the return flight, members of the squadron noted that smoke "could still be observed from 50 miles." During these particular attacks, lieutenants Edwin J. Weil, Herbert W. Pickering, Robert W. Cocks, Richard F. Kenney, Alvin D. Leach, and Edwin M. Wilson Jr. were all singled out for their hits on Japanese shipping. That day was also a highlight for air-to-air combat where gunners Anthony W. Brunetti and Robert R. Seneker were both credited with shooting down a Japanese Zeke. Only two members of the air group failed to return home from this strike: Lt. (jg) Edward Francis Hughes and Aviation Radioman Second Class Harold Milton Marrs, both officially listed as missing in action.[44]

One of the last missions CVG-11 flew from their base on Guadalcanal occurred on July 22, 1943. CVG-11 headed up the slot toward Kahili at Bougainville for an early evening strike against a Japanese transport and its destroyer escorts. As the transport came into view, pilot Bill Strahan remembered, "What a sight. That huge ship with several destroyers starting to circle and taking evasive action. Heavy anti-aircraft and dust trails from enemy fighters taking off from nearby Kahili Airfield. In came VB-11 with fighter escorts above and below ready to take on the Japanese fighters seen kicking up dust as they launched from nearby Kahili Airfield. As many times before in the previous months, VB-11 pushed over at 12,000 feet. Soon the troop ship was ablaze and CVG-11 headed home from another days work after spending only three or four minutes over the target."[45]

CONCLUSION

The Japanese evacuated Kolombangara in late September and early October. The American forces under Halsey and MacArthur previously decided to bypass the island, determining that an amphibious landing there gained the Americans nothing. The Japanese had planned for it to be a bloodbath for the American forces, but neither American leader intended to attempt an amphibious invasion against a heavily defended island unless it met a significant strategic objective, and Kolombangara did not. However, strategic concerns mattered little for the members of Eleven. The air group was headed home. On August 1 CVG-11 left Guadalcanal and boarded USS *Chenango*, USS *St. Louis*, and USS *Honolulu*. They arrived back at NAS Alameda two weeks later. Upon return to the United States, CVG-11 trained for the next assignment: carrier operations.[46]

On July 18 Mitscher sent a congratulatory note to the commander of Air Group Eleven: "The operations of the past three months have been noteworthy for the aggressive manner in which offensive and defensive missions have been executed. I desire to convey to the pilots and all personnel, air and ground alike, my most heartfelt, 'Well Done' for the outstanding performance of duty which has characterized the entire period of its service under my command at Guadalcanal. To the living, I say no unit has excelled you in exacting from the enemy the maximum toll for your honored dead."[47]

Mitscher also left the area of operations. During his operations at Guadalcanal, his forces had destroyed more than five hundred Japanese aircraft and wrested control of the skies over the Solomon Islands from the Japanese, but these operations took their toll. Mitscher had a bout of malaria, dropped to 115 pounds, and was in desperate need of rest and recuperation. Nevertheless, just like the men of Eleven, his time in the Pacific was not at an end. Like MacArthur had promised, they too would return.[48]

Dick Miralles noted in his diary that VB-11 made their last raid on July 27, 1943: "We made a raid on Munda Airfield, our troops have almost complete control." His next diary entry was made with a red grease pencil instead of his normal pencil entries. It read, "MY BIRTHDAY: TURNED 19." The next day, he noted that CVG-11 "Left for return to USA."[49]

What had CVG-11 accomplished in this, its first "cruise" at Guadalcanal? Bill Strahan recorded that "from April 23 to August 9, 1943. Carrier Air Group Eleven attacked the Japanese air, land and sea targets at Bougainville, Munda, Vanga Vanga, Vella Lovello, Ringi Cove, and Rekata Bay. We were part of the Allied Air Power in that area at that time. These consisted of Army Air Corps, Marine Air Corps, Navy Air Corps, and New Zealanders and Australians. Real cooperation and leadership prevailed." Fred Ashworth noted "only this, to finish on a brighter note. In August, I guess it was, we were relieved of our tour there on Henderson Field. We were just about as impatient to get going . . . and pretty proud of what we had accomplished, even though it was out of the mainstream of the Navy's carrier operations."[50]

By the time it departed Guadalcanal, VF-11 racked up an impressive fifty-five aerial victories. Three of the pilots made ace: Vern Graham, Charlie "Skull" Stimpson, and James Swope. Five men died in action: Lt. (jg) Chandler Boswell, Ens. Leroy W. Childs, Lt. (jg) John A. Cooke, Lt. (jg) Teddy Hull, and Lt. (jg) George W. Ricker. For their mine-laying prowess, VT-11 commander Ashworth received the Distinguished Flying Cross. Tragedy befell the unit in June when sixteen members of VT-11 plus the air group commander, Weldon Hamilton, died when their R&R transport crashed. While that was a crushing blow, the torpedo squadron had every right to be proud of the good work they had accomplished from mine laying to bombing. VB-11 and VB-21 conducted more than thirty strike missions. In addition to missions like anti-submarine, the squadron's primary mission was delivering bombs onto enemy positions, and seventy percent of all VB-11 and VB-21 sorties were attack missions. The "performance of Bombing ELEVEN was not only highly satisfactory in combat but that overcoming the obstacles of rugged advanced land operations is also a credit to its organization." The same could be said of the other squadrons as well. It was a record any unit could be proud of, but this was only the first act for CVG-11.[51]

Mark Peattie stated, "As serious as were the casualties among experienced Japanese navy flyers at the Coral Sea and Midway, it was the air combat over the Solomons that, by the summer of 1943, finally destroyed the combat-effectiveness of Japanese naval aviation as it had developed before the war." But the war was far from over and after a brief respite, CVG-11 would find itself back in the thick of aerial combat as the United States continued its inexorable march to the Japanese home islands.[52]

● INTERLUDE

CVG-11 boarded the escort carrier USS *Chenango* (CVE-28) in August and returned to U.S. soil on August 21, 1943. VF-11, VB-11, VT-11, and VB-21 now returned to the United States as part of a regular "training and reforming cycle." Any leave or rest and recreation would be relatively short. On September 25, 1943, the three squadrons were reformed and re-established. VB-21 ceased to exist as a separate organization and was officially incorporated into VB-11. The veterans of the Guadalcanal tour, men with combat experience, provided a cadre of experience for new members of the squadrons. However, not all the veterans would return to the Pacific for CVG-11's second tour. VF-11 members Frank Quady and Bill Leonard now had two tours each under their belts and found themselves headed to Admiral Mitscher's staff. Also finishing his second tour was VT-11 member and Midway veteran George Gay.[53]

The three squadrons of the air group called NAS Alameda home for their replenishment period. According to a history of VB-11, their new home station was less than ideal: "For the benefit of the uninitiated, Alameda is a damp, flat island of no particular pretensions that juts unapologetically from the Oakland shore into San Francisco Bay. Cold and raw in winter, it is a sort of meteorological magnet which draws to itself any and all storms, fogs, winds, etc. in the entire Day and thus it is not surprising that the Navy should have selected it for a Naval Air Station."[54] Surely, it was better than Guadalcanal. At least Alameda offered the nearby comforts of San Francisco and Oakland. Drinking establishments frequented by the men of Eleven included the Leamington, Berry's, Biff's, and Tiny's.

Some of the men of VB-11 and VB-21 transferred over to VF-11, wanting the chance to fly fighters. They included Lt. (jg) Bob Saggau, a former All-American football player for the University of Notre Dame, who noted, "It was actually very simple. We requested through official channels to transfer to VF-11 and were so authorized." The bomber flyers turned fighter pilots were not the only new arrivals to VF-11. Gone were the veteran F4F Wildcats, replaced with the newer F6F Grumman Hellcats. Lt. (jg) Gerry Coeur said,

"The Hellcat was the fastest thing the Navy had at that time. It was really just a joy to fly." When VF-11 traded in its F4F Wildcats for the newer Grumman F6F Hellcat, it unknowingly received one of the most iconic and important aircraft of the war. The Hellcat became one of the premier fighters of World War II. To call it the best is subjective, but the Hellcat was an excellent escort and an excellent air-to-air fighter. It proved to be easy to maintain, which meant more fighters were available for daily operations. Barrett Tillman points to three aircraft as being "instrumental" in the defeat of Japan. In 1942 and 1943, it was the Dauntless SBD. In 1945 it was the B-29 Superfortress, and from late 1943 through early 1945, it was the F6F Hellcat.[55]

In addition to the new Hellcats, VF-11 also gained a new mascot and a new commanding officer. A range instructor gave veteran pilot Gordon Cady a Boston bull terrier puppy. Commander Cady became VF-11's commanding officer on September 25, 1943. Cady named the puppy "Gunner" and immediately assigned the youngest pilot in the squadron, Blake Moranville, mascot duty. In August 1944 Eugene Fairfax assumed command of VF-11, replacing Cady. Fairfax was "well respected, and knew his work, he was the ideal naval officer."[56]

Over at VB-11, the replenishment and reorganization period began in earnest. Their history noted, "The days that followed were filled with activity of every sort—planes were accepted by the material officer, always a great hand at accepting things; familiarization flights were scheduled and, surprisingly enough, flown; officers and men reported in daily, fresh from training or exhausted from leave; the inevitable offices and files were established, and all the myriad pieces that comprise an active squadron began to fall into place." Lieutenant Commander Jacoby assumed command of the squadron.[57]

VB-11 also transitioned aircraft at this time, giving up the SBD Dauntless for the Curtiss-made SB2C Helldiver. Bill Strahan remembered, "We pilots of VB-11 really missed the reliable old SBD Douglas Dauntless we had flown at Guadalcanal. However, the SB2C was bigger, faster, had more range, and carried a heavier load."[58]

Lt. Cdr. Radcliffe "Pete" Denniston Jr. became commander of VT-11 at its reformation ceremony on September 25, 1943. Denniston, from Wauwatosa, Wisconsin, was a few weeks short of his twenty-eighth birthday when he took on the role of squadron commander. A graduate of Lawrence College in Appleton, Wisconsin, he joined the Navy in 1936 and served with VT-5 on the USS *Yorktown* at the Battle of the Coral Sea where he distinguished himself and earned the Navy Cross. As with VB-11 and VF-11, the torpedo squadron spent its time at Alameda "organizing departments . . . acquiring training aircraft and . . . routine area familiarization flights."[59]

VT-11 continued to fly the Avenger, although the squadron received newer versions of the aircraft. The aircraft's designation changed from TBF to TBM, indicating a change in manufacturer from Grumman to General Motors. Other than the designation, the aircraft were virtually identical. As Grumman phased out the production for the Avenger, General Motors took over.

Lt. Cdr. Clarence White had served as commanding officer of VF-11 since April 1943, shortly after the squadron's formation, and had led the unit throughout the first cruise on Guadalcanal; he turned over VF-11 to Gordon Cady in September 1943 after the first tour ended. Cady died attempting to land on the USS *Belleau Wood* (CVL-24) on August 30, 1944. Lt. Cdr. Eugene Fairfax replaced Cady as the new commanding officer. Fairfax arrived from flying the OS2U Kingfisher, an observation floatplane that looked as if it had been cobbled together from the parts of other aircraft. The fighter pilots of VF-11 were "less than enthusiastic" about having a non–fighter pilot as their new executive, but with training from some of the Guadalcanal veterans, Fairfax was soon just another member of the squadron, albeit one of the newer ones.[60]

Once reformed, each squadron had a commanding officer and executive officer, as well as officers in charge of operations, gunnery, flight (the squadron scheduler), radio, engineering, navigation, communications, material (supply), morale and welfare, athletics, administration, and education. Most squadrons also had two officers in nonflying billets: the personnel and intelligence officers. Additionally, the bomber and torpedo squadrons had radio and radar officers who oversaw the enlisted aircrews.

From September through January, the squadrons received new aircraft and new personnel to fill out their tables of organization and equipment. The cadre of veterans prepared the new squadron members as best they could for the fight ahead. January 1944 found the squadrons in their final training stages before shipping out to the Pacific in preparation for a deployment, hopefully this time on an aircraft carrier. VF-11 moved briefly to conduct night flying training from Crow's Point. All CVG-11 squadrons conducted their carrier training and landing qualifications on the USS *Copahee*. In March 1944, after six months on the West Coast, the group departed for Hawaii on the new USS *Wasp*, their first taste of life on the new *Essex*-class carriers. On April 4, 1944, the group arrived at Ford Island in Pearl Harbor and found the naval base had "now risen phoenix-like from the ashes." At Pearl and NAS Barber's Point, the squadrons continued "simulating attacks on everything and everybody in sight." Air Group Eleven remained and continued training in Hawaii for five more months. This included more carrier landings on the *Wasp*, USS *Kadashan Bay*, and USS *Ranger*. Air-to-air, air-to-ground, dive-bombing, and torpedo-dropping tactics were the orders for most of the days. By the time the group departed for combat in September 1944, most of the newer pilots had over three hundred hours in their respective aircraft, and many of the veterans of the Guadalcanal operations peaked at over one thousand. While the men might have complained about the training, and while it was certainly not as deadly as combat operations, the preparations for combat still cost lives; CVG-11 lost eighteen men between October 1943 and August 1944, all to training accidents.[61]

On May 2, 1944, the air group received a new hand: Lt. (jg) Joseph Hyland, a Long Island native who had attended Columbia University before joining the Navy in 1943. What made Hyland unique was that he attended the Massachusetts Institute of Technology's radar school, was then an instructor at the naval air navigational radar school in Gainesville, Georgia, and was attached to an airborne radar training unit in San Diego before he joined the squadron as the air group's radar officer. Since he was the group's only radar officer, members immediately gave him the nickname "Blip." It was Blip's job to train VB-11 and VT-11 radiomen in the fine points of radar search, navigation, and bombing. The radar was also useful on return trips after a strike. The *Hornet* had its own radar signal. Verg Bloomquist remembered that "if we were at the right altitude and right mileage, we could pick up that signal. Although Blip was a hard worker and spent hours training the radio operators the art of operating the radar, he spent an equal amount of time in the organization of extra-curricular activities. . . . His equal eagerness to imbibe a friendly glass soon pointed him out as life of any party at hand. His Irish eyes and wit necessitated a more appropriate nickname than 'Blip' and that moniker was soon changed to 'Shamus O'Toole.' "[62]

In September, the officers and enlisted personnel split up as they took different ships toward their final destination. The officers of Eleven were on the USS *General O. H. Ernst*, while the enlisted crews departed on the USS *Breton*, "a hell ship . . . a modern *Bounty*." Some of the mechanics departed Hawaii without their aircraft on board the USS *Wasp*. It was clear there was significant animosity between the "combat" men headed to war and the men of the transport crew: "It was clear that we were looked upon as unwelcome intruders—unwelcome, that is, until it came to the little matter of standing hatch watch and compartment watches."[63] The only relief in the monotonous torture was the ancient ceremony of crossing the Equator: "Polliwogs were duly summoned before the court of Neptunis Rex, composed of air group shellbacks, urged to confess their crimes and awarded suitable punishments." CVG-11 men were only too happy to depart the *Ernst* for their new home of the USS *Hornet* (CV-12): "As we shoved off, we gave the *Ernst* and her gallant crew a rousing bird."[64]

Weldon Lee Hamilton took CVG-11 to combat, leading the group from Guadalcanal and flying "up the slot." He had previous combat experience leading VB-2 and had received the Navy Cross. On June 8, 1943, Hamilton and fifteen other aircrew from VT-11 died when the transport aircraft they were on crashed during a rest and recreation break. *United States Naval Academy*

Guadalcanal, at the southeastern end of the Solomon Islands, was no island paradise. Kermit Enander of VB-11 remembered, "There was no fun in Guadalcanal. Zero. It was from the sack, to the line, to the chow hall, to the sack again. That was it." *Courtesy of George Retelas*

George Retelas, known as "the Greek" or "Rattle-Ass" to his squadron mates, looked every bit the ideal U.S. Navy sailor. Decades after World War II, his grandson found his diary, leading him on a search for members of the air group and ending in the creation of *Eleven: The Movie*. *Courtesy of George Retelas*

The USS *Hornet* (CV-12) was the newest and most advanced of a long line of ships bearing the name, the first being a ten-gun sloop in the Revolutionary War era. The veterans of CVG-11's first cruise found the accommodations on the *Hornet* much improved over those on the island of Guadalcanal. *Naval History and Heritage Command*

VF-11 pilots play cards while waiting in the ready room. Charlie Stimpson (*second from left*), the squadron's leading ace, earned the nicknames "Skull" and "Trigger Mortis" because of his cadaverous appearance and skill at aerial combat. *Naval History and Heritage Command*

A Curtiss SB2C-3 Helldiver of VB-11 banks over the carrier before landing in mid-January 1945. The aircrews of VB-11 flew both the Dauntless SBD and the Curtiss SB2C during the war, while VT-11 stayed with the TBM Avenger. *Naval History and Heritage Command*

James S. Swope and Charles R. Stimpson study reconnaissance photographs of Hong Kong prior to a mission. *Naval History and Heritage Command*

VF-11 pilots and mascot Gunner are briefed on the day's mission. Leading ace Charlie Stimpson sits on the aisle in the third row on the right. *Naval History and Heritage Command*

Crews wearing Chinese-American insignia prepare before departure for a strike against Hong Kong. *Naval History and Heritage Command*

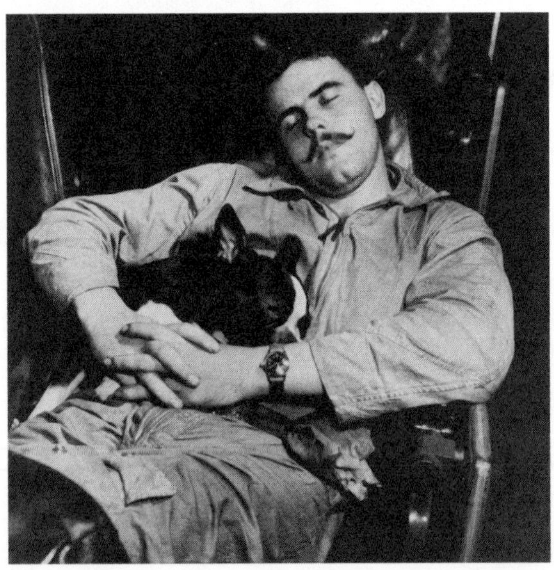

Blake "Rabbit" Moranville cradles squadron mascot Gunner during a quick nap in the VF-11 ready room. As the most junior member of the squadron, Moranville was responsible for Gunner's care. *Naval History and Heritage Command*

The "Murderers' Row" of *Essex*-class aircraft carriers of the U.S. Third Fleet anchored at Ulithi Atoll. *Left to right:* USS *Wasp* (CV-18), USS *Yorktown* (CV-10), USS *Hornet* (CV-12), and USS *Hancock* (CV-19). A much smaller escort destroyer can be seen passing the *Wasp*. This photo, taken from the USS *Ticonderoga* (CV-14), shows the folded wings of a number of F6F Hellcats. *Naval History and Heritage Command*

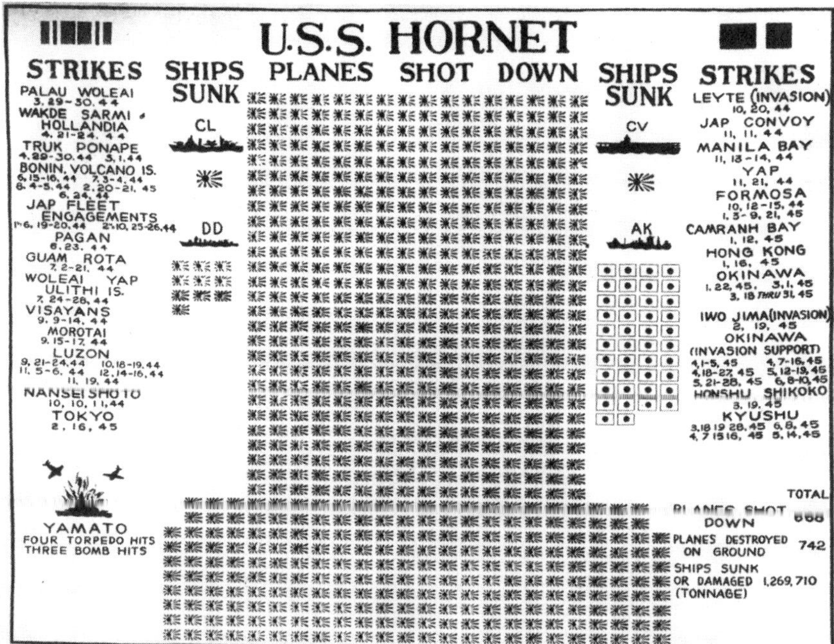

A final tally from the USS *Hornet*'s three cruises during the war. A similar graphic would have been painted on the island's superstructure. *NARA*

Lt. Cdr. Eugene Fairfax, VF-11 commander from October 1, 1944, to February 1, 1945, in his F6F Hellcat, which shows four aerial victory credits and the famous Sundowners emblem. During the war, he earned three Distinguished Flying Crosses. *Naval History and Heritage Command*

CHAPTER 4

THE *HORNET*, HALSEY'S RUN, AND LEYTE GULF

The war in the Pacific Theater was fundamentally different in the latter part of 1943 through 1945 than it had been from January 1942 until CVG-11 departed Guadalcanal in the summer of 1943. Although Coral Sea, Guadalcanal, and Midway were important turning points in the war, they were not culminating or decisive victories. If anything, they indicated that a decisive battle was more theoretical than possible or probable. While Colin Gray postulated that there are decisive operational victories—"a victory which decides the outcome to a campaign, though not necessarily to the war as a whole"—there remained few such engagements throughout the war. After each of the above battles, the air arm of the Imperial Japanese Navy and the land-based fighters, bombers, and torpedo planes lived to fight another day. Although the lifeblood of the Allied war effort—America's arsenal of democracy—began to pump vigorously throughout 1942 and 1943, there still was not going to be a decisive battle. World War II in the Pacific would be won through attrition at all levels. American forces were going to bleed the entirety of the Japanese military beyond its ability to resist.[1]

That being said, what the Americans could now bring to bear in the Pacific in 1944 was nothing short of extraordinary. Under Halsey's Third Fleet was Marc Mitscher's Task Force 38 and four separate carrier task groups, 38.1 through 38.4. Each carrier task group boasted four to five aircraft carriers. Each had at least two of the new *Essex*-class carriers, the first of which (the USS *Essex*) the U.S. Navy commissioned in December 1942. It reached the Pacific in May 1943. For example, when CVG-11 returned to the Pacific, Adm. John McCain's Carrier Task Group 38.1 included the *Essex*-class *Wasp* and *Hornet*; the light carriers *Monterey*, *Cowpens*, and *Cabot*; the heavy cruisers *Wichita*, *Boston*, and *Canberra*; and fifteen destroyers.

American naval forces now fielded aircraft far superior to anything the Japanese could hope to throw against them. American planes were more heavily armed, more technologically advanced, and more durable than those of their opponents. Self-sealing fuel tanks and armor meant that U.S. aircraft could take hits and remain aloft. The older Japanese aircraft, despite some advancements and updates, did not have such a luxury and often burst into flames with a good hit. Mark Peattie noted that Japanese planes, "which had caused such havoc . . . in the spring of 1942," were now just a "slow moving and weakly protected target for enemy fighters."[2]

Clark G. Reynolds noted "the characteristics of the new carriers and their aircraft. Instead of the slower Wildcat (F4F), VF-11 now flew the speedier Hellcat (F6F). Other fighters available to the allies included the gull-winged Corsair (F4U). These aircraft rose to meet the Japanese planes which had not been altered since Pearl Harbor." Now the Japanese were outclassed, outperformed, outgunned, and outmatched.[3]

Opposing American forces were the remnants of the Japanese combined fleet. Admiral Isoroku Yamamoto died in the April 1943 vengeance raid shortly before CVG-11 arrived at Guadalcanal and was replaced by the aggressive Admiral Mineichi Koga. He lasted roughly one year until March 31, 1944, when his Kawanishi H8K flying boat went down in a typhoon during withdrawal operations of the combined fleet from its Palau headquarters. Admiral Soemu Toyoda took Koga's place in May 1944. Japan's Third Fleet was now led by Vice Admiral Jisaburō Ozawa, who replaced Admiral Chūichi Nagumo in November 1942.

The naval forces of Japan also remained constrained by several factors. At a strategic level, Japanese forces were hamstrung by the lack of an indigenous industrial base and a rapidly diminishing set of conquered islands capable of providing Japanese industries the raw materials they needed to survive; the empire simply could not make up for losses in the same way the United States did. Newer U.S. aircraft were superior in nearly every category to anything the Japanese military could put into the sky. The Zekes, Kates, Vals, and Bettys so feared in 1941 and 1942 remained in service. Although in many cases updated and more advanced than their predecessors, they were in no way a match for the American aircraft they faced and proved to be a major liability for those who flew them. Also, the great sea battles and duels over the islands of the Solomons had sapped the Imperial Japanese Navy of its cadre of combat-experienced aviators. According to Clark G. Reynolds, "By the autumn of 1943, the Japanese fleet was not ready to fight a major battle." Yet it had little choice. It was clear to the IJN leaders that the only way to victory was a decisive battle and the destruction of the American fleets.[4]

The Japanese hoped that they might inflict a decisive defeat against the U.S. fleet when the latter landed in the Mariana Islands in June 1944. However, Filipino guerrillas recovered Chief of Staff Vice Admiral Shigeru Fukudome's briefcase after his plane crashed; the case contained a trove of documents, including the IJN's "Z Plan." These plans found their way to Gen. Douglas MacArthur's military intelligence service in Brisbane, Australia. MacArthur now had in his possession the Japanese navy's plan for its future operations. As a result, the Battle of the Philippine Sea, conducted June 19–20, 1944, cost the IJN two more fleet carriers, over seven hundred aircraft, the last of its veteran pilots, and, more importantly, the ability to conduct offensive operations. If Colin Gray was correct, the Battle of the Philippine Sea was indeed "a victory which decides the outcome to a campaign," as it put the Japanese empire on the path toward its final sunset. Again, CVG-11 was preparing for deployment and missed this important battle.[5]

● THE NEW USS *HORNET* (CV-12), THE *ESSEX*-CLASS CARRIERS, AND JAPAN'S DESPERATE SITUATION

The *Essex*-class aircraft carriers began to arrive in the Pacific in mid-1943. Twenty-four ships out of a planned thirty-two-ship build were completed, and although some received heavy damage in combat through the end of the war, the Navy did not lose even one. The USS *Essex* (CV-9) came first, commissioned in December 1942. By May 1943, she was in the Pacific. The *Yorktown* (CV-10) followed three months later, and then the *Intrepid* (CV-11). Each *Essex*-class ship typically carried thirty-six fighters, thirty-six scout/dive bombers, and eighteen torpedo planes (although exact numbers often varied). This started a steady stream of aircraft carriers of all sizes sent to the Pacific, each with their complement of aircraft. This included the heavy *Essex* carriers, medium carrier air groups, light carrier air groups, and escort carrier air groups. During the operations at Leyte, the U.S. Navy could boast of having thirty-four aircraft carriers of different types to the Imperial Japanese Navy's four.

Fighting Eleven was going back to the Pacific for its second tour, but this time the men were headed to the newest incarnation of a ship whose roots stretched back to the Revolutionary War, ironically with the same name as the carrier on which they initially planned to deploy in 1943. The first USS *Hornet* (1775), a ten-gun sloop armed with nine-pounder cannons, was part of the fledgling U.S. Navy until His Majesty's schooner *Porcupine* captured her in 1777. She was followed in 1805 by another ten-gun sloop that participated in the Tripolitan War. The third *Hornet*, a brig-rigged ship armed with eighteen "short" thirty-two-pounders and two "long" eighteen-pounders, fought in the War of 1812 alongside the USS *Constitution*. *Hornet* number four was a smaller schooner, and five was a side-wheeled steam-powered ship, followed by *Hornet* number six in 1865, a steam-powered side-wheeled ship that began life as the CSS *Lady Stirling*, until Union forces captured her off the coast of North Carolina.[6]

A converted yacht took the name in 1898 and participated in the Spanish-American War. Forty years later, the newest USS *Hornet* was ordered, laid down, and launched as CV-8 of the *Yorktown* class of aircraft carriers. From her decks on April 18, 1942, the sixteen B-25 Mitchells of the Doolittle raid launched to attack targets in Japan. Six months later during the Battle of the Santa Cruz Islands, Aichi D3A Val dive bombers and Nakajima B5N Kate torpedo bombers scored multiple hits, but *Hornet* remained afloat. The USS *Northampton* attempted to tow her from the battlefield, but another Kate got in a fatal shot that sent the *Hornet* listing. Admiral Halsey ordered the stricken carrier sunk, and she absorbed another nine American torpedoes, but

Hornet still refused to go down. *Hornet* was abandoned, and U.S. forces left the area. The Japanese destroyers *Makigumo* and *Akigumo* finally finished off CV-8 on October 27, 1942.[7]

The newest *Hornet*, CV-12, had a lot to live up to. Built by the Newport News Shipbuilding Company, the keel was laid down on August 3, 1942, and the carrier was launched a little over a year later, on August 30, 1943. Three months later the USS *Hornet* was commissioned into the U.S. Navy, the fourth of an eventual twenty-four *Essex*-class carriers. When completed, the *Hornet* was 872 feet long with a beam 93 feet across, and it had a standard displacement of roughly 30,000 tons. Her abbreviated shakedown cruise occurred between November 29, 1943, and February 1, 1944. The *Hornet* departed Norfolk on Valentine's Day 1944 already bearing the dazzle camouflage paint scheme that made it difficult for an enemy to estimate its range, speed, and heading, transited through the Panama Canal, and arrived in San Diego on February 27. She left three days later for Pearl Harbor, arriving on March 4.[8]

On March 20, the new *Hornet* crossed the 180th meridian and joined Task Force 58 at the Marshall Islands. From March through September, Carrier Air Group 2 (CVG-2) performed operations at Palau, Truk, Guam, Rota, Iwo Jima, and numerous other locations. Members of CVG-2 participated in the great Marianas Turkey Shoot on June 19, 1944, during the Battle of the Philippine Sea. By September, CVG-2's time in theater was over, and it was time for CVG-11 to board CV-12 and take its place on the line.[9]

LIFE ON THE NEW *HORNET*

After its transfer from Alameda to Hawaii and then on to the Pacific Theater, CVG-11 was back in the war for its second cruise from September 29, 1944, until February 1, 1945. The reconstituted CVG-11 deployed on board the new USS *Hornet* (CVG-12). The VB-11 history noted the crew's arrival to the new ship: "We mounted the accommodation ladder to the deck of the USS *Hornet* while the ships' band blared out a hearty welcome. We heaved a sigh of relief as we saluted the quarterdeck and stepped aboard. This is what we had trained twelve months and come 5,000 miles to see. The was our ship—the Happy *Hornet*—and we were here to stay." There is no doubt the accommodations were well above those found on Guadalcanal.[10]

An *Essex*-class aircraft carrier was a technological wonder of the age, with amenities undreamed of by the veterans of Guadalcanal. The VB-11 history noted, "The air-conditioned ready rooms and office spaces seemed luxury unheard of. . . . dinner music in the wardroom at evening chow once a week, a truly Ritz-like touch. . . . evening prayers over the speaker system nightly . . . reminding us all to pause for a moment to give thanks for the day past, to voice a hope for those to come. . . . Small points these, perhaps, but they go to make the character, the personality of a ship." One naval historian called the ships "the most significant class of warships in American naval history"—a bit hyperbolic, but the men of CVG-11 probably would not have argued the point.[11]

By the time the men of CVG-11 boarded the *Hornet* and began their second tour in September 1944, the carrier already had one cruise under its belt. The actual crew of the *Hornet*, not the members of the air group, were already running on a routine, had given the ship a good shakedown, and had taken it to combat for the first time. CVG-2 took the carrier and crew to war from June through September. VB-11, VT-11, and VF-11 boarded a ship with a seasoned crew. Leaving the island of Manus in October 1944, the unit participated not only in the Battle of Leyte Gulf, but also in several engagements both before and after the largest battle in history, including the air battles over Formosa.

● FIRST STRIKES

CVG-11 boarded the *Hornet* at the anchorage at Ulithi Atoll in the Caroline Islands. The atoll sat 360 miles southwest of Guam and 850 miles due east of the Philippine Islands, a magnificent parking spot for U.S. ships and aircraft out of reach of the Japanese navy. The Navy landed the Army's 81st Division there on September 23, 1944, and the Japanese had already removed all personnel, so "Naval Base Ulithi" rapidly developed into a U.S. Navy base used throughout the rest of the war. The atoll's importance lay in the flat-calm, crystal-blue azure water at its center. It was, and is, one of the largest coral reef lagoons in the world.

The atoll there was twenty miles long and ten miles wide, with over thirty small islands; the largest island was only half a square mile in area, and yet this developed into the world's largest naval base in 1944–45. Sometimes as many as six hundred ships filled the atoll and hundreds of aircraft parked on the four airfields constructed by the U.S. Navy Seabees. Such a conglomeration of ships in one area would have been unheard of just a year before, but after the defeat at Philippine Sea, the IJN no longer had the capacity to mount an assault on the base, nor could they hinder operations at Ulithi.

Other facilities at Ulithi included a submarine base, a repair depot, a seaplane base, and a long-range navigational signal post. In 1945 the Navy used the atoll as a major forward hospital location with eight different hospital ships rotating through the area and back to Pearl Harbor. From late 1944 through the end of the war, it was routine for hundreds of ships to be in the atoll on any given day. In March 1945, with five months of fighting left and plans for the invasion of Japan moving forward, there were between 650 and 750 ships in the atoll.[12]

After departing Ulithi, Capt. Austin K. Doyle, commanding officer of the *Hornet*, picked up the ship's intercom and informed the men of the ship and the newly added Air Group Eleven where they were headed and what they were about to encounter. Bill Strahan remembered him saying, "I'm gonna tell ya what we're going to do. . . . For security reasons I didn't say anything in port there, but now we're out and we're on our way. We're going to join Admiral Halsey's 3rd Fleet. We're gonna make strikes, we're gonna go right up next to Japan itself, at Okinawa."[13]

In the following months, CVG-11 participated in what might be described as a cornucopia of operations all across their operating area. In 1943 the air group was tied to their land-based stations. Ironically, by this point in the war, the USS *Guadalcanal* (CVE-60), a *Casablanca*-class escort carrier, was also operating in the Pacific Theater. Bill Strahan recalled, "The *Hornet* soon joined Admiral Bull Halsey's Third Fleet, and Mitscher's Fast Carrier Force (Task Force 38) with Task Groups 38.1, 38.2, and 38.3. Halsey's armada lost no time conducting a series of strikes against the Japanese, air, land, and sea forces. They started on October 10, 1944, with a strike close to Japan itself, Naha Airfield at Okinawa and the Pescadores Islands. Many strikes soon followed."[14]

The Ryukyu (Nansei) Islands sat between Formosa (Taiwan) to the south and the four main islands of Japan to the north. The Japanese considered the Ryukyus part of the Japanese homeland. For the first time since the Doolittle raid in April 1942, Japan came under aerial attack by forces of the United States. The Air Group Eleven squadrons participated in the first strikes against Okinawa. The first sortie consisted of strikes against Naha Harbor, Naha

Field, and surrounding docks and warehouses. Perhaps due to sheer surprise, Japanese resistance was light.

Admiral Matome Ugaki, commander of Japan's 1st Battleship Division—composed of the *Nagato*, *Yamato*, and *Musashi*—noted in his diary on October 3, 1944, a nearly perfect list of the U.S. Navy's Third Fleet, its senior officers, and its composition: "four groups, each made up of two regular carriers, two converted carriers, sixteen cruisers, and escort destroyers." He then listed the carriers in each group by name. It was a remarkable recitation of American naval power, and it is doubtful that even many in America had as complete a list as Ugaki had at his fingertips. Badly beaten, but not out of the fight, the Imperial Japanese Navy knew exactly what faced them going forward.[15]

Combat operations for Air Group Eleven began on October 10, 1944, with strikes against the islands of Nansei Shoto and the main Naha Airfield located there. These islands were part of the Japanese homeland island chain and included Okinawa. The *Hornet* and CVG-11 were to be the first naval strike against the Japanese homeland. The Japanese mainland was also soon to come under air attack from the AAF XXI Bomber Command under Maj. Gen. Haywood Hansell flying out of the China-Burma-India Theater. Japan's leaders no longer had the luxury of believing the Pacific Ocean, the Greater East Asia Co-Prosperity Sphere, or divine intervention was going to protect them.

In the operations that were to follow, getting from the ready room to the aircraft parked on deck was a process fraught with a peril of its own. Just getting to the flight deck, on a dark night with the aircraft carrier in complete blackout, was an adventure. As the flyers departed the ready room and walked on the catwalk, the preferred method was for each man to grab the flight bag or collar of the individual ahead of him. Caution had to be taken stepping over or out of a watertight door to ensure that he stepped high enough and simultaneously ducked low enough to get through the door; each door had a half-inch horizontal steel plate that was just the right height to cause damage to the shins, and the top of the door was a danger to taller crewmembers. The passageway from the ready room opened out onto the catwalk on the port side of the ship. This steel-grated walkway was eighty-five feet above the ocean. As the ship prepared for air operations, it might make a tight turn to put the carrier into the wind for takeoff. Depending on which way the ship turned, it often listed to port. This gave the pilots on the catwalk the feeling the carrier was rolling over them. To one side, the ocean yawed up toward them, and to the other, the flight deck lifted above them: a vertigo-inducing experience. One flyer noted, "Hanging out over the water on a catwalk, with the ship riding up and down on thirty-foot swells, produced a ride that could not be exceeded by the most spectacular rollercoaster." Once up on the flight deck, with each man still holding the man in front of him, the next obstacle was to find his particular aircraft in the dark, picking it out from "a flock of twenty-four look-alikes. . . . This left you staggering around on the flight deck in the dark, buffeted by prop wash, gagging on the exhaust gases, dodging the whirling discs of the thirteen-foot propeller blades, groping forward to find your airplane. We pilots were extremely careful where we put our hands and feet."[16]

After successfully finding his aircraft and climbing aboard, it was time for each flyer to get preflight and receiving instructions from the plane captain on deck, who ensured the pilots or crewmembers of the bomber and torpedo squadrons were in the right place, with parachutes on and strapped into the proper seats. The deck was awash as dozens of aircraft taxied into the correct position. Deck crews gave the needed taxi signals to clear enough area for the aircraft to unfold their wings. Deck crew and the men responsible for each aircraft pulled pins and release hooks on each wing, allowing the wings to swing into their correct positions. As a crewman held the wing, the pilot inside the cockpit engaged a lever that moved a pin down to lock the wing into position for flight.

Aircraft then maneuvered toward the middle of the flight deck and pointed down the deck in position for takeoff. Pilots locked their brakes and with their left hands moved the throttle all the way forward to the full power position. When the aircraft in front of them departed and the deck was clear, the launching officer swung his flag forward and down. This was the signal for the pilot to release the brakes, and the aircraft moved down the carrier's teak deck and lifted into the sky.

Ens. Paul Warren said, "We preset the rudder trim tab for 3¾ units of right rudder to correct the torque of the 2000 [horsepower] Pratt and Whitney R-2800 engine. Even with that, a little extra rudder was still needed to keep the airplane going down the center of the deck. It was reassuring when you generated enough speed to bring the tail up so you could see the flight deck over the engine." Pilots used roughly half the deck, about four hundred feet, for takeoff. However, some pilots quibbled whether the term "takeoff" was the best terminology here. Warren noted, "We just ran off the end of the deck at high speed and then started flying." Once airborne, the pilots made a quick right turn; this was necessary to clear the deck of the aircraft's slipstream turbulence and allow for a smooth takeoff for the next plane in line. Takeoffs occurred at roughly seventeen-second intervals, and an entire squadron or strike force could launch in a matter of a few minutes.[17]

On the morning of October 10, "Dawn had just broken over a calm sea. . . . Those of us who weren't on the first hop crowded onto the flag bridge to see the takeoff. The fighters and torps were already turning their engines. Their exhausts flamed and flickered in the semi-darkness." VF-11 launched first, followed by VT-11, and VB-11 last. The *Hornet* launched four separate attacks that day against shipping in Naha Harbor, the airfield collocated with the harbor, and the docks and warehouses of the Japanese base there. It was a successful first strike.[18]

VF-11 pilot Lt. John Ramsey wrote in his diary after the first strike that the fighters surprised the Japanese forces and they received no opposition in the air that day: "The bombers took the air field and destroyed all they could see, such as planes on [the] ground, buildings, storage areas, dumps, and shipping last." While the bombers were busy with the airfield and as the fighters had no opposition to take care of, the men of VF-11 dove down to find targets of their own: "My division put five rockets into a big Sea Plane tender and beached it on a rock. . . . We hit the place with four strikes and when we left all shipping, aircraft, and [illegible] had been destroyed or damaged."[19]

The first strike also had the first casualties. The youngest member of VF-11, Lt. (jg) Kenneth Chancellor Chase, scored a direct hit on a Japanese ship with a five-hundred-pound bomb but was shot down seconds later. While on Guadalcanal, the units of CVG-11 had lost men, but some of those successfully landed their aircraft or bailed out and were able to work their way back down the slot. As CVG-11 attacked the homeland of Japan, the same was not going to be possible—no friendly natives, no coast watchers to send word back to Henderson Field.

It was during the first days of attacks on the second cruise that a nearly disastrous event ended in only a funny war story to be related at later CVG-11 gatherings. A VT-11 plane returned without dropping its torpedo. When the TBM Avenger landed hard on the deck, the torpedo ripped away from its connections. On the deck of the *Hornet*, Bob Fitz remembered, "I mean that baby landed hard, and that torpedo went right through the front of the plane." Ens. George Stebbings recalled, "The torpedo came bouncing down and everybody's running for cover. I'm down on the catwalk. We're all ducked, and it's out there and it stopped and the wheel is spinning. And we had a Gunnery Officer named Satterlee, and he went out there with his tools and took it apart and stopped it and disengaged it." Both Stebbings and Bob Fritz remembered that if the torpedo had exploded on the deck of the *Hornet*, the result might have been catastrophic. The Mark 13 torpedo carried by the TBM Avengers had six hundred pounds of Torpex high explosives, and a detonation on the deck could have put the *Hornet* out of commission for some time. Fritz later joked that throughout their second tour and with all of the enemy aircraft they faced, "We were the only ones to torpedo the *Hornet*."[20]

Depending upon how badly an aircraft was damaged upon returning to the *Hornet*, it might end up either in the hangar below the deck for repairs or in the ocean. If maintenance personnel decided an aircraft was not worth saving, it was simply pushed off the rear of the ship. Lt. (jg) John Williss remembered that any aircraft that was about to meet its fate off the back of the ship was first cannibalized for parts by the deck crew. An aircraft "looked like a swarm of ants would get on it, pulling instruments out, pulling guns out, pulling ammunition out, anything that was salvageable and by the time they got to the end of the deck, everybody jumped off and they pushed the plane off the side."[21]

On October 11, during an attack against Aparri on the northern coast of Luzon, VF-11 "shot up several aircraft and all came home." The strikes were accomplished in conjunction with aircraft from Task Group (TG) 38.4, roughly sixty aircraft in total, and "were unopposed" by the Japanese. Then it was off to Takao, Formosa, the next day. The strike against Formosa occurred in the early morning hours before sunrise. It was dark as aircraft launched and attempted to form up in their strike packages. According to Lt. John W. Ramsey, the fighter director announced that Japanese aircraft were present in the traffic circle. This caused all manner of consternation as everyone expected "to get shot away not knowing from whence it would come." Flight leads restored order, and the strike package headed for Heito Airfield on Formosa where bombers and fighters alike dropped five-hundred-pound bombs and continued the attack with strafing runs. Again, no Japanese aircraft opposed the strike.[22]

Operations from October 12th to 14th were against Formosa with the express purpose of destroying "enemy aircraft and shipping on Formosa that might be used as a staging area for reinforcements to the Philippines." Japanese forces retaliated the night of October 12 and into the next morning, launching strikes against Task Group 38.1. The strikes did not damage the task force ships, but they did result in the "loss of a night's sleep by the entire ship's company."[23]

The loss of sleep did not hinder operations as strikes against Formosa continued on October 13, but there was a high cost to the air group's leadership. VF-11 lost another pilot on October 12 when Ens. George Edgar Grier Lindesmith did not return to the ship and was listed as missing in action. On October 13, air group commander Cdr. Frederick Schrader took off from the *Hornet* in an F6F-5 Hellcat as the leader of a group of twelve Hellcats headed to a strike mission against the Japanese installations and facilities on Formosa. As Schrader led VF-11, dove on the enemy facility, and strafed the Japanese seaplane base, his Hellcat aircraft was struck by anti-aircraft fire. The F6F crashed into the seaplane harbor's shallow water, and Schrader was killed in the crash. The ship's diary recorded, "His loss was a serious one since his leadership and work with the Air Group had been outstanding." The same day Schrader died, Ens. Leon Edsel Lee also went missing.[24]

The entire air group continued the strikes against Formosa for three straight days of unrelenting attacks. VF-11 provided a fighter feint toward Aparri on Luzon, while VB-11 headed toward Formosa. Heito and Reigaryo fields had aircraft assembly plants, with hangars making great targets for the bombers. Toko seaplane base and Takao harbor also came under attack. The first two days of strikes were fruitful, but the third night found Japanese forces marshalled and ready to respond as they attacked the *Hornet* and surrounding ships. VB-11 crewmembers remembered the sky was "alive with bogies" and that the recent attacks had "stirred up a hornet's nest" against the *Hornet*. The air group claimed credit for one Kawasaki Ki-61 Tony during the strike. The Ki-61s were more modern and heavily armored than the Zeros but by this point in the war were being flown largely by inexperienced and undertrained crews. However, Japan would shortly put the Tony to great use against American ships and B-29s as part of the "special attack units."[25]

Launching and landing aircraft remained dangerous activities. On October 13 a VF-11 Hellcat recovered on the *Hornet*. As its wheels struck the rear deck, its machine guns began to fire, wounding one sailor. At 0432 on October 14, the first patrol of the day, an F6F with Lt. E. E. Helgerson pitched into the water immediately after takeoff and was lost. Ens. W. H. Boring of VF-11 had a similar experience. A pilot had roughly forty-five seconds to escape a sinking aircraft—if the pilot made a good landing. During launch, Boring's engine unexpectedly cut off, and he crashed into the water. With the *Hornet* bearing down on him, he leaped from the wing of his stricken aircraft and made his escape. A fellow flyer wryly noted, "The Navy said this was the first time in history a fighter pilot had walked on the water."[26]

Despite being naval aviators and having a reputation to uphold, the fighter pilot sometimes made mistakes. It was rare, but not altogether uncommon, for a pilot to make a mistake of grandiose proportions, as occurred to Ens. Paul Warren. Returning from a patrol, Warren brought his division through a break in the clouds, lined up the aircraft carrier, and brought his division in for a safe landing. Ensign Warren hopped out of his aircraft with his flight equipment, chart board, and parachute and hurried over to the catwalk, which led to the ready room.

As he walked down the catwalk, the young ensign noticed something rather peculiar: "I arrived on the catwalk where, only two hours before, there had been a door. Now it was just a solid steel wall and the door had miraculously moved twenty feet farther down the catwalk." Warren, standing in front of solid steel, could not bring himself to believe the idea now taking root in the back of his mind. Instead, he tried reasoning with himself, holding out hope: "The maintenance crew must have really been busy while I was gone. They had obviously moved the door." He even reached out to touch the steel, hoping to find wet paint, but the wall was dry. Warren "looked up at the superstructure where the scoreboard was kept" only to finally accept that he and his fellow pilots were not on the *Hornet*. He had landed his division on the *Essex*. Fellow fighter pilots on the *Essex* decided that Warren should be "president for life" of the "I landed on the wrong carrier club."[27]

Around mid-morning on October 14, seven Hellcats of VF-11 launched to engage an incoming enemy raid. The Hellcats, under the direction of Lt. N. W. Dayhoff and Lt. Jimmie "Doc" Savage, climbed to twenty thousand feet and flew west on a heading of 275. Savage counted thirty-four planes ahead and dove on the unsuspecting Japanese. Flying in one of the Hellcats was Guadalcanal veteran Lt. Charles Stimpson, already an ace. In one engagement on April 16, 1943, Stimpson had earned four aerial victories in a single engagement. He later earned two more, making him an F4F Wildcat ace. He was about to enjoy even finer results over Formosa in the afternoon's attack.

Stimpson was one of eight Hellcats flying with division lead Savage. Their mission was a combat air patrol over *Hornet*. The F6Fs of VF-11 launched from the wooden deck and climbed to twenty thousand feet. The *Hornet* detected an incoming group of Japanese fighters and vectored Savage's flight to intercept. As they flew toward the Japanese, Savage found his compass was not functioning, and he turned the flight lead over to Stimpson. Approaching the Japanese formation, VF-11 saw it was a mixed formation of fighters and bombers. The two Hellcat divisions split, with Savage and his elements heading for the bombers and Stimpson's group hitting the fighters. The Japanese should have had a high level of situational awareness given the tactical situation, but it was a total surprise when the Hellcats dove on them from above. The fight was on. Stimpson rapidly dispatched two Hamps, and Lieutenant John Zink bagged another, but the Japanese were not going to be willing victims. They brought the score back to a more even level and shot down both Zink and Dayhoff.[28]

Savage's division had also found itself shot up in the uneven fight. Soon only three VF-11 Hellcat pilots remained in the fight—Stimpson, Blair, and Savage—but losses did not mean a disengagement from the battle. Stimpson and Blair entered VF-11's Cady weave. Enemy fighters attempted to engage the two Hellcats, but the weave worked perfectly; Stimpson claimed two more and Blair another, each falling victim to the tactic's protective feature. As soon as an enemy pulled into a six o'clock position, either Blair or Stimpson would be in place to take a deflection shot at it, and vice versa. Using this tactic, they fired on and saw another two enemy fighters go down smoking as "probable." This back-and-forth continued unabated, and Stimpson and Blair both racked up more kills. Another Zeke fought hard behind Blair, but Stimpson, a true Sundowner, turned into the enemy and brought it down with another quick deflection shot. In a few minutes, Skull Stimpson added his fifth victory of the engagement and became an "ace in a day." However, the Japanese fighter peppered Blair's aircraft, and black smoke and flames began pouring from it. Stimpson saw Blair ditch, but he did not see Blair escape the rapidly sinking aircraft. Meanwhile, Doc Savage fought for his life against the Japanese. His aircraft shuddered with the impact of bullets and took hits that disabled his instruments. Savage dove into a cloud bank and made his escape. Emerging below the cloud bank, the Japanese were gone, but Savage was lost. He made a guess and used dead reckoning to find his way back to the *Hornet*. He arrived two hours overdue, but alive.[29]

Despite Stimpson's ace in a day, the men of VF-11 lost five fighter pilots that day: Lt. N. W. Dayhoff, Lt. E. E. Helgerson, Ens. F. J. C. Blair, Ens. Henry Ptacek, and Lt. (jg) S. E. Goldberg. Helgerson's F6F taxied off the aircraft carrier and into the Pacific in the early morning launch operations. Blair, Goldberg, and Dayhoff were all engaged in the dogfight and failed to return to the *Hornet*. Blair's aircraft ditched, but he did not escape the sinking machine. "Nellie" Dayhoff, a VF-11 veteran of the Guadalcanal campaign, destroyed one Judy but was immediately jumped by Zekes and shot down. For the loss of five pilots and five aircraft, VF-11 received credit for fourteen kills and two probable. Zink, Stimpson, and Savage were awarded Distinguished Flying Crosses for their actions on October 14, while Dayhoff, Blair, and Goldberg received posthumous awards. In five days of operations, VF-11 had already lost ten men.[30]

The next day, October 15, the *Hornet* retired back toward Luzon. The air group was back in the air, and the *Hornet* was under constant attack by Japanese aircraft. Ramsey wrote that VF-11 was in the air "all day long, and many Jap planes were shot down." He also noted that despite the heavy attack, very few attacking aircraft ever got close enough to the *Hornet* to drop their munitions: "One 'Judy' . . . dive bomber just got through the screen and dropped a bomb about 50 feet off our starboard quarter and was shot down before he could get away."[31]

Ramsey pinned a translated report in his diary that detailed to the Japanese people the losses suffered by the American forces. This report listed as sunk "53 ships all types" and claimed that the Japanese fleet was now in "hot pursuit of a fleeing, panic stricken, and disorganized enemy task force." While both sides undoubtedly often exaggerated claims, the Japanese people received an endless stream of propaganda and deceitful news. However, the Japanese population itself was by this time well aware of the glaring difference between the unsophisticated propaganda they received and the overall reality of the ongoing war effort. As historian Richard Overy noted, "In 1944 it was impossible to disguise the reality of the war. . . . Behind a façade of national unity and confidence in victory, both leaders and led understood that the war was effectively lost."[32]

This feeling was shared by the Japanese military leaders in the field who fought desperately against the rising tide of American military, technological, and production might that threatened to overwhelm them. Shigeru Fukudome, the commander in chief of the 1st Combined Base Air Force and 2nd Air Fleet based in the Kyūshū-Okinawa-Formosa district, remembered, "Although I was thoroughly aware of the manifest inferiority of our airmen's military skill as compared with that of the enemy flyers, I was confident that, as far as the defensive fighting over Taiwan [Formosa] was concerned, the odds would be in our favor."[33]

Fukudome was incorrect. He was forced to watch, initially believing his pilots were making a good fight against the Americans, but his enjoyment turned to terror: "As I watched from my command post, a terrific aerial combat began directly above my head. . . . All those shot down were our fighters. . . . Our fighters were nothing but so many eggs thrown at the stone wall of the indomitable enemy formation. In a brief one-sided encounter, the combat terminated in our total defeat."[34]

The Japanese pilots put up a hellacious "all or nothing at Formosa" defense. Admiral Toyoda decided his last stand would be at Formosa instead of over the Philippines. Japan threw relatively raw, lightly trained pilots against the American forces. Clark Reynolds called it "another turkey shoot." Losses in the sky were high for the Japanese, but it was even worse on the ground. The air battles over Formosa cost the Japanese air arm over five hundred airplanes in a scant five days.[35]

During one of the strikes on Japanese ships at Takao Harbor, Bill Strahan earned a Purple Heart. He had just dropped his bombs and pulled out of his attack and was, in his words, "flying full speed towards our rendezvous point when my plane was hit by anti-aircraft fire. It felt like a bee sting. An anti-aircraft shell fragment had hit my right shoulder." Strahan initially thought he might have to ditch, so he flew in the direction of the rescue sub, but after noting everything with the aircraft seemed to be functioning in normal fashion, he flew back to the *Hornet*. A piece of shrapnel was pulled from the wound and a large bandage placed over it, and Strahan found himself back on rotation without missing a single mission. Strahan later recalled, "My squadron mates joshed me for receiving an easy Purple Heart."[36]

It is important to note that after receiving the anti-aircraft fire, Strahan made a decision to fly in the direction of a rescue sub. As the war dragged on and losses mounted, the U.S. Navy made every effort to rescue downed pilots. In later 1944 through the end of the war, it was routine for the Navy to station rescue submarines just out of reach of Japanese shore batteries. Strahan recalled, "If our pilots were wounded or his plane disabled by [anti-aircraft] or enemy fights, he could be rescued if he was able to land on the water near our submarine. It sure was a welcome sight to spot that submarine as we were approaching our target. Because we were inflicting such crippling damage to Japanese forces, we knew how there could be terrible consequences if we were shot down and captured."[37]

The Imperial Japanese Navy was now reporting wildly exaggerated claims of American losses. One report Ugaki received stated that on October 12–13, "six to eight carriers sunk" followed by "three to four carriers sunk." Ugaki knew this could not be true and wrote, "According to the above, the enemy carriers found yesterday ought to have been annihilated." Scouting reports from the next day found the American forces intact. Ugaki estimated that at best, five American carriers remained afloat. In fact, none had been sunk, and all continued daily operations. The Japanese forces had accomplished little other than to damage one light carrier and one destroyer. The translator of Ugaki's diary noted that all the initial claims "were widely accepted as accurate in Japan."[38]

● LUZON, OCTOBER 18–19

After Formosa, it was back to attacks on Luzon, including Clark Airfield, as part of Admiral Halsey's preplanned strikes to support the forthcoming invasion of Leyte and MacArthur's return to the Philippines. Task Group 38.1 moved into a position east of the island of Samar. The mission of the air group at this point was to "disrupt the Japanese aerial lifeline in preparation for the Leyte landings." Lieutenant Ramsey wrote in his diary about the briefing received on the evening of October 17: "We are to send fighter sweeps all over the Philippine Islands until all Japanese aircraft is [*sic*] destroyed in the air and on the ground." VF-11 made a good showing on October 18–19. Lt. Cdr. Bob Clements shot down a Tojo and an Oscar, and Ramsey bagged a pair of Tojos, while Lt. Dick Cyr had four confirmed and two probable.[39]

VB-11 members Warren Sailor and Duane Brash in an SB2C-3 were hit over Neilsen Field. Other aircraft observed one parachute, but neither man was ever recovered, and both were declared killed in action one year later. VF-11 lost two men during the attacks on October 18: Ens. George Anderson, whose Hellcat ditched short of landing on the *Hornet*, and Ens. W. DeRolf, who went down over Luzon. These two men made it twelve losses in eleven days just for VF-11. Despite the fact the United States had such clear technological and material superiority by late 1944, and despite all the hindrances the Japanese found themselves facing, this war was not one where the United States merely walked its way closer to the Japanese homeland every day. It remained a brutal war with losses mounting not just for CVG-11, but for all of the air groups prosecuting the war.[40]

VB-11 pilot William Strahan also had one of his many brushes with death over Luzon. As Strahan dropped his bombs during an attack on Clark Field, he pushed his throttles to full power to speed toward the rendezvous point with the rest of the squadron. He recalled as he turned toward the rendezvous that "my engine started to pop and bang and [I] had only partial power. I thought some of my cylinders in that big air-cooled engine had been shot out." His engine began to fail, and he started losing altitude. He became concerned that he might not have enough power to join the air group as they climbed over the mountains to fly back to the fleet. He knew he was in a bad position: "What a lonesome feeling. No rescue sub there in the plains of Luzon." He turned his aircraft east toward the mountains, skimming just above the treetops with partial power and hoping he might nurse his aircraft to a landing near some of the friendly Philippine guerrilla forces in the area—at the very least to avoid contact with Japanese forces. Strahan flew his SB2C through valleys and passes and finally spotted open ocean in front of him. He took up a heading toward the Third Fleet, now just able to hold the aircraft above the wave tops.[41]

Meanwhile, the ships of the Third Fleet had reports of supposed kamikaze pilots in the area. Strahan's low-flying aircraft certainly fit the description of an incoming enemy: "Suddenly, one of our fighters came swooping at me from above. He had been vector[ed] to this possible kamikaze by the ship's radar control center. Lucky for me, he recognized Bombing Eleven's identification on that SB2C." Strahan now had an escort back to the *Hornet*, and he was able to make a successful landing despite his engine problems. He learned later that the spark plugs had been changed on his plane the night before and had not been tightened with the torque wrench. This caused them to become loose and blow out when he applied full power. Strahan survived to fight another day, but it was far from the last danger he faced.[42]

The weather continued to turn foul during the late fall months. Sometimes pilots had difficulty finding their way back to their assigned carriers. While conducting operations off Formosa, the weather was so ruthless that air group commanders requested flight operations be suspended. Admiral Halsey growled out a message "to all ships and all hands: plenty of pilots, plenty of planes, plenty of targets, send them out." Bill Strahan remembered, "We were really flying on the edge of eternity in that horrible weather. We kind of got the feeling that it was downright dangerous to fly for Bull Halsey in such weather."[43]

The weather and the Japanese were not the only lethal threats facing CVG-11. Daily operations on the *Hornet* also invited death. Bill Strahan remembered fellow VB-11 pilot Raymond Gahan, who experienced a complete power failure as his SB2C left the deck of the *Hornet*: "His plane fell into the ocean in front of the ship and the *Hornet* passed over him. He told me later that all he could think of was those big screws that propel that ship as he bumped along under the keel. Well, a skipper ordered a hard right rudder. As the big ship swerved, Gahan and his rear seat gunner came out on the side of the ship and were rescued by a destroyer." Another incident occurred when an F6F of VF-11 landed: "A landing hook failed and an F6F fighter plane veered into the enclosure after the bridge where the Carrier Air Group Eleven's flight surgeon, Lieutenant Stanley Ogush, was stationed during flight operations. The big four bladed prop of that plane chewed the only entrance to that enclosure to bits." The flight surgeon survived but found a more concealed location on deck in future operations.[44]

● LEYTE GULF

The noose continued to tighten around what was left of the Japanese military, but the forces of imperial Japan still had one bluff left to play in this deadly game of poker with the forces of the United States. The first step in the fall of 1944 was the Leyte invasion slated for later October. The island of Leyte sat due west of the line of demarkation between MacArthur's and Nimitz's forces. The commanders needed to reach a decision about how current and future operations could be coordinated between the two commands and how the men and materiel available to each commander might be suitably used by the other. It was a complicated situation then, and eighty years of hindsight have not cleared the muddied waters much. The command structure looked this way: Admiral Nimitz remained the Supreme Allied Commander, Pacific Ocean Areas, and MacArthur retained command of the Southwest Pacific Theater. Under Nimitz was the AAF VII Air Force and the Third Fleet was under Halsey. Under MacArthur was the Seventh Fleet commanded by Vice Adm. Thomas C. Kinkaid and the landing forces of the Sixth Army.

Prior to the landings, members of MacArthur's and Nimitz's staff met to sort out the command relationships. To support MacArthur's landings at Leyte, the two commands agreed that Halsey's fleet would operate "in strategic support of the Leyte Operation, by destroying enemy naval and air forces threatening the Philippines area." However, Nimitz transmitted to Halsey in Operation Plan 8–44 added verbiage that altered the agreement in a subtle but important way. Nimitz added, "In case the opportunity for destruction of a major portion of the enemy fleet is offered or can be created, such destruction becomes the primary task." This order essentially gave Halsey carte blanche in carrying out operations against the Japanese fleet regardless of the forces on Leyte. In simple language, if Halsey determined that he could bring his forces to bear against a sizable portion of the Japanese fleet, he should do so, and this is exactly what Halsey did.[45]

However, recent scholarship continues to point out that Halsey made a mistake in seeking to create a fist by combining the entirety of his task groups into a single massive punch and going after the Japanese northern force. This included Vice Admiral Mitscher's Task Force 38 with Rear Adm. Frederick C. Sherman's TG 38.3, Rear Adm. Gerald Bogan's TG 38.2, and Rear Adm. Ralph Davison's TG 38.4. Vice Adm. John McCain's TG 38.1, the "most potent of the four task groups," according to Thomas J. Cutler, was in the process of sailing east to Ulithi. Trent Hone noted, "Halsey's decision to take his whole force north prevented him from winning a decisive victory over the IJN. He had sufficient force to defeat both the Center Force and the Northern Force simultaneously."[46]

To add confusion to an already foggy command situation, there were no less than six separate air arms operating in the vicinity of Leyte, Luzon, and the Japanese home islands. MacArthur had the air arm of Kinkaid's Seventh Fleet and the Southwest Pacific Air Forces under Lt. Gen. George Kenny. Nimitz had Halsey's Third Fleet, which is where the *Hornet* and CVG-11 fell. However, the XIV Air Force, operating under Maj. Gen. Claire Chennault, fell under Gen. Joseph Stilwell's China-Burma-India Theater and the XX Bomber Command under Maj. Gen. Curtis LeMay and XXI Bomber Command under Maj. Gen. Haywood Hansell. The XX and XXI Bomber Commands reported not to any commander in the theater, but directly back to Gen. Hap Arnold in Washington, DC, and existed for the sole purpose of carrying out strategic bombing missions against the Japanese homeland, not to provide support to any other forces in theater.[47]

After the attacks leading up to the Leyte invasion, Ramsey wrote that "we don't know exactly when the landings are to be made on the Island, but we are now wiping out Japanese aircraft to gain control of the air." The men of CVG-11 soon learned that MacArthur's return to the Philippines was to begin on October 20. The day before, the full complement of VF-11, VB-11, and VT-11 were in the air above Nichols and Clark fields. VB-11 and VT-11 each lost one aircraft, but the Japanese provided no meaningful aerial resistance, and the invasion began the next day. On October 20, 1944, the *Hornet* and CVG-11 were part of the naval armada in direct support of Admiral Kinkaid's Seventh Fleet with amphibious invasion landings on Leyte. Members of CVG-11 bombed and strafed Japanese troops behind the ridges that sheltered them from the ships' big guns. On October 20, VF-11 dropped napalm bombs along the invasion beaches in advance of the landings there. Samuel Eliot Morison noted of the landings on the island of Leyte, "This was an easy landing, compared with most amphibious operations in World War II—perfect weather, no surf, no mines or underwater obstacles, slight enemy reaction." On the afternoon of October 20 with Philippine president Sergio Osmeña at his side, Gen. Douglas MacArthur went ashore at Leyte. [48]

The landing's "A-day" took place beginning on October 20, with the U.S. Sixth Army coming ashore with a strength of four divisions. This included strikes by Halsey's task groups 38.1 and 38.4 hitting airfields in the Visayas and on the northern part of the island of Mindanao and also striking targets over the beaches and landing zones. After the support to the actual landings at Leyte and the protection of the landing and supply ships, Halsey dispatched the *Hornet* and the rest of TG 38.1 under McCain to the fleet anchorage at Ulithi for rest and refueling. The Imperial Japanese Navy then enacted the "*Sho*-1" (victory 1) plan to counter the landings at Leyte, continuing to seek a decisive naval battle with the United States. As Americans secured their footholds on Philippines invasion zones, the IJN planned for three separate naval surface forces to converge on Leyte Gulf and destroy Admiral Kinkaid's U.S. Seventh Fleet. To do this, the IJN needed to lure away Halsey's Third Fleet supporting the invasion force. On the same day the landings on Leyte took place, the IJN sortied the first of three elements to be used in the battle. This first element to sail was Vice Admiral Jisaburō Ozawa's northern force. This was the bait to pull Halsey away from the Seventh Fleet and included the heavy carrier *Zuikaku*—the only remaining of the carriers used to attack Pearl Harbor in 1941—and the light carriers *Zuihō*, *Chitose*, and *Chiyoda*. On October 21, the center and southern elements of the Japanese force departed Brunei.[49]

The rest of the American fleet now engaged in what collectively became known as the Battle of Leyte Gulf. In reality, however, Leyte Gulf was four separate actions: Battle of the Sibuyan Sea, Battle of the Surigao Strait, Battle off Cape Engaño, and Battle off Samar. Leyte Gulf is north of the Surigao Strait and west of Samar. The island of Leyte is west of the gulf. More than enough has been written on Halsey's actions during Leyte that it need not be covered here. Suffice it to say that the *Hornet*, along with the *Hancock* and

Wasp—the bulk of Task Force 38.1—was hundreds of miles east heading toward Ulithi when Halsey recalled them on the morning of October 24 around 0600. According to Cutler, this made "good tactical sense," since TG 38.1 had more carriers and therefore more planes of all kinds than any of the other task groups, but TG 38.1 at this point was too far away to do much good. Admiral McCain's task force was not able to get into a position to launch a strike against the Japanese center force until 1030 the morning of October 25, and even then was some 335 miles away in what historian Barrett Tillman noted was "one of the longest strike missions of the war." McCain remained unsure if any of the Japanese airfields at Leyte were now under American control. If this was the case, he could load his bombers and torpedo planes up with more munitions, but since he was unsure, McCain wisely decided to load the aircraft up with extra drop tanks and more fuel to ensure they would make it back to the task group. As Cutler notes, "A weak strike was perhaps better than no strike."[50]

One group of Japanese carriers came down from the north along the east coast of Luzon to lure Halsey's forces away from Leyte. Two other forces of battleships, cruisers, and destroyers came from their China Sea bases southwest of Leyte in a pincer-type movement designed to destroy Admiral Kinkaid's Seventh Fleet at Leyte. Bill Strahan of VB-11 recalled the *Hornet*'s response to the battle and remembered that CVG-11 struck at the weaker carrier force east of Luzon, but it was too far away to stop the other two forces. A group of older battleships that had been mostly restored to use after Pearl Harbor effectively destroyed the southern Japanese force. The third and most powerful Japanese force broke through and created havoc with Admiral Kinkaid's Seventh Fleet, but the Japanese admiral broke off the engagement and retreated, apparently while Halsey's forces were returning to Leyte. Carrier Group Eleven had been launched at maximum fuel range from the *Hornet* as it raced full speed toward the battle area.[51]

On October 24, the Japanese fleet converged on Leyte to oppose the landings. VF-11, VT-11, and VB-11 launched from 342 miles away, well beyond normal range, to strike the Japanese fleet. Not every aircraft that launched made the daring reach back toward Leyte. William Strahan recalled that he and his rear seat gunner, Aviation Radioman Second Class Robert W. Koster, were fortunate to survive the "Second Battle of the Philippine Sea." As he took off from the *Hornet*, his aircraft's oil pump failed and the oil pressure dropped to zero. With no oil flowing to the engine, oil temperatures exceeded their limits, and the engine locked up and failed. Strahan and Koster had no choice except to try "a dead-stick ditch wheels-up landing" with a fully armed plane into a heavy sea: "As we hit the big wave, my engine cowling broke loose and went over my cockpit and a wing buckled. The last I remembered was climbing out of the cockpit with my backpack and chute still on and the water coming up over my knees as the heavy plane quickly sank." Strahan blacked out, fell into the sea, and came to later in a life raft with Koster at his side as a rescue destroyer broke formation and swung around to pick them up.[52]

With Halsey racing back to Leyte, Admiral Kurita turned the Japanese fleet north to race away, and they were off the coast of Samar when VB-11 and VT-11 located them. Bombers broke away and the torpedo planes dove for the surface to make their coordinated runs. The history of VB-11 recounted the incident: "The eleven bombers poked their noses down and went into a screaming dive. Ack-Ack was all around them—featherly [*sic*] phosphorus blobs, bursts of red, blue, green—all the colors of the spectrum. To each pilot and radioman it seemed as though every ship in the fleet had selected his particular plane to shoot at. But they pressed the attack home, down, down, down til the altimeters read 1500 feet. Then bombs away and pullout for all you're worth jinking as you go."[53]

Enemy fighters attempted to intercept the VB-11 bombers, but the Hellcats of VF-11 pounced and drove them off or shot down any escaping stragglers. VB-11 scored hits on the *Yamato* battleship and two other cruisers. All of VT-11 squadron's aircraft returned, completing a 621-mile round trip, but the planes of VB-11 began dropping out short of fuel. Two ditched near American ships (Bill Armstrong, radioman Jim Betsekas, Lt. C. F. Schwab, and Ray Crawford), one landed at a newly won airfield on Leyte (George Ford), and two others landed on a different carrier while the deck crew of *Hornet* tried to get the decks cleared for landings. Six planes landed safely back on the *Hornet*.

A second sortie launched at 1245, though closer, did not fare as well on fuel. This group struck two more cruisers. Most of CVG-11 was now dangerously low on fuel, and the chances of making it back to the *Hornet* were nonexistent. CVG-11 needed somewhere to land as soon as possible. Luckily, American forces had just overrun and taken Tacloban Airfield on the eastern side of Leyte.

VB-11 TAKES TACLOBAN AIRFIELD

The "aerial landings" and taking of Tacloban were a direct result of CVG-11 launching at the limit of its available fuel in an attempt to get in the fight during the Leyte sea battles. By the end of the first day's landings on October 20, the 1st Cavalry Division of X Corps and Sixth Army had secured the airfield. Lt. Robert W. "Jack" Cocks participated in that day's strikes against the Japanese fleet. With the rest of the VB-11 strike, Cocks took off in his SB2C Helldiver from the teak deck of the *Hornet*. It was a strike at the extreme edge of the Helldivers' range in an attempt to reach the long-range strike battleships and cruisers attacking Vice Admiral Kinkaid's Seventh Fleet.

After the strike was over and VB-11 was finished engaging the Japanese fleet, many of the bombers in VB-11 were perilously short of fuel. They were not going to make it back to the *Hornet*, even with the aircraft carrier making a full head of steam toward the coast of Leyte. VB-11 members had two choices: fly until their fuel ran out and ditch their bombers, hoping to be picked up, or land on Leyte. Seven of the dive bombers headed for Leyte and Tacloban rather than ditch on the flight home and hope to be picked up by an American ship. Cocks had no interest in ditching and hoping to be rescued. His was the first aircraft to head for Leyte. Behind him, flying on a few gallons of remaining fuel, were twenty-seven other Navy dive bombers, not all of them from VB-11. The twenty-three-year-old Cocks decided to land on the newly seized Tacloban Airfield. Circling overhead, Cocks noted, "The [Tacloban] field was clear . . . but it was being worked on that day on the far end with Marston matting. . . . I went in first successfully, [and] saw that the crew that was working on that end of the field was too darn close to planes that were coming in too fast." Someone had to do something. Aircraft low on fuel were going to land at the field, and someone needed to get control of the situation lest there be significant injury to the men in the planes and the men on the ground.[54]

Only one airstrip had been loosely secured by American forces, and Cocks had no choice but to bring his aircraft in for a landing. Perilously low on fuel and fearful of coming under friendly fire, Cocks "made a big circle. Just slowly and letting everyone see the silhouette of our planes." As soon as he landed, Cocks jumped from his aircraft just as an officer from one of the Army units on the ground rushed up to him, yelling, "You gotta slow these planes down, they're landing too fast and they're gonna go into this bomb crater," as he pointed to the end of the runway where a large hole was still smoking. Cocks nodded, sprinted to the end of the runway, and "jerry-rigged some paddles and I took my shirt off so the white would show up, and I . . . never been a signal officer but I was concerned with all those planes coming in that they not go all the way down the runway and go in these shell holes, and, it just continued. . . . I think the total was 18 or 20 aircraft that came in that way."

As evening approached, the same officer told Cocks, "You're gonna get shot by the Japanese because they can see you better than anyone else." Cocks, still concentrating on other incoming aircraft, responded nonchalantly, "Well, if it happens, it happens. Let's get these planes in."[55]

The reality was even more harrowing than Cocks let on. The bomber pilot turned landing signal officer successfully guided every one of the twenty-seven aircraft following in his wake safely onto the battered and bombed-out airstrip. None of the aircraft received serious damage during the landing operation. Even as Cocks guided each aircraft into a safe parking spot and returned to lead in the next flyer, artillery continually fell around him, and enemy bombers flew overhead. Besides the other aircrews of VB-11, Cocks also saved several other aircraft, including some that had participated in the day-long series of strikes against the Japanese fleet off the coast of Samar Island and provided air support for General MacArthur's troops in their return to the Philippines. In the day's fight, several light carriers received damage to their flight decks, and Japanese forces sank two other vessels.

The planes turned to the only available landing place, the newly won airstrip at Tacloban in the northeast corner of Leyte Island. The U.S. Navy found the feat important enough to issue a press release:

> Seizing two pieces of wood and affixing strips of cloth, Cocks hurried to the end of the strip with his makeshift landing "paddles" and jockeyed several planes down to a safe landing. His chief concern was to line the planes up so as to land on a firm spot on the strip and to kill their airspeed to prevent their rolling down the strip too far into the soft dirt at the farther end. Employing approximately the same signals as the landing

> officer of a carrier, and with a few simple improvisations of his own he was able to get his instructions across to the pilots. As the early tropical dusk began to close in, Lt. Cocks saw that the Army engineers, working feverishly to set up boundary lights, would not be able to complete their work in time. He had a number of trucks lined up on both sides of the strip with their headlights directed down it. He also commandeered a small battery of floodlights, used for night construction work, and stood in front of them, stripped to his skivvy shirt so he could be seen more clearly. He was ready to bring the tired pilots in.[56]

For his efforts that day, Cocks was awarded the Legion of Merit by Adm. John McCain. His citation read,

> For exceptionally meritorious conduct in the performance of outstanding service at an advanced field during amphibious assault operations. After a long and hazardous mission, involving a major fleet engagement, he landed on the beach and, at the request of Army authorities, assumed the dirction of aircraft landing operations on a partially serviceable strip. He was instrumental in improvising an emergency lighting system and in the face of intermittent air attack, personally directed the landing by night of some 25 aircraft without a single casualty. He had no previous experience as a landing signal officer. This exemplary action prevented the destruction of many aircraft and injury to personnel involved, and further had the effect of keeping the field clear for full use the next day for air support missions, which assisted materially in preventing general destruction of the area by Japanese air attack.

October 26 found the members of CVG-11 minus the members of VB-11 on the island ready for a fight. The "Plan of the Day" stated, "Today will be a Field Day! Air Department dust off all overheads, removing any snoopers which may be adrift and sweep all corners of the Philippines, sending to incinerator or throwing over the side. . . . Gunnery Department will assist as necessary. Engineering, continue to pour on the coal. Medicos stand-by with heat rash lotion. Damage control, observe holiday routine."[57] The damage control line was somewhat tongue in cheek, indicating the ship itself expected no Japanese resistance or attacks, but the future held different plans. The aircraft that had landed on Leyte returned to the *Hornet* two days later. By then the Battle of Leyte Gulf was over.

During the Battle of Leyte Gulf, George E. Ford of VB-11 earned the Navy Cross. He had been with VB-11 from the start and served throughout Guadalcanal. A native of Orisi, California, Ford attended San Jose State before joining the U.S. Navy in 1941. Ford's fellow VB-11 member Jack Cocks said Ford was "a very solid character and nothing wild about him," and Bill Strahan said, "Everybody loved George Ford. He was a source of great respect. He was a very likable, capable guy." Ford did what was asked of him without great fanfare. He was exactly the type of pilot anyone might want under their command. However, on October 25, during the Battle off Samar, Ford distinguished himself with a bombing attack against the Japanese fleet battleship *Yamato*:[58]

> For distinguishing himself by extraordinary heroism in operations against the enemy while leading a carrier-based dive-bombing attack against a large enemy task force on 25 October 1944. With great skill he directed the attack upon enemy units, which resulted in the damaging of a battleship and two heavy cruisers. He himself scored a direct hit on an enemy battleship of the largest class, pressing home his attack with skill and vigor in the face of enemy anti-aircraft fire of the most intense character and enemy fighter planes. His courageous conduct and skillful leadership were at all times inspiring and in keeping with the highest traditions of the United States Naval Service.

The *Yamato* survived the attack by VB-11, but other bombers and torpedo planes that were still part of Halsey's TF 38 carrier planes hit the center force and decimated it— including the *Yamato*'s sister ship, the *Musashi*, hitting it with nineteen torpedoes and seventeen bombs.

AFTER LEYTE

Despite Halsey's decision to chase the Japanese fleet away from Leyte, the Battle of Leyte Gulf was a disaster for the Japanese forces, but the conflict remained far from over. For the men of CVG-11, this meant more daily operations in support of the tightening noose around the empire of Japan. After the loss of

Commander Schrader on October 13, the air group needed a new commanding officer, and CVG-11 received thirty-two-year-old Cdr. Robert Emmett Riera. Riera, a 1935 graduate of the Naval Academy, earned the Navy Cross at the Battle of Leyte Gulf as part of VB-20, attached to the USS *Enterprise* (CV-6), during action against units of the Japanese fleet. His citation noted that during two days of the battle, Riera was

> leading his squadron on a search and attack mission when an enemy task force was sighted and his division was assigned the Japanese battleship MUSASHI as a target, Lieutenant Commander Riera defied the withering barrages of anti-aircraft fire to lead his division low over the hostile warship and release his bombs at perilously low altitude to score direct hits which started fires and contributed materially to the infliction of extensive damage on the Japanese vessel. The following day he again led his division against an aircraft carrier in the face of withering barrages of anti-aircraft fire to dive low over the hostile warship and release their bombs at perilously low altitude to score direct hits which started fires and contributed materially to the infliction of extensive damage on the Japanese vessel.[59]

After arriving as commanding officer of CVG-11, Riera moved from flying the SB2C to the F6F.

Following the Battle of Leyte Gulf, "the *Hornet* ranged through the Philippines, supporting landings, attacking enemy installations and on several occasions turning back Japanese convoys trying to reinforce their Philippine garrisons. The war was far from over."[60]

Clark G. Reynolds noted that the operations to come in the winter of 1944–45 eventually "led many historians to succumb to hindsight in minimizing the potential strength of the Japanese fleet air forces in October 1944," but this hindsight ignores the fact that possible Japanese forces included several repaired and new aircraft carriers. Even as late as 1944, the Japanese fleet could sally forth a formidable opposition.[61]

CHAPTER 5

MINDORO

Stepping Stone to Luzon

"Leyte and then Luzon." This was the message General MacArthur conveyed to President Roosevelt in the summer of 1944. Admiral Nimitz agreed; Admiral King did not. After Leyte, King wanted the next invasion to be on mainland China at the island of Formosa. Invading Formosa continued the Pacific "leapfrog" strategy—seen earlier with the bypassing of Rabaul—and brought the American forces closer to mainland Japan than did liberating islands in the Philippines chain. MacArthur would have none of it. He was not going to bypass the Philippines or its people. He was going to return as he said he would. This disagreement broke into two camps, the "Luzonites" and the "Formosans." The outline of the plan for the entire Pacific War strategy in June 1944 noted "advance to FORMOSA, either directly or via LUZON." All of this was being done to "establish bases for a final assault upon Japan."[1]

On September 29–30, Admiral King met in San Francisco with Nimitz, Rear Adm. Forrest P. Sherman, Army Gen. Bolivar Buckner, and Army Air Forces Lt. Gen. Millard Harmon to settle the matter. The assembled stars convinced King that no invasion of Formosa was possible before June 1945, while MacArthur stated he could take the Philippines in December 1944.

The Luzon campaign objectives included the destruction of the Japanese air forces in the Philippines, continued isolation of the Philippines, the containment or destruction of the Japanese fleet, and the reoccupation of Luzon and the destruction of the Japanese ground forces there. To take Luzon, the first step was taking back Mindoro, which was slated for December 15, 1944. After the end of the Leyte campaign, the United States and the Allies now had control of the air over the islands of Leyte and further extended their umbrella of air cover toward the Japanese home islands.[2]

● NOVEMBER

In November and December 1944, the squadron continued to work toward the occupation of Leyte, striking targets on Luzon in support of the landings on Mindoro from December 13 to 16. However, perhaps even more deadly than the action in the air was the typhoon that Halsey sailed the fleet into, resulting in the loss of three ships, two of which were destroyers escorting the *Hornet*. The men of CVG-11 watched one of their ships roll under a wave, never to be seen again; the crew on the *Hornet* rode out the storm, and operations continued. In November, the *Hornet* moved from Admiral McCain's TG 38.1 to Rear Adm. G. F. Bogan's TG 38.2. Bogan, a 1916 Naval Academy graduate, had already commanded the USS *Saratoga* and was sent to the United States to work for Admiral King, but he found his way back to active operations in the Pacific in early 1944.[3]

● ● *November 5–6, Luzon*

The *Hornet* task force turned back for operations around Luzon on November 1. Four days later, CVG-11 from the *Hornet* destroyed a Japanese convoy of troopships and destroyers in Ormoc Bay as they tried to reinforce Leyte. Other strikes hit Clark Field. The Japanese aircraft at Clark had been "heckling our forces on Leyte," and the order went out for the *Hornet* task group to "to give the Luzon airfields another going over in an attempt to reduce his air interference." The morning dawned with the *Hornet* steaming on a course of 275 at twenty-two knots in TG 38.1 with the other carriers and escort destroyers. Up front on picket duty, the destroyer USS *Boyd* (DD-544) opened fire on a surfaced Japanese submarine, which quickly submerged and disappeared.[4]

VF-11 launched at 0614 on its morning sweep. Gene Fairfax led a flight of eleven F6Fs off the *Hornet* followed by eight more fighters, eleven VB-11 bombers, and eight VT-11 TBMs. In total, Fairfax was the overall lead for an attack that included dozens of other aircraft from three of the other 38.1 carriers, including fifty-two Hellcats from the *Hornet*, *Wasp*, and light carrier USS *Monterey* (CVL-26). The various elements of the combined air armada formed up and headed west away from the task group en route to Manila, some 160 miles away. The carriers stayed close to the coast, allowing the attack maximum time over the target.[5]

The F6Fs from the fighter squadrons spread out and set to strafing the aircraft parked at Tarlac Field. VF-11 members noted that some of the Japanese aircraft were already damaged and shot up, and it was possible they were to serve as decoys and bring the fighters down into a Japanese anti-aircraft artillery (AAA) ambush. The VB-11 history noted that there were so many aircraft on the ground and that the "enemy's dispersal system" placed the aircraft so far apart that "three strikes were none too many." Giving credence to the ambush, VB-11 also noted that the AAA was especially thick, but that the fighters and bombers continued their low-level attacks with aplomb.[6]

After Tarlac had been given its due attention, Fairfax led VF-11 and the other fighters to the airfield at Mabalacat, where the Japanese were in the process of scrambling some very intact fighters and bombers. Blake Moranville throttled up his fighter and barrel-rolled in a descent, making a slashing overhead attack against a G4M Betty bomber. His bullets struck true, but his pass shot him out in front of the Betty, and he did not see if he had earned the victory. Following Moranville down over the field, Ens. Eddie Kearns observed the bomber crash. However, the bomber was not the first aircraft to go down over Mabalacat.[7]

CVG-11 and the other squadrons entered another cinematic dogfight with Zekes, Oscars, and Tojos. Blake "Rabbit" Moranville, after his pass on the G4M, yanked his stick back and pulled up from his low-level attack. Upon reaching four thousand feet he unloaded into a Nakajima Ki-44, which started spilling smoke as it spiraled to the earth. His guns jammed during the shoot-down, so he disengaged from the combat to try to gain some space and clear his weapons. As Rabbit worked to clear the jam in his machine guns, he saw another Ki-44 fleeing low on the deck. Both the Ki-44 and Moranville's Hellcat were outside the general melee and were easy prey. If Moranville stayed where he was, he might fix the jam and return to the fight, or he might fall victim to the Tojo. He had two choices: make the attack from a position of advantage and with a disabled machine gun, or try to get his guns functioning and perhaps lose situational awareness of the Tojo. His aggressiveness prevailed, and Moranville made a diving pass at the enemy. Only one of Rabbit's machine guns spurted fire at the enemy. The Ki-44 turned to flee the bullets flying by his cockpit and impacting his aircraft. The Tojo's wing clipped the ground, and the aircraft tumbled into nonexistence in a spray of dust and machine parts.[8]

In a matter of minutes, Moranville downed three enemy fighters, but the rest of the squadron was still embroiled in the dogfight occurring above. It proved to be a nearly one-sided fight. VF-11 only lost one aircraft and pilot that day. An attacking Ki-43 Oscar got behind Ens. William M. Mann and opened fire, and Mann's belly tank burst into flame. Mann's wingman, Lt. William R. Sisley in his older F6F-3, turned into the Ki-43 in a desperate bid to defend Mann, but he was simply too far away for an accurate shot. Sisley fired valiantly, but his older "dash three" Hellcat could not make up the distance fast enough. The Oscar broke off the attack, but it was too late to save Ensign Mann and his stricken aircraft.[9]

While other fighters flew north to hunt over other Japanese airfields, Lt. Doc Savage, Lt. Charlie Stimpson, Lt. (jg) Walton Boring, Lt. Daniel T. Work, and Ens. John E. Olson remained over Clark. Savage recalled that day's fight. He noted that several Japanese "fighters were tally-hoed below and Lt. Charlie Stimpson's and my divisions acted as high cover while Lt. Cdr. Bob Clements and a division from VF-14 off the *Wasp* went down a few thousand feet and engaged them, quickly shooting down four enemy airplanes. Things were quiet after that, and Bob came back up to 15,000 feet and joined Charlie and me," but the fight was far from over. In a few more minutes, Ensign Olson, flying on his first combat mission, called out that a Japanese fighter was on his tail. Savage turned sharply away from Olson, bleeding speed to allow Olson and his pursuer to pass to his front. As Olson and the Japanese fighter passed, Savage threw his stick in the other direction, now falling in behind Olson and a Japanese Oscar. Savage opened up out of range, but it was enough to shake the enemy, who broke away from trying to shoot down Olson. The Japanese fighter "turned and twisted, diving for the deck, and I followed, waiting for a good shot. He straightened out momentarily and I settled down dead astern." Savage was in a perfect six o'clock firing position with the Oscar right in his gunsights, and he depressed the trigger. No sooner had the bullets left his gun than another Hellcat dropped down from above, making an overhead run against the Oscar; it was Olson. Olson's Hellcat passed vertically between the Oscar and Savage. Although momentarily surprised, Savage remained on the tail of the Oscar: "I settled down again and put the pipper on the elevator and fired a good long burst, Pieces started coming off the 'Oscar' and he flamed immediately, hitting the ground and disintegrating."[10]

Eight Tojos rained from the sky, two each for Lieutenant Commander Fairfax, Lieutenant Swope, Ens. Jack M. Suddreth, and Lt. (jg) Marvin P. South. Five other VF-11 members accounted for three more Ki-44s and two Ki-43s. The day saw a total score of twenty-six aerial victories in the two extended dogfights over Clark. Never one to miss out on bringing down a "rising sun" and with his proficient dogfighting skills on display, "Skull" Stimpson shot down an additional three aircraft that day. Stimpson was inarguably the best dogfighter in VF-11; counting his victories at Guadalcanal, he finished the war with sixteen confirmed victories, the highest in VF-11.

The bombers of VB-11 joined in the aerial fight. Pilot Doug Logan shot down a Zeke after dropping his bombs. Logan pulled out of his dive and found the Zeke right in his crosshairs. He depressed the trigger and sent the Zeke down. Shortly after that, gunners Jim Kufeldt and Al Pierce shot down another enemy, each earning half a kill. Bill Strahan received the Distinguished Flying Cross for a direct hit on a destroyer sunk in that engagement.[11]

Lt. Francis Joseph Grassbaugh, known as "Grassie" to the other members of VT-11, was the unit's operations officer. He was born on November 7, 1916, and was thought to be lost in operations over Clark Field on November 5, 1944, two days shy of his twenty-eighth birthday. In the TBM Avenger with him were his radioman Homer Johnson and gunner Norman Morgan. Observers saw two parachutes from the stricken aircraft, so hope remained that one or more of the crewmembers survived. Grassie as the operations officer was also the "father confessor" of the squadron. The men of VT-11 recalled his "easy-going manner and calm evaluation," which always served to smooth out any problems as they arose. His efficiency in performing his duties as operations officer kept VT-11 functioning smoothly. The squadron did not learn until Christmas Eve that Grassie survived being shot down over Luzon, but the two enlisted crewmen did not.[12]

While heading back to the *Hornet*, VB-11 pilot Ed Wilson and his gunner Harry Jespersen ran out of gas and ditched. They were quickly picked up by an escort destroyer and given "the customary bell-hop service" back to their home on the *Hornet*. Fellow VB-11 pilot Bill Strahan noted that the normal "reward" for the return of a pilot picked up by a destroyer was five gallons of ice cream. The destroyer pulled alongside the carrier, lines were passed, and when the aircrew was safely back on board, the ice cream was sent over in the same basket.[13]

Transferring between ships was part of the routine for the sailors of World War II, if not something enjoyed by the pilots who certainly preferred their ready room and bunks to the other ships of the fleet where they were merely "guests." After the events of November 5–6, VF-11 pilots Lt. John Ramsey, Lt. James Swope, and Ens. Brainerd Beckwith departed the *Hornet* via basket to the destroyer USS *Maddox*. They were to transfer from the *Maddox* to an escort carrier, pick up some replacement F6Fs, and fly back to the *Hornet*. Instead they found themselves guests of the *Maddox* crew for the next four days, riding out a typhoon, and then "spent the remainder of the three days griping" as the destroyer and other members of the task force chased reports of a Japanese battleship in the area. The three pilots were returned via basket to the *Hornet* on November 11, without any replacement Hellcats. No sooner had they arrived back on the *Hornet* than all three of them were briefed and launched for an air patrol.[14]

● ● *November 11, Ormoc Bay*

On Armistice Day, November 11—something the men of CVG-11 felt to be "a grim and rather stale joke"—VB-11 attacked a Japanese convoy headed to Ormoc Bay, a large body of water on the western side of the island of Leyte. VB-11 launched twenty bombers, but another air group beat them to the convoy, and the five transport ships were already ablaze. VB-11 turned its attention to the escorting destroyers, sinking one and damaging the other. The VB-11 history noted, "The convoy was literally obliterated," and pilots Ed Smith, Bill Strahan, Abie Fite, Art Dunlap, and Bill Armstrong were singled out for their "excellent hits" despite intense anti-aircraft opposition. In all, four troop transports, four destroyers, four smaller destroyer escorts, and three other ships fell victim to the combined attacks of VB-11 and other strikers.[15]

Attacks and strikes continued every day as the U.S. Navy relentlessly attrited Japanese forces in the region. It was clear in late 1944 that American and Allied forces were on the offensive everywhere in the Pacific, but Japan's defeat was not recognized at this stage in the war, nor were daily operations in any way mundane, routine, or even easy. Death stalked all combatants. Sitting in his room on November 12, Lt. John Ramsey pulled out his well-worn leather diary with the Sundowners emblem on its cover. He wrote that the day had been one of rest and relaxation, but closed that day's entry with "We are due for some hot A.A."[16]

● ● *November 13–19 over Luzon: Manila Bay and Subic Bay*

After Ormoc Bay, the air group's operations in November against Japanese reinforcement convoys dwindled. The VB-11 history noted that "it was decided to break up the Japanese reinforcement attempts at their source." The target was the harbor of Manila Bay. Strikes continued on November 13–14.[17]

In two days, the air group carried out six strikes. Lieutenant Ramsey's thoughts proved prescient. At approximately 0815 on November 13, during the first strike of the day and in his twelfth strike as commander of VT-11, Lieutenant Commander Denniston made a glide-bombing attack against shipping in Manila Harbor. The AAA was indeed fierce that morning. Denniston's TBM Avenger was hit and he transmitted, "Plane hit, am going in."

Only one parachute was observed, so there was initially hope that at least one of the crewmembers survived. Denniston, Aviation Radioman First Class Glenn Allen Faulk, and Aviation Ordnanceman Third Class Clint Thomas Steed Jr. were never heard from again. The loss of young Steed hit his friend Bob Fitz particularly hard. Just as they were called to the planes for the day's strike, Fitz asked Steed to borrow his comb. Fitz recalled, "I don't know why I wanted to comb my hair because I gotta put my goggles and hat on and all," but he ran the comb through his hair and hollered at Steed to wait a minute and take the comb back. Steed shouted over his shoulder, "Give it to me when I get back." Fitz carried that comb for many years after the war ended. Denniston had been the commanding officer of VT-11 for over a year. The squadron commander's aircraft was one of two lost on November 13.[18]

Many years later, Verg Bloomquist related a story relayed to him about the three missing American airmen from VT-11. In the telling, an unknown F6F fighter pilot from an unknown squadron was shot down a few days later near Manila Harbor. Coming down under his parachute, he was unlucky enough to get tangled in a tree, his feet rocking uselessly several feet off the ground, too high to release himself without injury. The pilot heard voices in the distance, but remained caught in the tree unable to conceal himself or make a run for it. The approaching group turned out to be Chinese guerrillas, who then helped him down out of his predicament..As it turned out, the guerrillas were aware of three other deceased airmen not far from his location. Walking a short distance, the group came to a clearing, where the pilot clearly saw three dead Americans. The pilot, signaling to the three dead Americans and to his dog tags, indicated he wanted to retrieve the tags from the corpses. The guerrillas set off to attend to the macabre task while the pilot sat down and rested. Bloomquist related the story he had been told: "They came back and said that their tongues had been cut out and some of their fingernails had been pulled off. But they got the dog tags and brought 'em back and gave them to the leader. And the leader handed them to the fighter pilot." The dog tags turned out to be those of Denniston, Faulk, and Steed.[19]

Also shot down were Ens. Burton Oberg and crewmembers Aviation Machinist's Mate Third Class Robert Verne Burgess and Aviation Ordnanceman Third Class Dowd Howaker. VT-11's history noted that a small degree of "retribution" was felt with the forty thousand tons of shipping sunk or damaged during the two days' strikes.[20]

VB-11 also participated in the two days of attacks against Manila Bay and the big island of Luzon, noting, "We played havoc with the merchant vessels anchored there." As noted with VT-11 attacks, VB-11 "had to dive through a regular curtain of fire to get at the fat targets inside the breakwater," but the bomber pilots did not suffer any downed planes. Meanwhile, up above the bombing, VF-11 provided air cover. The Sundowners shot down only three Japanese bombers, indicating the scope of Japan's ability to provide adequate air cover to its bases in late 1944. Ramsey noted the fighters covered the air from 1,500 to 20,000 feet in low and high cover, flying along "in and out of clouds and smoke from the burning ships in the harbor." The next day was much the same: "two strikes and a VF sweep." When the *Hornet* left on November 14, the harbor was "a regular graveyard of burnt and sunken ships. It was a most gratifying sight."[21]

Retiring from Manila Bay and the big island of Luzon, the *Hornet* moved again for refueling operations. It is a testament to naval logistics that the task forces of Third Fleet were able to continue prosecuting the war without the need for extended rest or refueling in harbor. After a few days of refueling and resupply, the *Hornet* and CVG-11 were back off to Luzon to give the island "a thorough one-day going over."[22]

According to the records kept from CVG-11, the strikes on November 19 added little of value to the campaign. The VB-11 history noted, "We hit shipping in Manila Harbor, installations at Olongapo in Subic Bay [which turned out to be vastly overrated as a target] and had one final go at our old stomping ground, Clark Field. It was a busy day, but good targets were scarce and we were able to add little to our running score." After the strikes, the *Hornet* retired back to the anchorage at Ulithi.[23]

Operations since the *Hornet* returned late to the fight at the Battle of Leyte Gulf proved profitable for the air group. VF-11 decimated Japanese air resistance over Luzon on November 5–6. The torpedo and bomber squadrons also had "field days" with Japanese shipping in the middle of the month. Bill Strahan summed up the operations saying, "Admiral Halsey took his mighty Third Fleet into the China Sea. We flew strikes east against Formosa, Luzon,

Clark Field, Manila, and Subic Bay. We flew west all along the China coast destroying tankers and targets. Passed Hong Kong and French Indochina. All this in preparation for the Lingayen Gulf invasion at Luzon."[24]

The *Hornet* and CVG-11 remained at Ulithi for the next three weeks. The U.S. Navy Seabees had performed miracles in the two months since conducting the build-up of the base. In addition to all the needed naval facilities mentioned previously, the Seabees had created a resort worthy of any vacation seeker: "The largest island, Mog Mog, was set aside chiefly for recreation purposes and everyday those who had no duty aboard were free to go ashore and explore its wonders. There was swimming in the warm, clear waters of the lagoon, too shallow to accommodate an uninvited shark. Softball diamonds and volleyball courts called lazy muscles, inactive after long weeks afloat. Best of all, ice-cold beer in the shade of the whispering palms made the island a popular resort for all hands."[25] The beer was available at "Flag Bar" or "Crowley's Tavern," and the only complaint seemed to come from the men waiting for a boat to go ashore or return aboard, as the base was chronically short of transport craft—no surprise given the amount of men and shipping in the atoll at any one time.

During the interlude at Ulithi, VB-11 lost over twenty personnel to reshuffling of billets inside of active Navy bomber squadrons to "further streamline carrier bombing squadrons and to conform more closely with current strategic needs." It was an unexpected blow to a unit that had already gone through so much since operations began. The history of VB-11 said "it was difficult to say goodbye to those who had shared our ups and downs for so long." Shuffling affected VF-11 as well, with twenty-six pilots transferred to other units, but these ranks were filled at Ulithi with other pilots transferring into the squadron. One of the new arrivals was Lt. Cdr. Fritz E. Wolf. He had joined the Navy right out of college, but in the summer of 1941 Wolf voluntarily resigned his commission in order to join the American volunteer group in China under Maj. Gen. Claire Chennault. Thus, the naval aviator became a member of the famed Flying Tigers.[26]

DECEMBER

As December began, CVG-11 went through a series of command changes due primarily to the loss of squadron leaders in the ongoing operations. Lt. Cdr.

Edward J. "Bud" Kroeger assumed command of VB-11. He had been at Pearl Harbor on December 7 and later participated in the Battle of Midway. Flying with VB-6 from the USS *Enterprise*, Kroeger served as wingman for VB-6 commanding officer Dick Best. Thus, Kroeger was in the thick of the fight on June 4, 1942, where he dropped his munitions on the Japanese flagship, the carrier *Akagi*, with a one-thousand-pound bomb, thereby contributing to its demise. Later in the same afternoon, Kroeger participated in the sinking of the *Hiryu* and also attacked the *Soryu* before returning to the *Enterprise*. VT-11 was without a commander after the death of Lieutenant Commander Denniston. Lt. W. J. Engman served temporarily as the commanding officer, but he was replaced by Lt. Cdr. John A. Fidel, a classmate of Fairfax's at the Naval Academy in the class of 1939. During his time as a midshipman he participated on the track and tennis teams and was on the staff of the Naval Academy yearbook, the *Lucky Bag*. Fidel was a recent convert to naval aviation, having only attended flight training from June 1942 until April 1943. In January 1944 he became executive officer of Torpedo Squadron 80, based on USS *Ticonderoga* (CV-14), until his transfer to be commanding officer of VT-11 in December 1944.[27]

On December 12, after three weeks in the paradise of Ulithi, the *Hornet* and the rest of the ships in the task group sortied forth once more. As the task force got underway, training commenced with a series of drills including zigzagging and emergency maneuvers during a simulated attack. The ship launched fighters, bombers, and torpedo planes to begin shaking off the rust from their time in port and to prepare for the combat that lay ahead of them. At 1405 as the ship launched another round of aircraft, a plane from VT-11 piloted by Lt. (jg) James Hooper knifed over after launch and crashed into the water. The pilot did not appear to have attempted to make a water landing; the aircraft just plowed, right wing first, into the water. Inside the Avenger were radioman Robert Trobaugh and gunner Wilfred Leblanc. Hooper and Trobaugh both extricated themselves from the aircraft, but Leblanc was never seen again. Even routine training and practice operations had the ability to turn deadly in the blink of an eye. The *Hornet* headed once more for the airfields over Luzon to ensure that any enemy resistance there could not interfere with the landings on Mindoro, which began on December 15.[28]

● ● *December 14–16: Subic Bay and Luzon Again*

Halsey's Third Fleet sailed south of Luzon off the island of Mindoro where their aircraft supported MacArthur's and Kinkaid's landings on December 15. From December 14 to 16, Halsey supported the landings, and his aircraft, including CVG-11, made attacks against Luzon. On December 16 Halsey recovered his air fleet and turned east for refueling operations. Edwin "Big Ed" Wilson described his pre-strike planning preparation in a diary entry that clearly demonstrates the amount of work needed to prepare for a strike and get off the *Hornet*'s deck for a "typical day" that December:

> rudely awakened by the telephone at 0645. Duty Officer informed me to get my breakfast and hustle up to the ready room. . . . Hustled up to the Ready Room at 0730 to get ready for Charlie Strike. Put on my belt with extra thirty-eight Cal. ammunition, my dog tags and then my flight suit with the pockets filled with copious quantities of miscellaneous life-saving gear. My leg pockets are so full I have to take my shoes off to get my flight suit off. I would sink like an anchor in the water with all the gear we carry. Donned my shoulder holster, got my navigation board and started putting down all the necessary flight information. About this time Jonesy [Lt. A. M. Jones, USNR] our ACI Officer got up on his soap box and gave us all the rescue calls for subs and seaplanes plus all nav codes (shackle, ZB approach and recognition). Jonesy . . . then gave us our targets. The teletype started ticking away giving us our 0830 position (Point Option), course and speed. So we immediately started working our navigation, course to target and the return trip to base. Working like beavers, because they no more than give us Point Option then they usually say, "Pilots Man Your Planes." Quickly put on my Mae West, back pack (with all its emergency contents), grabbed helmet and plotting board. While those not on the hop and ground wished us luck and told us to "give 'em hell."[29]

Prior to the bombers and torpedo planes taking off, the *Hornet* launched a series of F6Fs to provide an air patrol over the ship. One of the first Hellcats into the sky on December 16 was that of Lt. (jg) John A. Zink. Immediately after launch, Zink and his wingman Lt. (jg) M. J. "Bull" Hayter received a report of an unknown aircraft flying over the fleet. Flying "in the soup" of the poor weather above the fleet, Zink and Hayter flew back and forth without finding anything. Just as they were about to break away, Zink saw a Yokosuka P1Y Ginga Frances orbiting and observing the fleet below. Zink thought, "This is my chance." He pushed the throttle forward and went after the larger and slower enemy: "I didn't even call it in—I caught a little hell for that. I was the first one there and I was right on his tail. The Frances was a good aircraft, but not quite fast enough to outrun a Hellcat on supercharger. He went down easy, so to speak."[30]

Hayter also joined in on the kill. Later, back on the *Hornet* the two pilots argued over who should get credit for the kill. Apparently, it was VF-11 custom to not share kills, so the two men were having a heated exchange when air group commander Fairfax showed up. To settle the dispute, Fairfax made the two men flip a coin. Zink won the coin toss and got credit for the kill.[31]

VB-11 pilot Ed Wilson had flown with the same radioman, Harry R. "Jep" Jespersen, since Bombing Eleven was commissioned in October 1942. They flew off Guadalcanal together and now off the *Hornet*, and Wilson considered him his "good luck piece."[32] VB-11 put in work on December 15 striking targets at Floridablanca west of Manila and south of Clark Air Base. Wilson's was the seventh aircraft in the squadron to dive down on the target that day. He remembered that the first six aircraft had already "really plaster[ed] the assigned areas," so he kicked his rudders over to attack a large shed. Wilson dropped four bombs and hit the shed to little effect; neither Wilson nor Jep witnessed any secondary explosions. As he pulled out he saw six new Japanese fighters parked on the ground. Wilson conducted a "wing over and came back strafing with my two 20 mm cannons. Went down the line putting rounds in at least five of them but none burned, apparently all degassed."[33]

The members of VB-11 strafed and bombed targets of opportunity on their flight back and landed back on the *Hornet* at 1300. Wilson noted that this was his fourteenth strike since commencing operations. However, all the members of CVG-11 would put combat operations out of their minds for the next seventy-two hours because they were about to face something just as dangerous as any Japanese attack. None of them knew they were about to do battle with Mother Nature.

TYPHOON COBRA

The typhoon arrived on December 17, and Halsey ordered the Third Fleet ships to stop their ongoing refueling efforts as winds picked up to over thirty knots. Halsey turned the fleet to the northwest in an attempt to escape the storm. However, rather than escape it, he was sailing toward its heart. Later in the afternoon, Halsey brought the fleet around to the southwest, but this only placed his fleet on a parallel course to the storm throughout the night of December 17 and into the following morning. Halsey biographer Thomas Alexander Hughes noted that the admiral "was now matching wits with nature, and losing." Winds reached a peak speed of over one hundred knots, and the sea had waves over seventy feet high. For reference, the distance from the *Hornet*'s deck to the waterline was typically fifty to sixty feet.[34]

The typhoon, soon to be known as Typhoon Cobra, was having its way with the Third Fleet. Halsey radioed MacArthur that no air support was coming December 18 or 19, and he ordered the fleet to find their own course out of the storm, the fleet equivalent of "every man for himself."

The members of Eleven remembered the typhoon just as clearly as they remembered combat. Verg Bloomquist recalled, "Some of the waves were coming up over the flight deck. The flight deck is 65 feet off the water." Bob Fitz noted, "A ship as big as the *Hornet*, when that thing would go down into the water in that typhoon, it would go down in the water, whoom! And the whole rear end, all the screws would come out of the water, and that thing would shake all over. That ship would just shake all over and rattle, and make some of the worst noise."

Bloomquist and Bill Corley, tired of riding the storm out in the ready room, decided to make their way topside and were wrapped around the railing on the *Hornet* holding on for dear life. Shortly after they arrived on deck, the hatchway they had just exited banged open; another sailor came on deck just as a wave broke over them. The sailor disappeared into the ocean. Bloomquist and Corley had no time to even think about the man overboard because just then, one of their accompanying destroyers nosed down into the waves: "the Tin Can went down bow first and we kept waiting for it to come up. Never did come up." The men wisely decided to make their way back to the ready room, where they learned the destroyer they just saw disappear had indeed sunk. Oddly enough, the official history of VB-11, no doubt written with hindsight, noted that it was "fun to go aloft in the island and watch the fury of the gale." The same history did note that "it was far from fun for the poor wretches who were being tossed like milkshakes in the cans and light cruisers."[35]

Strahan noted, "I got a glimpse of the typhoon from a sheltered position on the flight deck. The foam from the huge waves was flying horizontal like [a] winter blizzard in the Midwest. When the *Hornet* was on the crest of a huge wave, other nearby ships were in the trough. Moments later, those ships were riding high on the mountainous crest and the *Hornet* was in the trough." Robert Cocks remembered, "The *Hornet* would roll and almost, it feels like it was on its side. And then it would pitch up and down with enough violence that it bent the support girders of the flight deck and the forward part of the ship."[36]

The storm began to settle by the evening of December 18, but the Third Fleet was scattered, literally, to the winds; it now covered 2,500 square miles of ocean. During the typhoon Halsey lost three destroyers: USS *Spence* (DD-512), USS *Hull* (DD-350), and USS *Monaghan* (DD-354). Only seventy men from those three ships were recovered, with a total of almost eight hundred men lost. Although other ship losses accounted for more deaths, when combined, the three-ship loss during Typhoon Cobra was only exceeded by the loss of the USS *Arizona*, USS *Indianapolis*, and USS *Corregidor*. Besides the loss of the three destroyers, "four escort carriers, a light cruiser, seven destroyers, two destroyer escorts, a fleet oiler, and a fleet tug were badly damaged."[37]

When the typhoon ended, *Hornet* returned with the rest of the task group to Ulithi for repairs and to take stock of the losses from the storm. Nearly eight hundred sailors perished in the storm, three destroyers were lost, thirty ships were damaged, and dozens of aircraft were ripped off the decks and out of the hangars of the carriers. At Ulithi at the same time were five of *Hornet*'s sister ships: the *Essex*, *Wasp*, *Yorktown*, *Hancock*, and *Ticonderoga*. The Navy released a publicity shot titled "Murderers' row, Third fleet carriers at Ulithi Atoll in December 1944." The *Hornet* spent the remainder of 1944 at Ulithi as the fleet tended its wounds.

The *Hornet* spent Christmas and New Year's at Ulithi. It was not home. Loved ones were thousands of miles away. However, the men put to work to celebrate the holiday as well as they could: “Mail and presents from home came aboard by the sackful. . . . Industrious souls did a magnificent job of decorating the ready room and all hands gathered here for the two-hour jubilee show broadcast over the ship’s speaker system. Christmas Eve brought a happy hour with songs, stories, skits, a tree, and Santa Claus himself, who came in on radar, his sled towed by sea horses. The ship provided a magnificent feast and nothing was left undone that would make us feel more in the holiday mood.”[38]

CHAPTER

HUNTING SEASON

Luzon, Formosa, French Indochina, and War's End for CVG-11

The New Year dawned, and CVG-11 moved into its final act. In January, no one knew the war was entering its final stages. Few knew the Japanese people were about to reap the whirlwind of the most destructive strategic bombing campaign in history, and even fewer knew the United States was closing in on a new and destructive weapon that might end the war on its own. This is all to say that the sailors, soldiers, airmen, and marines in the Pacific only knew the war was likely to continue for an indeterminable amount of time, and many guessed what only the senior leaders knew: that the invasion of Japan itself, the Japanese home islands, was to begin sometime in 1945.

On the *Hornet*, the final command team was in place: CVG-11 under the command of Lieutenant Commander Riera, VF-11 under Lieutenant Commander Fairfax, VB-11 under Lieutenant Commander Kroeger, and VT-11 under Lieutenant Commander Fidel. They were all part of Capt. Austin Doyle's USS *Hornet*. Above the *Hornet* was Rear Adm. Jocko Clark's Carrier Division 5, then Rear Adm. Gerald Bogan's Task Group 38.2, part of Vice

Adm. John McCain's Task Force 38. At the head of all of this was Third Fleet under Adm. William Halsey. McCain's TF-38 had three main body task groups, each with three heavy carriers and one light carrier. There were fourteen different air groups. On board the *Essex* and *Wasp* the two carriers carried ninety-one fighter aircraft and fifteen TBM Avenger bombers each. The *Independence* and *Enterprise* comprised a smaller unit: Task Group 38.5, which Halsey and McCain created as a night-flying, night-striking group. As naval historian Samuel Eliot Morison noted, it was "the most powerful naval striking force the world had ever known."[1]

Halsey and McCain were on the offensive: "The year 1944 had been one of victory from the Marshalls to the Philippines, they were determined that 1945 would see the final and complete liquidation of Japanese Sea Power." In a sense, Admiral Nimitz kept Halsey on a short leash in the first weeks of 1945, and the Third Fleet struck targets in direct support of the landings in the Lingayen Gulf. After that, however, Nimitz gave Halsey the okay to enter and conduct operations in the South China Sea.

As 1945 began, the men of CVG-11 found themselves pressing the attack and hunting Japanese forces in the air, at sea, and on the ground throughout their area of operations, which included the familiar Philippines and also French Indochina. In January 1945 the squadron struck ships and targets on Formosa and Luzon in support of the invasion of the Lingayen Gulf, Luzon. The squadron participated in operations in the South China Sea (the first time an American task force had entered these waters since the beginning of the war), striking targets at Cam Ranh Bay and a convoy off Qui Nhơn, French Indochina, shipping at the Pescadores Islands, and Hong Kong.

Halsey's plan of attack called for strikes against Formosa on January 3–4, refueling the following day, a strike on Luzon on January 6, reattacks on either or both locations on January 7, refueling the next day, and strikes on Formosa again on January 9, which was when the landings in the Lingayen Gulf began.

January also found the Third Fleet dealing with Japan's expanding kamikaze attacks, although the *Hornet* during the cruise of CVG-11 was relatively lucky in this regard. Halsey noted shortly after the invasion of Luzon early in January that "Luzon is now a bloody battleground. The enemy is fighting to the death to destroy our expeditionary forces and kill the embarked American soldiers. Many ships have been hard hit in the past two days. Every undestroyed enemy aeroplane is a potential threat to our comrades and a threat to its success."[2]

Bill Strahan remembered that the near-daily strikes wore the pilots down to exhaustion, making them complacent in their response to the alarms of general quarters: "I recall how totally exhausted we pilots were on return from those flights. . . . I had just dozed off when general quarters sounded. Bong, bong, bong. Kamikaze attack." Strahan and several other pilots rolled over and ignored the alarm, too tired to move. Lying in bed, he heard the large compartment door to the area of the officers' room clang shut as someone sealed it. Strahan and every man in that compartment were now locked below decks with no way to get topside. Strahan later found out that his roommate, Howard Bose Erwin, was on the hangar deck and witnessed a kamikaze shot down by the *Hornet* gunners as it headed toward the carrier. Strahan later said, "After that scary experience and my own foolish decision, I was never too exhausted to go to the assigned area when general quarters was sounded."[3]

At midnight on January 3, the *Hornet* steamed on a course of 287 at twenty-five knots. The pilots were roused, fed, briefed, and inside their aircraft before 0600. Eight VF-11 Hellcats launched first on a reconnaissance sweep over the city of Tainan on Formosa. They were followed at 0715 by twenty-four more Hellcats: twelve in a combat air patrol and twelve as strikers. At 0910 the first launch of nine VB-11 bombers and five planes from VT-11 took place. As soon as the second strike launched, the first strike was back overhead, ready for recovery. The strikes on January 3 were a disappointment for all involved. Lieutenant Ramsey noted, "Today was a very bad day for flying, even for the birds." The weather at the target was especially bad with cloud cover stretching from nine thousand feet down to the water. Strikes on January 4 were much the same, and the weather refused to cooperate again. Fighters strafed and the bombers did the best they could under the circumstances, but the pilots in all squadrons were happy to turn away from Formosa and head back to Luzon, where they hoped the hunting might be better.[4]

January 6 saw better results all around. The Japanese fighters chose to engage in a dogfight with members of VF-11, and six Zekes jumped a flight of Hellcats, but the results were all in the favor of the Sundowners, with two victories and two probable. The weather returned on January 7, an "impenetrable, insurmountable wall of cloud." The weather was the ultimate enemy this day, claiming the lives of four members of the air group. VF-11 pilot Lt. (jg) John Sims disappeared into a cloud bank and was never seen again. Lt. (jg) Richard Glen Aubel of VB-11 and his radioman Marion Russell Young were seen through a break in the clouds to be spinning out of control, but they too disappeared without a trace. Also gone was Ens. James Houston Bethel Jr. from Massies Mill, Virginia. He was engaged in a fight with an enemy Oscar at very low altitude and crashed into the water; the plane was seen burning on the surface, but there was no trace of the young pilot.[5]

FORMOSA

On January 9 the *Hornet* and other members of the task group launched more strikes against Formosa. The war diary of VT-11 noted they "had a field day," and VB-11 called it the "ever-rewarding Takao Harbor." Floating in Takao Harbor, as if waiting on American naval airpower, were nearly fifty Japanese ships. VT-11 and VT-7 dropped torpedoes on Japanese tankers, which "broke apart like a piñata hit with a baseball bat." The VB-11 history noted the missions that day were "without doubt one of our most productive strikes."[6]

As the strike on January 9 was coming to a close, Lt. (jg) Gordon Woolfolk Bell's TBM Avenger was hit by anti-aircraft fire over the southern tip of Formosa. In the aircraft with him were Aviation Machinist's Mate First Class Claude Ellsworth Haley and Aviation Radioman Second Class Laurence Ernest Sawyer. After the TBM went down, fellow pilots circled overhead. George Stebbings saw Claude Haley in a life raft with another unconscious or wounded member of his crew. No pilot above could tell if it was Bell or Sawyer. Stebbings and others watched helplessly as Haley frantically attempted to row the life raft out to sea to save himself and his crewmember, but a strong wind was blowing the small raft toward the shore where Japanese troops waited on land. None of the crew was ever seen again.[7]

Also killed on the January 9 attacks was Aviation Radioman Second Class Roger Balcombe from Cosmopolis, Washington, also of VT-11. His crewmates remembered that as the TBM's pilot, Lt. David W. Mangum, made strafing runs over their target, Balcombe was hit. The TBM's gunner, Roy Eddington, jumped down to render aid, but the bullet had sliced Balcombe's belly open, and he died on the flight back to the *Hornet*. The next day he was buried at sea. The ship's diary noted, "1400: Half Masted Colors—held funeral services for BALCOMBE, ROGER ARM2c." A contemporary newspaper proved more loquacious in reporting the afternoon's events:

> Roger Balcombe was buried in the clothing in which he bravely died, in his flight suit, bearing on the shoulder a shield blazoning stars of two nations—the United States and China. The sailmaker sewed him into his canvas shroud, weighting it with a five-inch shell that his plunge might be swift and final. Six shipmates brought him to the forecastle, where the roaring blowers for once were stilled that yet living ears might hear the prayers said over Roger Balcombe's body. The captain came, and stood hatless beside a man who died serving him and, through him, the nation. The band softly played "Abide with Me," and the rushing sea murmured its immemorial dirge below. His shipmates tipped the board and the cold flesh that was yesterday alive slid from under the flag and fell into the sea. Soft and sweet the bugler sounded Taps, and the Marine guard fired three volleys into the sky, a vestigial touch of superstition: for once the funeral volleys were meant to drive off the devils from entering ears laid ajar by grief. The band played "Nearer, My God, to Thee," and the ship turned again to its work of death, in whose interest Roger Balcombe died.[8]

● FRENCH INDOCHINA AND RABBIT'S RUN

CVG-11 and the crew of the *Hornet* were flying high. Despite losses and death, the men knew they were putting in good work and felt as if their strikes were having tangible effects on the war effort and the destruction of the Japanese empire. After Formosa, "we looked around for new worlds to conquer. Someone suggested the South China Sea. There ought to be targets a-plenty, fat and unsuspecting, along the shores of China and even Indo China [*sic*]." January 12 was CVG-11's first strike against French Indochina, hitting Japanese shipping in Cam Ranh Bay. VB-11 members called it a "banner day." The Japanese occupied Indochina militarily before World War II but allowed the French to continue to govern the colony. These strikes were part of a larger coordinated effort where, starting in December 1944, attacks on Japanese targets in what is today Vietnam were made by Halsey's Third Fleet, B-29s of the XX Bomb Group flying out of India, and elements of the Fifth and Thirteenth Air Forces.[9]

Despite VB-11's proclamations about the banner day, VT-11 and VF-11 both suffered losses. Lt. (jg) William Maier led VT-11's strike that day in TBM-1C Avenger Bureau Number 73322. As he pulled up and away from his attack run, his plane exploded. Shortly after his loss, the squadron learned that Maier was to receive the Navy Cross for actions during Leyte Gulf. Also killed in the explosion were Aviation Ordnanceman Second Class Edward Speckner and Lt. (jg) Joe Hyland, the group's radar officer. The squadron's war diary said, "To him goes much of the credit not only for the radar efficiency of squadron radioman but also for the sustained good humor of all hands." Little was written of Speckner in the same diary other than to note his date of death, that he hailed from Kentucky, and that he received an air medal for the action that cost him his life.[10]

Lt. Blake "Rabbit" Moranville was already an ace with six confirmed victories. His awards to this point on VF-11's second tour included the Distinguished Flying Cross and several air medals, but the thing Moranville seemed most proud of was his assignment as the guardian and caretaker of the squadron's mascot, Gunner.[11] On the afternoon of January 12, a flight of four Hellcats lifted from the deck of the *Hornet*. The crews were Lt. Jim Swope, division leader, and his wingman Ens. Charlie Boineau, and Moranville and his wingman Ens. Eddie Kearns. The flight of four headed for the city of Saigon to attack targets at the Japanese airfield there. Moranville was on his second strike of the day—the earlier flight had been to Cam Ranh Bay to attack shipping and any other targets of opportunity. He had made four successful passes when Kearns shouted over the radio, " 'Hey Rabbit, you're on fire! Bail out!' I was quite surprised because I had felt no explosion and had no indication that anything was wrong but since my altimeter indicated that I was at fifty feet I was not about to bail out. I did pull up though and almost immediately my wind screen was covered with oil so then I knew that I had a problem."[12]

Moranville's engine was bleeding oil and overheating. The aircraft was only at an altitude of 1,500 feet so the chance of parachuting to safety was slim. Rabbit decided his best option was to ditch the aircraft: "Besides I had practice landing the Hellcat but had never practiced jumping with a parachute." Moranville scanned the area around him and was pleased to see it was mostly rice paddies. He picked out a long rice paddy clear of any obstructions, tightened down his shoulder straps, pulled back his throttles, and dropped the tail hook, hoping it would "give me an indication of when I was about six feet from the ground." His fighter cleared a dike at the end of the paddy; he dropped his flaps to slow him down, and he settled gently into the field: "Although I knew it was going to be muddy I didn't realize quite how wet it would be. After a very short slide the aircraft came to a stop and I immediately got out."[13] Moranville ended up being one of six Americans, part of Task Force 38, shot down over French Indochina that day.[14]

Moranville was immediately approached by many locals but was having difficulty in gaining any help from them: "I heard one of the young boys say something in English. . . . I immediately zeroed in on him and attempted to get him to help me. I'm really not sure how much English he did understand but he did indicate that he didn't dare help because the Japanese would kill him. This was not said outright but he said, 'Japanese' and drew his hand across his throat as though to cut it." Shortly thereafter, a "little old lady grabbed my sleeve and indicated that I should follow her and started walking down the dike." He was taken to a small hut and given some mango juice and a couple of bananas, and then taken on foot to another village.[15]

The first night after being shot down, Moranville was led from village to village before settling in what he believed to be a church. That evening around nine o'clock he was approached by what appeared to be a French civilian who offered him a swig of cognac and a warning that Japanese troops knew he had crash-landed and were currently searching for him. Moranville departed with his new companion in the latter's car.[16]

After departing the village with the Frenchman, his companion stopped the car and told Moranville they would probably encounter Japanese patrols along the way. He said that if a Japanese patrol stopped them, Moranville should feign that he was asleep in the passenger seat and should not under any circumstances wake up. The Frenchman was correct; Japanese troops stopped them several times along the route. Moranville kept his eyes shut and tried to control his breathing. In reality, he "never even slept a wink!"[17]

Having survived encounters with local Japanese patrols while feigning sleep, Moranville "awoke" the morning of January 13 in Saigon and was delivered to a French military headquarters and interrogated at length by two French officers. They informed Moranville that the best course of action to protect him from the Japanese was to place him in a local French prison until other arrangements might be made for his safe return. The prison in question turned out to be for women, and he was thrown into a large room segregated into smaller cells by iron bars and with no privacy for any of the inmates. Moranville, being the only male prisoner, was constantly stared at by the other inmates. The next day he was moved to "Maison Centrale de Saigon," the city's larger prison, where he joined Lt. (jg) Elmer Stratton, an F6F pilot from the *Hancock*; 2nd Lt. Joseph Lynch, an F4U pilot from the *Essex*; and Ens. Peter Lambros, a TBM pilot from the *San Jacinto*, and his two crewmen Ordnanceman Edward Santopadre and Radioman Richard Fetzer.[18]

Moranville noted that the "Maison Centrale was an old time French prison surrounded by walls with pieces of glass embedded in the concrete along the top and barbed wire strands above that. The cell blocks and the Administrative Offices surrounded a very large and beautifully landscaped court yard." The Americans found themselves assigned to a section of the prison that was somewhat isolated from the general population and other prisoners. Their section consisted of three cells, which opened onto a very small walled-in breezeway, so they did have access to fresh air.[19]

The six men stayed three to a room and had a central "living room" area and a breezeway outside for exercise, but they were kept isolated from the other inmates. Their French "captors" fed them adequately three times a day and in the evenings allowed them out in the courtyard to enjoy the evening air. However, while in the courtyard, groups of French prison officials or dignitaries—none of the captives were quite sure—watched over them from a balcony above while enjoying cocktails. The Americans dubbed this "going to the Zoo to watch the Americans." They also received "gifts" from an unknown source including cigarettes, cologne, books, magazines, playing cards, a radio, and even alcohol (mostly rum, but also gin and scotch). While reading the magazines, one of the aviators noted some of the words had been underlined. The captives discovered a message: They were being watched by members of the Free French resistance force attempting to plan an escape or otherwise help the Americans back to friendly forces. Moranville noted that the Japanese collaborating Vichy French prison officials had many opportunities to turn them over to Japanese forces, but by this point knew the Japanese were going to lose the war. A set of coffins left by the front door of the prison by the French resistance with the message "This is for you as soon as the war is over" also helped secure the Americans' safety.[20]

The incarceration began to wear on the American flyers and they grew bored: "When the French incarcerated us the only thing they took from us was our service revolver so we had our flight suits and all of the equipment we carried. One of the things I always carried was a miniature Very pistol." The sole purpose of this small pistol, only about six inches long, was to shoot a single flare. It was a simple device to operate. One inserted the flare cartridge in the tube, cocked the hammer, and pulled the trigger, and a flare shot into the sky, attracting the attention of aircraft in the area to a downed aircrew. For reasons known only to himself, Moranville decided to fire the pistol one evening: "It had been months since I'd seen one fired and I'd forgotten how loud the explosion was and how far the flare flew."

Moranville was strolling in a central open courtyard when he took the pistol from his pocket and pulled the trigger: "The explosion of the cartridge was deafening inside the walls and of course the flare flew up and up and over the wall. We all knew that shortly all hell was going to break loose so we returned to our cells on the double." Five minutes later, their guard burst into their room, screaming, "What have you done? What have you done?" Moranville and the other prisoners feigned ignorance and objected that they had done nothing wrong and had been sitting idly in the room. The guard grew flustered by their declarations of innocence and continued yelling at the Americans, "Do you know where the fire landed? It landed in front of my house, and the Japanese officer who lives next door came running to see what the explosion was." Fortunately, the Japanese never solved the mystery of the explosion and apparently forgot the incident. However, the French did not forget. The next morning they ransacked the cell, taking the prisoners' flight suits and any other equipment they could find.[21]

Roughly a month into their imprisonment, the prison commandant, Captain Jacques Beauvallet, called Moranville into his office. The young lieutenant was told that local Japanese forces knew there were Americans inside the prison and they wanted to interrogate them. Moranville thought for a few minutes before telling the commandant, "Tell them that you don't have us. If the Japanese knew where we were, they'd be here in a minute to take us and there'd be nothing you could do to stop them." This apparently pleased the commandant, who was walking a thin line between placating the Japanese and saving his own life from the French resistance when the Japanese inevitably departed.[22] A relatively recent study noted that "Capt. (later General) Jacques Beauvallet paid a personal price for protecting the naval fliers in Saigon. He was horribly tortured by the Japanese who were trying to find out what happened to the Americans he saved."[23]

A few weeks later, the French officials had enough of keeping the Americans in Hanoi and knew the Japanese planned an imminent invasion of the prison to seize the Americans. The six flyers were loaded onto a truck shortly before midnight and driven off the premises. Their movement north was far from safe as the truck routinely stopped at bridge crossings or ferries while Japanese forces moved ahead of them. The truck was covered by canvas but was open to the back. The Americans experienced several close calls on their way north. In one instance, the truck became stuck in mud and Japanese troops aided in pushing the truck out. Moranville, sitting dead silent in the rear, observed several Japanese troops "looking in at us while they were pushing the truck. . . . Here they were pushing the truck out of the ditch and the six of us were just sitting there not doing anything to help. I guess the driver explained us to the Japanese as mentally retarded troops with communicable diseases."[24]

By this point, Moranville and the other Americans had lost all track of time. They eventually arrived at a French Foreign Legion camp at Ba Vi, twenty miles from Hanoi. Here they joined two other American enlisted aircrew from a shot-down B-25, whom Moranville identified as Sergeant Pope and Sergeant George Uhrine, both injured in their parachuting fall from their aircraft. The conditions at the camp were deplorable for the American flyers, but more pressing problems soon presented themselves.

On the night of March 9, 1945, the Americans heard nearby explosions. The next morning the commandant announced that the Japanese had attacked a French army camp during the night, driving through the camp and tossing hand grenades into the barracks where the soldiers were sleeping. All over the country, the Japanese were moving against French forces. The commandant then made an astounding announcement: they were either free to go or they could join the French and march north. "The decision to go along was immediate and unanimous," and the Americans each received an old rifle and thirteen rounds of ammunition. They joined the rest of the garrison on the parade field, where "they very formally played the French anthem and lowered the French flag and proceeded to march out of camp. There were about 250 Legionnaires and us eight Americans."

Shortly after marching out of the camp, the legionnaires entered mountainous terrain. Several legionnaires and Sergeant Uhrine could not continue and had to be left behind. Moranville remembered, "At sunset when it was becoming dark the troops started marching again through the jungle and we were forced to leave Sgt. Uhrine behind along with quite a few Legionnaires who were also unable to hike the terrain. It was an extremely emotional situation when we departed. It was impossible for Uhrine to go along but there was no logical reason for any of us to remain with him. It was a pure matter of probability that whoever stayed would certainly be captured and possibly be killed by the Japanese."[25] Thus, as Moranville and four others continued with the legionnaires, George Uhrine was left behind. Another legion member found him later and attempted to take him north to China on horseback. Both men were captured by Japanese soldiers within sight of the Chinese border. Uhrine made a final desperate gamble and pretended to be a Hungarian legionnaire. Rather than being executed, the Japanese threw him into Hanoi's Hoa Loa prison. He survived the war.[26]

As Moranville and the others wished Uhrine good luck and godspeed, they fell well behind the column of the foreign legion soldiers as they marched off. The long goodbye saved their lives. They trudged along in the wake of the legionnaires when, at around 1700 or 1800, the French troops crossed a rice paddy: "All of a sudden it was lit up like daylight by bamboo torches around the perimeter of the paddy. Small arms fire erupted and there was shooting all over the rice paddy. Fortunately we Americans were still together at the rear of the column when the shooting started."[27]

The foreign legion walked directly into a Japanese ambush. A single legionnaire ran back looking for the Americans, and together, the one legionnaire and five Americans made a desperate run for it. They evaded the Japanese for the rest of the night, and they eventually met up with the fifty or so survivors of the ambush. The trek continued for several more days and although no more Japanese were sighted, they did meet up with fresh-looking French soldiers armed with American weapons. These soldiers, loyal to General Charles De Gaulle, were ready to give the Japanese a fight: "They were wiring all the bridges with explosives in order to destroy them to slow the Japanese advance. They were also building barricades to fight from behind."[28]

Moranville and the other Saigon prisoners finally arrived at Dien Bien Phu and met up with U.S. Army intelligence officer Lt. Edmund N. Carpenter: "When the 50-odd men reached their destination at Dien Bien Phu on March 22 it was the end of a near-epic journey. They had walked 300 miles in 13 days across some of the roughest geography in Southeast Asia." All they had to do now was hold out until the weather cleared and a C-47 would fly in, pick them up, and take them to the safety of the U.S. Army in Kunming, China. The weather broke five days later. Moranville finally returned to the safety of an American base, albeit not his aircraft carrier. After a journey of about two and a half months that started when he departed the *Hornet* on the afternoon of January 12, it looked like Rabbit Moranville was going to survive the war. Dien Bien Phu fell to the Japanese two days later.[29]

Admiral Halsey's Third Fleet sailed with virtual impunity in the South China Sea—a feat that would have been unheard of only a year earlier. His biggest hindrance to conducting operations was not the Japanese, but the weather. Possible targets abounded in this area. Hainan Island sat directly south of mainland China's Leizhou Peninsula, shown on the maps inside the ready rooms of the USS *Hornet* as the Luichow Peninsula. At the southern tip of the island of Hainan sat the Yulin Naval Base. East of Hainan up the Luzon Strait sat Hong Kong. If a pilot flew north out of Hong Kong and followed the Pearl River he would arrive at Guangzhou, also known as Canton, the capital and largest city of Guangdong province in southern China. The Pescadores Islands are an archipelago of ninety islands and islets in the Taiwan Strait, located approximately thirty-one miles west of the main island of Taiwan across the Penghu Channel. On January 14, TF 38 sat nearly in the middle of the South China Sea and the Luzon strait. Having made the January 12 strikes against French Indochina, the task force was nearly equidistant east of Hainan Island, south of Hong Kong, west of Luzon, and southwest of Formosa. It could strike at any one of these targets with only a day's sail.[30]

The men of CVG-11 were certainly proud of their record so far, but the operations in January held special meaning. They knew they were in Japan's back yard. They noted the Japanese felt the South China Sea to be "practically home waters, where his ships could come and go at will . . . bearing the mineral spoils of his captured colonial empire." Where would Halsey strike next?[31]

On January 15 CVG-11 attacked shipping targets around the Pescadores, but weather was again the main enemy combatant. The weather also forced attacks under the cloud cover, giving good opportunity for Japanese AAA to engage them accordingly. VB-11 flyer Bose Erwin's aircraft was shot up, but he made it back to the safety of the fleet and had a good water landing near one of the picket destroyers, USS *Maddox* (DD-731). The seas were rough due to the storm, and the rescuers on the destroyer were having difficulty getting Erwin and his radio operator, William Malloy Rivers Jr., out of the water. At some point in the ordeal Erwin was knocked unconscious. A sailor finally tied a line around himself and dove into the choppy seas. He was able to get to the unconscious Erwin, but Rivers had disappeared, claimed by the sea.

● JANUARY 16, HONG KONG

Another memorable and solemn day for CVG-11 came on January 16, when the air group was sent out of Hong Kong and up the Pearl River to Canton. Unbeknownst to the men in the combined strike package of TF 38, the final casualties of the war for CVG-11 were to occur on this day.[32]

Zink said the raids against Hong Kong were "more of an aggravation raid than anything else. We were in and out." At this late stage in the war, the Japanese air arms of both the Imperial Japanese army and navy were simply shells of their former selves. Too few experienced pilots remained, and those who now filled the seats had too little training and flying hours to even be mildly competent in their aircraft. In one engagement over Hong Kong, VF-11 fighters dove on a group of four A6Ms escorting an L2D transport aircraft. Although the Japanese pilots saw the incoming F6Fs, they did not react like the seasoned Japanese pilots of 1942 and 1943. Instead, according to historian Steven K. Bailey, "they reacted like inexperienced aviators. . . . The rookie pilots tried to outrun the far more experienced American aviators on the deck. With ruthless efficiency, the *Hornet* pilots lined up behind each of the fleeing A6Ms and dispatched them with well-aimed bursts from their six .50-caliber wing guns." Gone too was the L2D, left alone and an easy target as its escort fled in terror.[33]

On that same day, VT-11 took another two losses during the four strike sorties flown. The first two strikes of the day damaged a dockyard and a ship sitting in a slipway. Their history noted, "The third, a torpedo strike, is one that will not soon be forgotten by any of the squadron personnel." The AAA was, again, intense and Lt. (jg) Edwin William McGowan's TBM was hit during his torpedo run and went down with crewmembers Aviation Ordnanceman First Class Charles Henry Cunningham of Bisbee, Arizona, and Aviation Radioman Second Class Lawrence Cornelius Schiller of Cameron, Texas. These proved to be the last losses VT-11 suffered during the war.

VF-11 also got in on the action by damaging and setting afire a ten-thousand-ton oiler, scoring twelve hits using the unguided high-velocity aircraft rockets. Skull Stimpson's division rocketed and strafed the oil storage area setting it aflame, and Lt. Robert "Cactus" Flath's pilots strafed the Kowloon docks. Ens. Richard Wilson, a twenty-one-year-old fighter pilot from Illinois, fell to the intense anti-aircraft fire that day. No one saw his F6F go down or heard any radio communication that he was in trouble; he was last seen "starting attack on ships in Hong Kong Harbor." He simply disappeared. He became the seventeenth, and last, Sundowner killed during the deployment.[34]

Ens. Matt Crehan's F6F was also struck by AAA; he rolled over and bailed out. Luckily for Crehan, his division leader, Lt. Cdr. Bob Clements, was circling over Tamkan Island nearby and saw him bail out. Other members of VF-11 had already departed the area, so Clements, noting that the downed aviator was not floating in his survival raft, which had escaped him and floated away, radioed to a VB-11 bomber pilot to have his gunner drop an additional raft. The

Curtiss SB2C circled low and dropped a second life raft to Crehan, but this one failed to inflate upon hitting the water and sank straight to the bottom. Clements, no doubt growing angry, maneuvered around in his own cockpit, extracted his own life raft, and dropped it to Crehan. This one worked, and soon Crehan was seen in the relative safety of the raft. Still circling overhead, Clements strafed nearby fishing boats and sampans until his ammunition ran out. He radioed for a rescue submarine to come in and pick up Crehan, but the shallow waters prevented the submarine from getting close enough to shore. Clements remained overhead until he was dangerously low on fuel; his chances of making it back to the *Hornet* were rapidly receding. He had thirty gallons of fuel remaining when he departed the area and "sweated all the way back to *Hornet*," no doubt thinking that if he had to ditch his Hellcat, he no longer had a life raft. His wheels hit the deck of the *Hornet* with his fuel gauge showing empty.[35]

Further searches found no sign of Ensign Crehan or any sign of F6F wreckage. The ship's log marked him down as killed in action. It was not until many months later after CVG-11 returned home that Clements discovered that Crehan had in fact survived. The source was no less than Crehan himself, who informed his executive officer he had been pulled from the water by some friendly Chinese—perhaps even those Clements had attempted to scare off by firing at them—who then helped him make his way to Kunming, China.

No sooner had Crehan arrived in China when he ran into the recently arrived Lt. Blake Moranville, who recalled, "When I arrived in Kunming I was fortunate to meet up with Matthew Crehan another Sun Downer from VF-11 who had been shot down four days after me while on air strikes over Hong Kong. Of course we were delighted to see each other and traveled back to the states together."[36]

After Hong Kong, it was back to Formosa on January 21, where VF-11 damaged five auxiliary ships totaling 25,000 tons plus two destroyers. In what was to be VF-11's final aerial combat against the Japanese, Lt. William R. Sisley led his division into another formation of Zekes and Judys. Sisley and Lt. (jg) Thomas S. Williams each downed a Zeke, and Ens. Zebulon V. Knott took down a Judy. Ens. Robert McReynolds was credited with a probable Zeke. VF-11 also lost one final F6F Hellcat: Lt. Cdr. Fritz Wolf made a successful water landing immediately after launch upon seeing his oil pressure drop to zero. He was rescued by a nearby escort destroyer.[37]

The air group's final mission, another strike against Okinawa, came on January 22, 1945. During the strike, VF-11 Ens. Paul Warren was on the receiving end of small arms fire, which shattered his windscreen and peppered his face and eye with Plexiglas shards. He flew his Hellcat back to the *Hornet* with only one eye to guide him, and the *Hornet*'s medical staff—after removing eight pieces of Plexiglas from his eye—believed that he would never fly or see out of that eye again. However, the human body is a miraculous object; Ensign Warren's eye recovered, and he ended the war as a flight instructor at the naval airbase at Melbourne, Florida.

Since Warren was CVG-11's final casualty, it is worth mentioning that the bullet that broke his windscreen was not Japanese AAA, but was from the rifle of a farmer. That day Warren flew with Lt. Robert Flath, from Stanley, North Dakota. Warren was a fellow North Dakotan from Parshall, only forty miles away. Flath and Warren flew together for months before learning how close their hometowns were and that Warren's dentist was Plath's uncle. On that day's mission, targets seemed scarce. The two elements flew along railroads looking for a train or other target to strafe. Nearing Naha, Flath decided to pull the division up. The incident was later related in the *Chicago Daily Times*, authored by war correspondent Keith Wheeler. Flath

> banked sharply, roaring away from the tracks and beginning to climb. Paul's section heeled over and followed through as though all four aeroplanes were wired together. As they ripped across a rice paddy "Cactus" saw out of the corner of his eye a farmer standing a few feet below. Straw hatted, overalled and barefooted, the farmer stared up and "Cactus" thought he shook his fist. He had flashed from sight when "Cactus" heard a sharp "splat" and saw a small hole come through his fuselage. Seconds later Paul called him by radio. "The goddam clodhopper hit me!"
>
> "Whaddya mean clodhopper? Who hit you? Where?" Cactus answered.
>
> "That farmer. Didn't ya see him? He had his old gopher rifle and hit me. Splattered glass in my face—the doggone independent operator," Paul yelled.

> "Hit me too," Cactus said. "What's he think he is, anti-aircraft? Where's his union card?" Cactus howled. And so the two outraged North Dakotans went back and burned the farmer's barn, scared his chickens out of a month's production.[38]

CVG-11 took to the skies a final time on January 22, 1945; the Sundowners, Pegasus, and Little Butch attacked a cargo ship, possibly the 2,073-ton *Hikosan Maru*, which sank. CVG-11 and the USS *Hornet* lost forty-four personnel during their deployment, including nineteen air crewmen. At the end of its cruise, the combined loss of aircraft from all causes—shot down or pushed over the side of the carrier—was eighty-six planes or, as Barrett Tillman pointed out, 103 percent of its original complement.[39]

For the entire month of January Mitscher's Task Force 38 of Halsey's Third Fleet had ranged all over the Philippine Sea and South China Sea. The first week of January found Task Force 38 east of Luzon, performing strikes in advance of the landings there. From there it sailed north off the coast of Formosa to hit Tainan, Takao, on the island, and over to the Pescadores, then down the Luzon Strait to the coast of French Indochina, striking against Quinhon, Cam Ranh Bay, and Saigon before turning north again for Formosa, Hong Kong, and Hainan Island. TF 38 was seemingly everywhere all at once, and the forces of the Japanese empire seemed unable to stop it. The war would not end for another seven months, but for CVG-11, their second tour and their contribution to the war had ended.[40]

After the attacks on January 22, the *Hornet* departed once again for Ulithi. Rumors flew among the members of the aircrew: Was this another break in the action, or were they going to be relieved? Over at VB-11, "rumors flew thick and fast. . . . A 'tote' was established on the ready room blackboard to try and keep abreast of the rapidly changing odds." The men of VT-11 placed bets, and "hundreds of dollars changed hands on the day the scuttlebutt was confirmed." CVG-11's tour was done. Once anchored in Ulithi, the men knew this tour was over. They still did not know if they would see action again on a third cruise. Okinawa and the Japanese homelands still lay in the future. A little over a year had elapsed between the air group's first and second tour. Might the war last well into 1946 or even 1947? Would the Sundowners, Pegasus, and Little Butch return for another tour—perhaps this time with attacks on Japan itself? For now, all of that was in the future: "We were relieved. We were going home. Late in the afternoon we transferred to the USS *Kasaan Bay*, and at this writing we are proceeding steadily eastward over calm seas. Two days should find us in Pearl Harbor. Perhaps another ten in Frisco. Nobody much cares. The important thing is, we are on our way."[41]

Although the air group was leaving, there was significant fighting left to be done. Even as CVG-11 departed the Pacific, MacArthur began his assault on Manila. The U.S. Sixth Army landed at the Lingayen Gulf, and XIV Corps marched south toward the capital city with orders from General MacArthur to "Get to Manila!" Units from the 1st Cavalry Division and the 11th Airborne Division moved toward the city. The Battle for Manila deteriorated into the severest city fighting fought by American forces during the entire Pacific War. The Philippines campaign did not end until the surrender of Japan in August 1945. The march toward Tokyo and unconditional Japanese surrender continued.

● THE ODYSSEY OF GUNNER AND THE RETURN HOME

After Blake Moranville was shot down, the little terrier Gunner became inconsolable, refusing to eat and sniffing every returning pilot, looking for signs of Rabbit. *Hornet* Capt. Austin K. Doyle wrote, "We can't tell him that his master is safe. It is really pathetic."[42] Gunner beat Moranville home. Upon their return to the United States in February 1945, members of VF-11 delivered Gunner to Rabbit's parents at their Guide Rock, Nebraska, home. Gunner became something of a celebrity himself. Having already made the papers in the small Nebraska town, the entire city knew who he was. Gunner quickly adapted to his new home and freedom from the confines of the *Hornet*. He even joined Blake's father, the local veterinarian, on house calls. His reunion with Blake was covered from Nebraska all the way to Australia:

> When word was received that Lt. Moranville was coming home, everyone was excited. The family was to meet Blake at Hastings College where Blake's sister, Eleanor, was enrolled. Gunner went along too. Doc parked the car near Eleanor's dorm and when he saw Blake and

Eleanor approaching, he let Gunner out of the car. Blake whistled with no response from Gunner. Then suddenly, the little dog picked up Blake's scent and from about 30 yards, he charged and landed on Blake's chest, the tiny screw of a tail wagging with happiness and the tongue washing Blake's face. Gunner was content to live the rest of his life with Doc Moranville. He preferred his perch in Doc's car to the seat of an airplane. He became the father of "Trixie" and these two Boston Terriers brought years of enjoyment to every-one who came in contact with them.[43]

CONCLUSION

THE RETURN

CVG-11 left the Pacific Theater on February 1, 1945, and thus missed the operations around the invasion of Okinawa and the end of the war in August. Between two combat cruises from 1943 to 1945, CVG-11 participated in numerous operations, conducted hundreds of strikes, and downed more than 150 enemy aircraft in aerial combat. VT-11 and VB-11 attacked targets up the slot from Guadalcanal and at Okinawa, the Philippines, Formosa, Hong Kong, and French Indochina, and all the way north to the Japanese stronghold of Okinawa and the Ryukyu Islands. In the process the air group destroyed over 100,000 tons of Japanese shipping. None of the squadrons participated in the major battles of Coral Sea, Midway, or the Philippines and only arrived late to Leyte Gulf. However, the actions of CVG-11 are emblematic of the overall naval air war in World War II. Dozens of squadrons stood on the line every day from 1942 to 1945. Not all of them were at major battles, but they all contributed to the defeat of Japan.

During World War II, three different air groups flew into combat and called the USS *Hornet* home. From April through September 1944, Air Group Two (CVG-2) was the first group to take the new *Hornet* to war. Air Group Eleven replaced Air Group Two in September 1944. During the second cruise, Japanese fighters, bombers, and anti-aircraft fire tested the air group every day. As the cruise continued into late fall and winter, the danger of kamikaze attacks against American fleets operating in contested waters increased by the day. The men of the air group and the carrier also contended with foul weather over the intended targets or rough seas and typhoons back on the ship.

Barrett Tillman noted that the pilots of VF-11 were extremely proud and boasted during and after the war that no members of VB-11 or VT-11 lost their lives or their aircraft to enemy fighter planes. Ground fire, mechanical failure, or any number of other gremlins in the aircraft might be inevitable, but not once in their second tour did a Japanese fighter ever get on the tail of or shoot down a CVG-11 torpedo or bomber plane. The VF-11 veterans of Guadalcanal helped ensure this record through hard work, training, and the lessons they passed to the new members of the fighter squadron who arrived throughout the second cruise.

By the end of their combat operations in January 1945, the pilots and aircrews of Air Group Eleven laid claim to numerous statistics, victories, and accomplishments. These numbers were painted on the ship's island superstructure. The large mural noted 105 enemy planes downed in aerial combat and a further 272 planes attacked and destroyed while sitting on enemy airfields. The bombers and torpedo planes attacked and sank 100,000 tons of enemy shipping and damaged more than one hundred Japanese ships. These actions came at a high cost, but CVG-11 certainly gave more than they received. On February 1, 1945, Air Group Seventeen replaced Air Group Eleven in the anchorage at Ulithi. Although they did not know it at the time, the war was over for CVG-11. The air group departed the Pacific and arrived in Alameda on February 24, 1945. For all the above operations, CVG-11 received the Presidential Unit Citation.[1]

The war in the Pacific Theater regardless of location was a carrier war. This was abundantly clear to American naval leaders on December 7, 1941. As Mark Peattie noted, "In a thunderclap, the Japanese navy itself had brought such a realization and such a decision to the United States Navy in the opening hours of the war. At Pearl Harbor the obsolescent American battle line had been critically disabled, thus freeing the United States Navy from its reliance on the capital ship and from whatever lingering faith it might have had in its preeminence." Conversely, "the Japanese Navy was slow to give up its prewar big-gun/big-ship convictions. The Japanese continually sought out the decisive fleet engagement with the aircraft carriers screening for the main battle line and never recognized that history had already sailed on by into a new naval way of war."[2]

● THE *HORNET*

Even with the departure of Air Group Eleven, the war was not over for the USS *Hornet*. The ship now took Air Group Seventeen to war. VT-17, VB-17, and VF-17 had exploits worthy of their own books. On board the *Hornet*, VF-17 added 161 more victories to the *Hornet*'s total and produced another twelve aces. Overall, the two combat tours of VF-17 ended with 313 victories, the second most of any U.S. Navy squadron, behind only VF-15. If VF-11's famous Sundowners emblem is one of the most recognized of World War II, VF-17's famous Jolly Roger insignia could not be far behind. VB-17 and VT-17 hit targets and supported the invasions of Okinawa and Iwo Jima. They also struck Nansei Shoto, Kyushu, and Tokyo itself. Of special note, the TBMs of VF-17 participated in striking and sinking the mighty battleship *Yamato* on April 7, 1945, and placed at least one torpedo into the battleship; the ship's record claims four torpedoes and three bombs hit the *Yamato*. When the *Hornet* departed the Pacific on June 19, 1945, it claimed 668 planes shot down, 742 aircraft destroyed on the ground, and over one million tons of shipping damaged or sunk.[3]

During the war, the ship earned nine battle stars for Pacific service in World War II, and each of her air groups received a Presidential Unit Citation. After the war, the Navy altered the designations of its carrier air groups. Air groups belonging to the *Essex*-class carriers became CVAGs; those organized for the newer and even larger *Midway*-class carrier became CVBGs. Air groups for light carriers of the *Independence* and *Saipan* classes became CVLGs. Finally, the World War II escort carriers were now CVEGs. Thus the USS *Hornet's* air group on CV-12 became CVAG-12. On September 1, 1948, the U.S. Navy changed its designation and nomenclature again, and CVAG-12 became CVG-12 for the second time.

The USS *Hornet* went on to serve the U.S. Navy for two and a half decades after the end of World War II. Despite her wartime record, her most famous accomplishment came on July 24, 1969. The USS *Hornet* picked up the Apollo 11 command module *Columbia* and its three crewmembers, Neil Armstrong, Edwin Aldrin, and Michael Collins, from the Pacific Ocean southwest of the Hawaiian Islands. Four months later, on November 24, the *Hornet* also recovered the Apollo 12 crew of Pete Conrad, Dick Gordon, and Al Bean and their command module *Yankee Clipper*. The USS *Hornet* decommissioned on June 26, 1970. CV-12 remains one of the four surviving *Essex*-class aircraft carriers of World War II, the others being the *Yorktown* (CV-10), *Lexington* (CV-16), and *Intrepid* (CV-11), all of which serve as museums. Today the *Hornet* sits on the southernmost pier of the former Naval Air Station Alameda in California and is operated as the USS *Hornet* Museum. In her hangar sit a number of aircraft including the World War II–era Grumman TBF Avenger and an F4F Wildcat. On Veterans Day 2014, a new exhibit memorializing Carrier Air Group Eleven opened to the public at the museum. In the display, one of the doors is adorned with the VF-11 Sundowners image and inscribed with Blake Moranville's name along with six rising sun flags denoting his aerial victories.[4]

● THE FALLEN

On a 152-acre plot on a conspicuous plateau, surrounded by skyscrapers and modern buildings of the city on Luzon, sits the Manila American Cemetery and Memorial. The cemetery in the Philippines occupies the area formerly on the receiving end of attacks by the members of Air Group Eleven in 1944 and 1945. The cemetery contains 17,206 graves. This grim statistic marks the site as containing the largest number of graves for U.S. servicemembers killed during World War II. The cemetery also contains a wide terrace composed of limestone columns inscribed with the names of 36,286 missing servicemembers. These "Tablets of the Missing" are updated with golden rosettes when one of the missing's remains are recovered and identified. Of the 36,286 names, only 439 now have rosettes.[5]

Between training, the Guadalcanal campaign, and the second cruise, 103 members of Air Group Eleven made the ultimate sacrifice. Over half of these, fifty-four in total, remain listed as missing in action, with their names carved in the limestone of the Manila American Cemetery. In four months of flying off the USS *Hornet*, CVG-11 lost more than three squadrons' worth of aircraft and more than forty men listed as killed, missing in action, or wounded. Another sixteen men, all of VT-11—along with the air group commander Lieutenant Commander Hamilton—had their remains returned home after their R&R aircraft crashed in June 1943. The rest of the remains can be found at cemeteries all over the United States.

● THE SURVIVORS

First, Alexa von Tempsky Zabriskie deserves mention. She opened her home to more than twenty thousand aviators during the war. The number is accurate, as a wall etched with the visitors' signatures that used to stand in the foyer of the home now resides at the National Naval Aviation Museum in Pensacola, Florida. Fighter ace and squadron commander Jimmy Flatley, a frequent visitor, said she was a "one woman USO." In 1945 Adm. John H. Towers presented her with the Asiatic-Pacific Area Theater Ribbon as a "special tribute in recognition of her service to the United States Navy." In his letter accompanying the award, Admiral Towers noted, "The facilities she provided gave combat weary personnel a period of rest and relaxation from the violence of war. Her wholehearted and unselfish efforts provided comfort and entertainment which were of inestimable value in restoring the health of thousands of officers and enlisted personnel of the Navy and Marine Corps. In so doing she gave material aid to the United States Navy in the war against the enemy. Her loyalty and devotion to duty were in keeping with the finest attributes of United States Citizenship."[6]

Alexa also received a letter from none other than Adm. Chester Nimitz: "I really should be congratulating you for the magnificent job you have done throughout the war in keeping up the morale and spirits of so many thousands of our officers. To have entertained twenty thousand officers in your home is indeed an outstanding record and I commend and congratulate you for it. . . . With kindest regards and great aloha." Alexa von Tempsky Zabriskie died on July 15, 1975.[7]

Hundreds of men served with CVG-11 during its two cruises in World War II. For those whose stories contributed heavily to this book, it is worth mentioning what became of them. At least five officers from the original group eventually attained flag rank and served the Navy as admirals: Ashworth, Cousins, Leonard, Ramsey, and Wilson.

Much of the information in this book with regard to VT-11 outside of the squadron's after-action reports and histories came from the remembrances of Vice Adm. Frederick Lincoln "Dick" Ashworth, the VT-11 squadron commander and two-time Navy Cross recipient. Ashworth led one of the more interesting careers after he departed VT-11. In November 1944 Ashworth joined the Manhattan Project, America's top-secret program for development of the world's first atomic bomb. It fell to Ashworth to recruit and train the men who would assemble the bombs in-flight on the unknown number of missions against Japan. In the winter of 1944, Ashworth walked the halls of the new Pentagon—itself built by Manhattan Project military lead Maj. Gen. Leslie Groves—looking both for skilled workers and men who could keep a secret (a sign outside the project's offices in New Mexico read "what you see here, what you hear here, what you do here, when you leave here, let it stay here"). Ashworth's code word "silverplate" gave him access to recruit highly desirable individuals even if their bosses protested. It also fell to Ashworth to pick a suitable base in the Pacific to conduct the bombing operations. Ashworth returned to the Pacific in February 1945. Entering the office of Adm. Chester Nimitz, the commander of U.S. Naval forces in the Pacific, Ashworth handed him a letter that explained the mission of the atomic bomb project. From there, Ashworth traveled to Tinian Island, the site chosen for the 509th Composite Bomb Group to conduct operations. The world remembers the first bombing mission of the aircraft Enola Gay piloted by Colonel Paul Tibbetts well. Less well known was the second mission, against the tertiary target of Nagasaki. On August 9, 1945, inside the B-29 Bockscar, Ashworth, the "weaponeer" for the flight, entered the bomb bay and armed the "Fat Man" device. During the flight, Ashworth also monitored the electronics of the bomb. Following war's end, Ashworth continued to rise through the ranks of naval officers. He ended his service to the nation as the commander of the United States Sixth Fleet, holding that post and the rank of a four-star admiral from September 1966 to April 1967 and finally as the commander in chief, U.S. Atlantic Fleet. He retired in 1968 and moved to Santa Fe, New Mexico. He died on December 3, 2005, at the age of ninety-three and is buried in Santa Fe. His alma mater, the United States Naval Academy, also has marker a honoring him in their cemetery.[8]

Lt. Charles R. Stimpson remained the Sundowners' top ace and ended the war with sixteen aerial victories, earned during the unit's two cruises on Guadalcanal and the USS *Hornet*. He was one of only four Navy flyers to earn ace status in both the F4F Wildcat and F6F Hellcat. His actions earned him a Navy Cross and three Distinguished Flying Crosses. He left active duty in 1945, but stayed in the reserves for another twelve years. He never left the San Diego area and despite jobs in hotel management, he stayed active in San Diego's aviation community. An obituary noted, "He was widely known as the genial, popular host of The Inn at Rancho Santa Fe, California." He died on August 20, 1983, at Miramar Naval Air Station, shortly after a performance by the Blue Angels.[9]

Lt. James S. Swope remained in the Navy and flew just about every jet the Navy developed after the war. He commanded Air Group 15 off the USS *Coral Sea* during Vietnam, flying both F-8 Crusaders and A-4 Skyhawks. Returning home from Vietnam, he became commanding officer of Naval Station Mayport, Florida. He finally retired from the Navy in April 1971. He died on June 26, 2000.[10]

Lt. (jg) Horace B. Moranville, keeper of Gunner, also made a career of the Navy and retired in 1964. He married Mary Sherwood in 1946, and they had two sons together. He moved to Monmouth, Illinois, and attended Monmouth College, where he earned bachelor's and master's degrees in education before joining the faculty of the Oregon College of Education; he remained there for the next two decades before retiring as the dean of students in 1985. He died on July 11, 2000, at the age of seventy-seven. He and Mary had been together for fifty-four years when he passed.[11]

Lt. (jg) Vernon E. Graham, another VF-11 ace, returned home and left the Navy behind. After the war Graham took up coaching and teaching in Colorado before he headed back to California and Stanford University where he earned a master of arts degree in guidance counseling. After graduation,

Graham and his wife moved to Santa Maria in 1950, where he spent the next thirty years as a teacher, counselor, and principal at the high school level. After retirement, he continued teaching home- and hospital-bound students. At the age of eighty-six he passed away on January 2, 2006.[12]

VF-11 diarist John Ramsey stayed in the Navy. Throughout World War II and the Korean conflict, Ramsey was awarded four Distinguished Flying Crosses and eleven air medals. In Korea he served as VF-111 squadron commander from 1951 to 1952. In spring 1948, the United States reorganized its fighter squadrons, and the lineage of VF-11 transferred to VF-111, as did the squadron insignia. So when Lt. Cdr. Ramsey took VF-111 to combat in Korea, it was with one of the most recognizable units in the history of the Navy: the Sundowners. Again, he flew Grumman aircraft into combat, but this time it was the F9F Panther. In Korea he earned a Bronze Star for destroying an anti-aircraft locomotive and bridge in the same mission. Later in his Navy career, Commander Ramsey graduated from the Naval War College and served at the North Atlantic Treaty Organization 7th Fleet. In 1958 Commander Ramsey was given a special assignment on board the USS *Oriskany* to handle upgrades to the ship and as executive officer of air operations to train air groups for future combat operations. Ramsey retired from the U.S. Navy in December 1963, died on January 2, 1988, and is buried in Retrop Cemetery in Oklahoma.[13]

A detailed write-up about the postwar life of William "Bill" Strahan would likely need a book of its own. His obituary noted,

> In 1946, he married Grace King (also from Wadsworth). In 1953, when Bill and Grace were expecting the fifth child, Bill left the Navy at the rank of Lieutenant Commander to honor the request of family so that his children could live close to both sets of grandparents in the Midwest. His degree was in Agriculture, and he went into dairy and crop farming. He also did soil analysis and topography maps for the University of Illinois Extension Service to aid farmers in crop rotation. He worked for Investors Diversified Services, and he was a realtor in Illinois and Wisconsin. In 1987, at age 69, Bill joined the U.S. Peace Corps and served in Nepal as a Crop Extension Specialist. During those years, Bill and Grace raised eight kids. Bill & Grace Strahan later resided in Wisconsin for many

> years until moving to Chugwater, Wyoming, in 2008, expecting to live a quiet life of retirement. Bill was in for a few surprises, though. . . . In 2011 at the age of 93, Bill went on the "Honor Flight" for Wyoming WWII veterans, from Cheyenne to Washington, DC. It was an unforgettable and uplifting experience that went way beyond his expectations. His was indeed a life well-lived, a life of honor. Bill's size 16+ feet have left indelible footprints upon this earth.

Bill Strahan entered this world on March 8, 1918, and died on November 23, 2019, at the age of 101.[14]

Rear Adm. Eugene George Fairfax, the commanding officer of VF-11 on the *Hornet,* made a career of the Navy. In May 1946 he returned as commander of VF-11 for a second time. He served in the Night and All-Weather Attack Squadron 33 (VC-33) and twice commanded a U.S. Navy ship: the USS *Passumpsic,* a fleet oiler, and the USS *Ticonderoga* (CV-14). Other assignments included chief of staff of Carrier Division 1 and deputy of Joint Task Force 2, and in 1966, he was promoted to rear admiral. He then became the commander of Anti-Submarine Warfare Group 5, an assignment that took him back on board the USS *Hornet.* Gene and his wife Juliana had five children. After retirement in February 1972, the family moved to Albuquerque, New Mexico, and never moved again. Juliana died in March of 2000. Gene Fairfax spent his remaining days looking after twelve grandchildren and fifteen great-grandchildren. He passed away on April 5, 2013, and is buried in Santa Fe, New Mexico.

Robert W. Cocks of VB-11, who was personally responsible for the landing of more than two dozen aircraft perilously low on fuel at Tacloban Airfield, continued his education after the war. Cocks earned a bachelor's degree from the University of Arizona and two master's degrees and a doctorate in criminal administration from the University of Southern California. For many years, he served with the Los Angeles County probation department and launched programs to readjust parolees into the work environment. He and his college sweetheart Dorothy married and had four children; they were together for nearly fifty years before her death. He died on May 4, 2017.[15]

Bob Maxwell, who survived a mid-air collision and successfully found his way back to Guadalcanal, was only with VF-11 for its first tour. His second tour was with VF-51, where he saw action at Marcus and Wake Islands, the Marianas, Palau, the Bonin Islands, Luzon, Formosa, the Philippine Sea, and Iwo Jima. During those actions he shot down seven Japanese aircraft, becoming an ace with VF-51. Returning home from the war, he married Marjorie Louise Saulpaw in August 1945. Maxwell returned to the University of Wisconsin and received his bachelor's degree in business administration in 1947. He then spent thirty years in sales based out of Columbia, South Carolina. His obituary noted: "a loyal Gamecock fan, Bob attended all home games and was a member of the Gamecock Club for over 65 consecutive years." He died in March 2016 at the age of ninety-six and is buried in South Carolina.[16]

Many of the enlisted crew who served as radiomen or gunners in the TBM/F Avengers or in the SBDs/SB2C of VB-11 contributed greatly to this book. Again, for their contributions two bear mentioning here.

Vergil E. Bloomquist, radioman in VT-11, had served on the *Wasp* before joining VT-11 on the USS *Hornet*. He left the Navy after the war. He married his wife, Mary Ellen, in a triple wedding ceremony: "The girlfriends accepted, and they all married at the same time in Carson City, Nev." He lived in Independence, Missouri, for the next fifty years and worked for DuPont for twenty-seven of those years. In 2017, as part of the research for *Eleven: The Movie*, Bloomquist flew in a TBM for the first time in seventy-two years. He recalled much later in life, "No 19 year old should have to see the things [I] saw." He survived those things and lived until the age of ninety-seven before passing away in 2022.[17]

Kermit "Tim" Enander served as a mechanic for VF-11 on Guadalcanal. His second tour found him stationed on Guam. He left the Navy after the war ended and married Violet Gill, whom he met on a bus, and they spent the next sixty-two years together. He taught high school typing and accounting for twenty-five years and was instrumental in organizing the first Sundowners reunion in 1988. An article about his participation in World War II noted it was easy to find Tim in a crowd as he always wore his VF-11 ball cap. He passed away in 2018 at the age of ninety-six. He is buried at the National Memorial Cemetery of the Pacific in Honolulu, a few miles from VF-11's training area prior to its departure for Guadalcanal.[18]

These were the men of Carrier Air Group Eleven. Their 103 victories did not make them the top-scoring fighter unit for the Navy in World War II; in fact, they were seventeenth on that list at the end of the war, just above average. VB-11 and VT-11 hit shipping throughout the Guadalcanal "cruise" and while on the *Hornet* sank a Japanese carrier, ten destroyers, and four dozen other ships of various kinds. Many other units sank more ships or total tonnage. Throughout the war, the air group lost 103 individual men: officers and enlisted, either killed or missing in action. That being said, CVG-11 is representative of every air group that served at least one combat tour in the Pacific in World War II. There were other units exactly like them throughout the theater, some more successful, some less, but it is important to remember the contributions of all the air groups that contributed in their own way to the defeat of the enemy. The generation that served in and fought World War II is all but gone now, enshrined only in the ways in which we choose to remember them. Moreover, their stories are worth remembering.

APPENDIX A

Rosters of Officers and Enlisted Personnel during Guadalcanal and USS *Hornet* Tours

One might argue that there is no need to include a comprehensive list of the men who piloted the aircraft of CVG-11 or of the enlisted personnel who manned the guns and operated the radio and radar. I have chosen to do so for the following reason: In the pages above, I had only so much room to include the story of Air Group Eleven, and each of the men below deserves to have their name inscribed for posterity; after all, they were there too, even if I did not mention them. I hope that any family members or friends will find opportunities for further research below. Any roster of any unit throughout the history of the U.S. military can only ever be a snapshot in time. Inevitably, for a myriad of reasons a name might not appear on a particular roster. I have attempted to use the full name of the individuals, but where a full name was not available, I used initials and, as a final resort, last name only. For the officers on board the USS *Hornet*, I have the ship's roster of officers from December 1944.

CVG-11 COMMANDING OFFICERS

Lt. Cdr. Paul H. Ramsey	October 10, 1942
Lt. Cdr. Weldon H. Hamilton	February 8, 1943
Lt. Cdr. Eugene G. Fairfax	August 15, 1944
Commander R. Emmett Riera	October 13, 1944

FIRST TOUR: GUADALCANAL

For the enlisted aircrew of VB-11 and VT-11, an AMM designation denoted an aviation machinist's mate, commonly called a gunner, and an ARM was an aviation radioman. A *C* designation (as in ACRM) denoted a higher ranking enlisted chief position. The designation was followed by the enlisted rate: 1c (first class), 2c (second class), and so forth. Other designations include aviation electrician's mate (AEM), aviation metalsmith (AM), chief aviation pilot (CAP), chief boatswain's mate (CBM), photographer's mate (PhoM), parachute rigger (PR), painter (Ptr), seaman (S), and airman apprentice (AA).

CAG

Lt. Cdr. Weldon H. Hamilton

Lt. Cdr. John Hulme
Lt. (jg) David A. Burr
Lt. Joseph S. Gestal Jr.

VB-11 Roster

Lt. Cdr. Raymond B. Jacoby
Lt. Ralph W. Cousins
Lt. Paul J. Knapp
Lt. (jg) Lloyd W. Bertoglio
Lt. (jg) Frederick K. Blatchford
Lt. (jg) Milton J. Bonar
Lt. (jg) John A. Cooke
Lt. (jg) Charles W. DeMoss
Lt. (jg) Monroe S. Doss
Lt. (jg) Robert C. Dye
Lt. (jg) Raymond P. Gahan
Lt. (jg) Hugh M. Gray
Lt. (jg) Richard R. Harding
Lt. (jg) Edward F. Hughes
Lt. (jg) William H. Kenah Jr.
Lt. (jg) Richard F. Kenney
Lt. (jg) Alvin D. Leach
Lt. (jg) William H. Mackey
Lt. (jg) Edward McCarty
Lt. (jg) Winfield S. Orndorf Jr.

Lt. (jg) Johnny W. Patterson
Lt. (jg) Herbert W. Pickering
Lt. (jg) Arthur W. Powell
Lt. (jg) Joseph Riley
Lt. (jg) Robert J. Saggau
Lt. (jg) Carl F. Schwab Jr.
Lt. (jg) Edward M. Smith
Lt. (jg) James Gilmore Steussy
Lt. (jg) Lester J. Toler
Lt. (jg) Tutwiler
Lt. (jg) Linzee Wallis
Lt. (jg) Edwin J. Weil
Lt. (jg) Edwin Wilson Jr.
Ens. Albert B. Fite
ARM1c Anthony W. Brunetti
ARM1c Charles J. Young
ARM2c Paul A. Brinegar Jr.
ARM2c William P. Carey
ARM2c Kenneth G. Day
ARM2c William Eads
ARM2c Myron L. Henry
ARM2c Kenneth W. Hinkle
ARM2c Glenn W. James
ARM2c Harry R. Jespersen
ARM2c Robert W. Koster
ARM2c Melvin J. Kufeldt
ARM2c Thomas J. Landerville
ARM2c Reese A. Magill
ARM2c Harold M. Marrs
ARM2c James W. McCorkle
ARM2c Alvah K. Mettler
ARM2c Richard E. Miralles
ARM2c Joseph F. Poole
ARM2c John B. Rasmussen
ARM2c William Malloy Rivers Jr.
ARM2c John P. Rucker Jr.
ARM2c George M. Saint
ARM2c Robert R. Seneker
ARM2c Chester H. Shipley
ARM2c Leslie M. Smith

VF-11 Roster

Lt. Cdr. Gordon D. Cady
Lt. Cdr. Raymond William Vogel
Lt. Cdr. Clarence M. White Jr.
Lt. Walter J. Hiebert
Lt. William Nicholas Leonard
Lt. Frank B. Quady
Lt. Lester Seneca Wall
Lt. Charles V. Wesley
Lt. (jg) Chandler G. Boswell
Lt. (jg) Cyrus George Cary
Lt. (jg) John A. Cooke
Lt. (jg) E. M. Coppola
Lt. (jg) Robert N. Flath
Lt. (jg) Vern W. Gaston
Lt. (jg) Robert L. Gilbert
Lt. (jg) Vern E. Graham
Lt. (jg) Terry H. Holberton
Lt. (jg) Teddy L. Hull
Lt. (jg) Edward H. Johnson
Lt. (jg) Alfred. A. Jones
Lt. (jg) William J. Masoner
Lt. (jg) William Robert Maxwell

Lt. (jg) R. B. Ogilvie
Lt. (jg) Chester A. Parker
Lt. (jg) A. T. Pimentel
Lt. (jg) John G. Pressler
Lt. (jg) John W. Ramsey
Lt. (jg) George W. Ricker
Lt. (jg) Charles H. Schild
Lt. (jg) Lowell E. Slagle
Lt. (jg) Charles R. Stimpson
Lt. (jg) James S. Swope
Lt. (jg) Kenneth T. Viall
Lt. (jg) Henry S. White
Lt. (jg) Dan T. Work
Ens. Leroy W. Childs
Ens. W. Dan Hubbard
Ens. Dan R. Hubler
Ens. Claude M. Ivie
Ens. B. J. Martin

VS-11 Roster

Lt. Cdr. Hoyt D. Mann
Lt. Timothy J. Gallivan
Lt. Tony F. Schneider
Lt. Ried W. Stone
Lt. Harry Wood
Lt. Max E. E. Woyke
Lt. (jg) Gene C. Anderson
Lt. (jg) John W. Aulson
Lt. (jg) David A. Beck
Lt. (jg) James H. Bell
Lt. (jg) George K. Bomberger
Lt. (jg) Kilmer S. Bortz
Lt. (jg) David E. T. Braden
Lt. (jg) James S. Brown
Lt. (jg) John R. Campbell
Lt. (jg) Richard F. Cyr
Lt. (jg) Raymond L. Earl
Lt. (jg) Howard G. Ervin Jr.
Lt. (jg) Freidrich G. Fleig
Lt. (jg) Harry A. Fredrickson
Lt. (jg) Ralph Hein Jr.
Lt. (jg) William H. Huber
Lt. (jg) J. C. Hogue
Lt. (jg) Charles T. Larsen
Lt. (jg) Warren P. Lutey
Lt. (jg) John C. McCollum Jr.
Lt. (jg) Austin Morris
Lt. (jg) Everett E. Newman
Lt. (jg) George M. Rounds Jr.
Lt. (jg) John I. B. Pyne
Lt. (jg) Warren H. Schoen
Lt. (jg) William L. Strahan
Lt. (jg) Norman E. Thurmon
Lt. (jg) Jesse James Walker Jr .
Lt. (jg) Thomas J. Warren
Lt. (jg) William A. Wright
Ens. Josiah “Joe” Hodges Compton
Ens. Joseph J. Eisenhuth
ACM(AA) William G. Tinker
ACM(AA) Robert A White
ACMM William A. Ortman
ACMM Carter E. Parker
ACMM(AA) Richard C. Underwood
AMM2c George R. Adaza

AMM2c Milton N. Albritton
AMM2c David Arnbrister
AMM2c Elio Bertolini
AMM2c Stuart R. Cain
AMM2c John W. Foster
AMM2c Dale W. Hansen
AMM2c John R. Hitch
AMM2c Andrew J. Ruegamer
AMM2c Eugene Van Glover
AMM3c Edward Leon Abbott
AMM3c Ernest L. Alfaro
AMM3c Stanley E. Anderson
AMM3c Joseph P. Brady
AMM3c Charles E. Burke
AMM3c Orlando J. Caprarese
AMM3c Charles E. Condon
AMM3c John B. Dobson
AMM3c James T. Durand
AMM3c John J. Gardner
AMM3c Ross D. Isel
AMM3c Clarence H. Leever
AMM3c Michael Soriano
AOM1c James H. Hadeland
AOM1c Robert F. Merrell
AOM1c James A. Van Ausdal
AOM3c James H. Reynolds
ARM1c Leslie D. Anderson
ARM1c Arthur H. Shanks
ARM1c Wayne Young
ARM2c Ervin G. Bailey
ARM2c Robert E. Barber
ARM2c Lloyd I. Barker
ARM2c William E. Evrard
ARM2c Kaini R. Henderson
ARM2c Cyril F. Huvar Jr.
ARM2c Leonard F. Lindsey
ARM2c Eddie L. Maney
ARM2c James McMillan
ARM2c Richard E. Miralles
ARM2c Orville L. Pimley
ARM2c Jack Soderling
ARM2c Isadore A. St. Martin
ARM2c Steve R. Walker
ARM2c Paul J. Watson
ARM2c Charles E. Welch
ARM2c Robert E. Wheelhouse
ARM2c Travis B. Williams
ARM3c William J. Buckley
ARM3c Mitchel T. Burchfield
ARM3c James E. Cotton
ARM3c Waino Laatikainen
ARM3c Jack A. Lilley
ARM3c George Molloy
ARM3c Douglas J. Naylor
ARM3c Theodore Schevon
ARM3c Dale E. Shover
ARM3c Ose M. Veesey
ARM3c John W. Wade
CBM(AA) Clayton G. Boettger
C3c Francisco C. Delgado
PR3c Harry C. Vanderhoof
Ptr3c Harry J. Howard Jr.
SD2c Ignacio M. Reyes
Sea2c Herman H. Haslag
Y2c William C. Krug

VT-11 Roster

Lt. Cdr. Frederick L. Ashworth
Lt. David Bonterese
Lt. Howard U. Bush
Lt. Virgil Flynn
Lt. (jg) John P. Ayres
Lt. (jg) Donald R. Burke
Lt. (jg) Carroll C. Campbell
Lt. (jg) R. L. Edwards
Lt. (jg) George H. Gay
Lt. (jg) John W. Shong
Lt. (jg) Melvin L. Tegge
Ens. Thomas B. Adams
Ens. Paul E. Babel
Ens. Harry T. Brown
Ens. Raymond B. Cook
Ens. William C. Hirsch
Ens. Edwin E. Hughes
Ens. John C. Livezey
Ens. William J. Slone
Ens. Robert J. Snell
Ens. Martin J. Stack
Ens. James L. Sweetser
Ens. William R. Weiss
Ens. William H. Winner
ACEM Walter P. Hanchak
ACMM John S. Fryer
ACMM Ralph T. Stuart
ACRM Paul E. Bos
ACRM Robert J. Brown Jr.
AEM2c Vincent J. Bevinetto
AEM2c James A. Gardner
AM1c Casey J. Szepieniec
AM1c Gordon W. Washlake
AM1c Nelson L. Whitehead
AM3c Robert J. Bragg Jr.
AOM1c Robert F. Weston
AOM1c Jack F. Young
AOM2c Clayton R. Lancaster
AOM2c Willie R. Miller
AOM2c Charles E. Wandell
AOM2c Robert A. Willis
AOM2c Harold I. Wilson
AOM2c Wayne L. Wood
AOM3c Lloyd G. Cramer
AOM3c Robert A. Demonte
AOM3c Dorwin A. Downey
AOM3c George M. Grossman
AOM3c Preston J. Keeler Jr.
AOM3c George R. Merritt
AOM3c Clint T. Steed Jr.
ARM1c Raymond S. Combs Jr.
ARM2c Robert H. Barnes Jr.
ARM2c William A. Combs
ARM2c William E. Corley
ARM2c Robert E. Dobyns
ARM2c Thomas A. Fanger
ARM2c Glenn A. Faulk
ARM2c John W. Fike
ARM2c Joe L. Harper
ARM2c Ordien F. Herr
ARM2c Charles R. Johnson
ARM2c Homer R. Johnson
ARM2c Paul T. Kortum
ARM2c William T. Owens
ARM3c Stanley A. Bloom
ARM3c Paul J. Chleborad

ARM3c Derrill L. Clark
ARM3c Carl L. Cobb
ARM3c Theodore L. Coleman
ARM3c Alley B. Conrad
ARM3c Reginald L. Drake
ARM3c Jack R. Ellison
ARM3c Anton F. Ganje
ARM3c Jess W. Jordan
ARM3c Ellwin A. Teal
AMM1c Julian F. Cannon
AMM1c Harold A. Medlock
AMM1c Leroy C. Moon
AMM2c Raymond J. Adams
AMM2c Leslie E. Arnese
AMM2c Carroll C. Barber
AMM2c John H. Carroll Jr.
AMM2c Clarence A. Dabler
AMM2c Roy O. Eddington
AMM2c Louis K. Hill
AMM2c Jacques B. Laperche
AMM2c Darrell F. Lee
AMM2c Walter H. Markowich
AMM2c Ruble H. Mize
AMM2c Verle C. Moore Jr.
AMM2c Henry E. Noth
AMM2c Marvin M. Ransom
AMM2c Richard E. Ream
AMM2c George Retelas
AMM2c Herbert J. Wait
AMM2c Henry A. Wright
AMM3c Robert J. Bowington
AMM3c Gordon S. Corradetti
AMM3c Howard E. Crain
AMM3c Mortimer J. Dennehy
AMM3c Claude E. Haley
AMM3c Frederick L. Keenan
AMM3c Michael J. O'Malley
AMM3c August G. Meyer
AMM3c Gustave O. Perlich
AMM3c Verlyn W. Perry
AMM3c James E. Pryor Jr.
AMM3c Fred L. Rhodes
AMM3c Bernard G. Robinson
AMM3c James F. Rommelfanger
AMM3c James F. Smith
AMM3c Laurence E. Stauch
AMM3c James W. Tinsley Jr.
AMM3c Clark H. Way
AMM3c Edward J. Wheeler
CAP(AA) Sidney W. Quick
PhoM3c Charles S. Ball
PR2c Raymond J. Schmitt
S2c David Bigham

SECOND TOUR: USS *HORNET*

The USS *Hornet* had an additional 150 officers in ten different departments: administration, air, gunnery, engineering, navigation, communications, supply, medical, and a marine detachment. Additionally, there were between two thousand and three thousand enlisted crew on the carrier.[1]

CAG

Cdr. George T. McCutchan
Cdr. Paul H. Ramsey
Cdr. Robert E. Riera
Cdr. Frederick R. Schrader
Lt. Cdr. John Hulme
Lt. Cdr. Charles E. Kerlee
Lt. John M. Griffith
Lt. Henry C. Higginbottom
Lt. Robert W. Holt
Lt. George Huiner
Lt. Stanley W. Ogush
Lt. (jg) Robert M. Hermann
Lt. (jg) Robert J. King
Ens. Clyde L. Waters

VB-11 Roster

Lt. Cdr. Edwin John Kroeger
Lt. John R. Campbell
Lt. Robert W. "Jack" Cocks
Lt. H. D. DuBois
Lt. Raymond L. Earl
Lt. H. G. "Bose" Ervin
Lt. George Edward Ford
Lt. A. M. Jones Jr.
Lt. Richard F. Kenney
Lt. J. H. Rounsaville
Lt. Carl F. Schwab Jr.
Lt. Edward M. Smith
Lt. William L. Strahan
Lt. Edwin M. Wilson Jr.
Lt. E. M. Yoder
Lt. (jg) Richard Glen Aubel
Lt. (jg) William H. Bourne
Lt. (jg) Charles H. Cardon
Lt. (jg) Robert E. Gallatin
Lt. (jg) Joseph A. Hayes
Lt. (jg) Douglas W. Logan
Lt. (jg) Kevin P. Lynch
Lt. (jg) Dwain C. Oakley
Lt. (jg) George W. Russell
Lt. (jg) Reuben E. Schultz
Lt. (jg) A. C. Wiley
Ens. Orlando E. Ynserni
ACEM Joseph McBride
ACMM Lewis T. Hanson
ACMM James H. Lovern
ACMM Kenneth E. Schott
ACRM Albert H. Cox
ACRM Albert E. Story
AEM2c Gerald W. Klingler
AM1c Herbert W. Jones
AMM1c Richard D. Bruno
AMM1c Jean L. Crump
AMM1c Uel K. Hawkins
AOM1c Howard H. Winters
AOM2c Maynard O. Hamlin
ARCM Cornelius C. Van Poll
ARM1c Donald E. Bolt
ARM1c Armando M. Chavez
ARM1c William Eads
ARM1c Lynn K. Fuller
ARM1c Myron L. Henry
ARM1c Harry R. Jespersen
ARM1c Robert W. Koster

ARM1c James M. Kufeldt
ARM2c Gene C. Barday
ARM2c Gaylord T. Bond
ARM2c William S. Brown
ARM2c John R. Cetanyan
ARM2c John C. Cowsert
ARM2c Maurice Cravey
ARM2c Raymond J. Crawford
ARM2c Arthur F. Cronin Jr.
ARM2c Kenneth G. Day
ARM2c George Eliopulus
ARM2c William T. Emanuel
ARM2c Edward P. Emmons
ARM2c James M. Fitzgerald
ARM2c Leonard R. Gilson
ARM2c Charles W. Homan Jr.
ARM2c Orion D. Hudson
ARM2c Raymond J. Kipp
ARM2c Leon Krzemien
ARM2c Arnold E. Landry
ARM2c Irwin M. Lanning
ARM2c Richard C. Minter
ARM2c John D. Owens
ARM2c Dale S. Peterson
ARM2c Alvin F. Pierce
ARM2c Moulton J. Rice
ARM2c William M. Rivers Jr.
ARM2c Pat R. Shields
ARM2c Leo H. Suhor
ARM2c Jessie J. Taylor
ARM2c William L. Weber
ARM2c Walter H. White
ARM2c Marion R. Young
ARM3c Francis L. Anderson
ARM3c James J. Betsekas
ARM3c Duane F. Brash
ARM3c Johnnie Lubo
ARM3c Richard W. Mosher
ARM3c Arthur J. Motulewicz
ARM3c Dean F. Ostler
ARM3c Edward J. Pickard
ARM3c Roger A. Warbelton
ARM3c John G. Watson
ARTıc Walter A. Tufly
CPhomM Leo J. Delamore
PR2c Henry R. Anthony
Y1c William C. Barlow
Y1c Earle T. Moran
Y3c Bill E. Kelly
Y3c Johnie L. Crosswhite

VF-11 Roster

Lt. Cdr. Edward H. Bayers
Lt. Cdr. Robert E. Clements
Lt. Cdr. Eugene G. Fairfax
Lt. James S. Brown
Lt. Richard F. Cyr
Lt. Robert N. Flath
Lt. George A. Griffin
Lt. Terry H. Holberton Jr.
Lt. Howard E. Maring
Lt. Arnold R. Meyer
Lt. R. W. Moore
Lt. G. L. Morris Jr.
Lt. Edward S. Ogle
Lt. John W. Ramsey

Lt. Robert J. Saggau
Lt. Jimmie E. Savage
Lt. William R. Sisley Jr.
Lt. Charles R. Stimpson
Lt. James S. Swope
Lt. Jack S. Welfelt
Lt. Oscar H. West Jr.
Lt. Henry S. White
Lt. Daniel T. Work
Lt. Walter O. Zoecklein
Lt. (jg) Walton H. Boring
Lt. (jg) Gerald T. Coeur
Lt. (jg) William G. Eccles
Lt. (jg) Adrian J. Engle
Lt. (jg) Lawrence S. Hardy Jr.
Lt. (jg) Melvin J. Hayter
Lt. (jg) Paul F. Hintze
Lt. (jg) Clifford W. James
Lt. (jg) Norton L. Jeffers
Lt. (jg) Robert McBride
Lt. (jg) Richard K. Meade
Lt. (jg) Horace B. Moranville
Lt. (jg) Clarence L. Parsley
Lt. (jg) John P. Sims
Lt. (jg) Marvin P. South
Lt. (jg) John T. Willis
Lt. (jg) John A. Zink
Ens. Brainerd K. Beckwith
Ens. James H. Bethel Jr.
Ens. Paul Bilbao
Ens. Charles E. Boineau Jr.
Ens. Harold E. Brookens
Ens. James R. Byerly Jr.
Ens. Frederick R. Chapman
Ens. Earl G. Clouser
Ens. Matthew J. Crehan
Ens. Frederick W. Crowell Jr.
Ens. James J. Crowley
Ens. Dean R. Dewitt
Ens. Charles Dikoff
Ens. Gaylord E. Edling
Ens. Neil W. Eft
Ens. Robert P. Farley
Ens. William L. Garlic
Ens. Raymond Grosso
Ens. Albert R. Groves
Ens. Orliss L. Jacobsen
Ens. Basil V. Jesmer
Ens. William E. Kearns
Ens. Paul E. King
Ens. Zebulon B. Knott Jr.
Ens. William J. Koressel
Ens. Tadeusz Lepianka
Ens. Richard K. Lewis
Ens. Wesley E. Lizotte
Ens. James Mansfield
Ens. William H. Martin Jr.
Ens. James J. McCarron
Ens. Robert McReynolds
Ens. Appleton T. Miles
Ens. Howard H. Moore
Ens. Alexander W. Morris III
Ens. James A. Mudd
Ens. Robert A. Nelson
Ens. Wade H. Nowlin
Ens. John E. Olson
Ens. Frank C. Onion Jr.
Ens. Sterling J. Richardson

Ens. Jack H. Robcke
Ens. Kester M. Roberts
Ens. Henry M. Rowland Jr.
Ens. Leslie B. Sahm
Ens. Clarence D. Smith
Ens. Hugh E. Smith
Ens. Howard J. Stockert
Ens. John M. Suddreth
Ens. Thomas W. Tidwell
Ens. Thomas C. Tillar
Ens. Allen P. Tonsfeldt
Ens. Robin C. Vance
Ens. Kenneth K. Walker
Ens. Paul C. Warren
Ens. John R. Whiteside
Ens. Thomas St. C. Williams
Ens. Richard E. Wilson
Ens. James P. Wolf

VT-11 Roster

Lt. Cdr. John A. Fidel
Lt. Thomas B. Adams
Lt. David C. Chamberlain
Lt. Wilbur J. Engman
Lt. Leroy H. Grau
Lt. James L. Hooper
Lt. Norman V. Lewis
Lt. Melvin L. Tegge
Lt. (jg) Gordon W. Bell
Lt. (jg) James R. Bowman
Lt. (jg) John M. Davis
Lt. (jg) Lawrence E. Helmuth
Lt. (jg) Joseph M. Hyland
Lt. (jg) William Maier
Lt. (jg) Edwin W. McGowan
Lt. (jg) Bernard S. Meyer
Lt. (jg) Jack V. Perry
Lt. (jg) Lewis Richfield
Lt. (jg) Nicholas Satterlee
Lt. (jg) Royal C. Schendel
Lt. (jg) Joseph W. Sobien
Lt. (jg) Walker White Jr.
Ens. Frederick O. Baker
Ens. Jay M. Cooper
Ens. George D. Stebbings
AMM1c Michael D. Collins
AMM1c William E. Corley
AMM1c Gordon S. Corradetti
AMM1c Roy O. Eddington
AMM1c Claude E. Haley
AMM1c Frederick L. Keenan
AMM2c E. Morgan Norman
AMM3c Curtis L. Pederson
AMM3c Charles T. Riley Jr.
AOM1c Preston J. Keller Jr.
AOM1c Clayton R. Lancaster
AOM1c Robert A. Willis
AOM1c Harold I. Wilson
AOM2c Charles H. Cunningham
AOM2c Robert A. De Monte
AOM2c Ralph M. Hameetman
AOM2c Wilfred W. Le Blanc
AOM2c Robert D. Leist
AOM2c Gayle K. Marz
AOM2c Jimmie L. Richards
AOM2c Robert D. Shongo

AOM2c Edward P. Speckner
AOM2c Clint T. Steed Jr.
AOM2c Joe M. Valenzuela
AOM2c Gordon G. Willis
AOM3c Leon D. Paul
ARM1c Thomas A. Fanger
ARM1c Glenn A. Faulk
ARM1c Homer R. Johnson
ARM1c Jess W. Jordan
ARM2c Raymond J. Arendt
ARM2c Fred J. Baker
ARM2c Roger Balcombe
ARM2c Sammy C. Black
ARM2c Louie E. Blankenship
ARM2c Vergil E. Bloomquist
ARM2c Raymond L. Brever
ARM2c Henry A. Butterworth
ARM2c Theodore A. Clay
ARM2c Paul J. Chleborad
ARM2c Robert A. Crawford
ARM2c Albert J. Day
ARM2c Denzil D. De Graffenreid
ARM2c William A. Culp
ARM2c Curtis S. Dugan
ARM2c Lawrence G. Collett
ARM2c Richard J. Nelson
ARM2c Laurence E. Sawyer
ARM2c Robert L. Trobaugh
ARM2c Fred F. Wilson
ARM3c Leonard J. Ekenstan
ARM3c Raymond E. McKnight
ARM3c Earl L. Pike
ARM3c Wayne M. Pitcher
ARM3c Laurence C. Schiller
ACMM Raymond S. Combs Jr.
ACMM Leo Estes
AEM1c James A. Gardner
ACEM Walter P. Hanchak
Sea1c Robert C. Fitz
ACM Gordon W. Washlake
ACOM Clarence C. Herzer
ACRM Whitney H. Kennedy
AP1c David W. Mangum
ACRT George J. Stumph
PR2c Joel L. Warren
Y1c Robert C. Hardin
Y3c William C. Pringle Jr.

APPENDIX B

CVG-11 Missing in Action, Killed in Action, Killed in Training[2]

The names below come from the CVG-11 Memorial Honor Roll, 1942–1945. Throughout the war, 103 members of Air Group Eleven made the ultimate sacrifice. This work would not be complete without recognizing their sacrifice.

November 18, 1942 . . Ens. Earl Otto Krieg, USNR, Forest Park, IL, VF-11, training

January 26, 1943 . . . . ARM3c Wayne Maurice Anderson, USN, Marvin, SD, VT-11, training

March 16, 1943 . . . . . Ens. Robert Wayne Baumgartner, USNR, Volusia, FL, VF-11, training

March 25, 1943 . . . . . Lt. (jg) Herbert Bronson Shonk, USNR, Westchester, NY, VB-11, training

March 25, 1943 . . . . . ARMC Francis Freeman Brown, USN, San Diego, CA, VB-11, training

May 6, 1943 . . . . Ens. Leroy Winston Childs, USNR, Hood River, OR, VF-11, MIA

May 19, 1943 . . . . Lt. (jg) James Loring Sweetser, USNR, Portland, ME, VT-11, MIA

May 19, 1943 . . . . AOM3c Lloyd George Cramer, USNR, Hoskins, OR, VT-11, MIA

May 19, 1943 . . . . AM1c Nelson Lee Whitehead, USN, Marietta, OH, VT-11, MIA

May 21, 1943 . . . . Lt. (jg) Harry Thomas Brown, USNR, Borger, TX, VT-11, MIA

May 21, 1943 . . . . ARM2c Joe Lewis Harper, USNR, Great Falls, MT, VT-11, MIA

May 21, 1943 . . . . AMM3c James Walter Tinsley Jr., USN, Dallas, TX, VT-11, MIA

June 5, 1943 . . . . ARM2c Howard Ely Crain, USNR, Farmersville, CA, VT-11, KIA

June 5, 1943 . . . . Lt. (jg) Robert Jefferson Snell, USNR, Meridian, MS, VT-11, MIA

June 5, 1943 . . . . AOM2c Wayne Lowell Wood, USNR, Coleharbor, ND, VT-11, MIA

June 5, 1943 . . . . ARM2c Reginald Leon Drake, USN, Battle Creek, MI, VT-11, MIA

June 5, 1943 . . . . Lt. (jg) David Allen Beck, USNR, Baxley, GA, VS-11, MIA

June 5, 1943 . . . . ARM2c Kaini Robert Henderson, USNR, Chicago, IL, VS-11, MIA

June 8, 1943 . . . . Lt. Cdr. Weldon Lee Hamilton, USN, Coronado, CA, CAG-11, R4D5 crash

June 8, 1943 . . . . Lt. (jg) Paul Edward Babel, USNR, Pawtucket, RI, VT-11, R4D5 crash

June 8, 1943 . . . . Lt. Donald Randall Burke, USNR, Hollywood, CA, VT-11, R4D5 crash

June 8, 1943 . . . . Lt. (jg) William Robert Weiss, USNR, Gainesville, TX, VT-11, R4D5 crash

June 8, 1943 . . . . Cpt. Sidney William Quick, USN, New Orleans, LA, VT-11, R4D5 crash

June 8, 1943 .... Lt. John Clifford Livezey, USN, Leonia, NJ, VT-11, R4D5 crash

June 8, 1943 .... Lt. Virgil Edmund Flynn, USNR, Milbank, SD, VT-11, R4D5 crash

June 8, 1943 .... ARM2c Robert Haywood Barnes Jr., USNR Montevallo, AL, VT-11, R4D5 crash

June 8, 1943 .... PHM2c Charles Sterling Ball, USNR, Kahoka, MO, VT-11, R4D5 crash

June 8, 1943 .... ARM2c Ordien Fenmore Herr, USNR, Webster, SD, VT-11, R4D5 crash

June 8, 1943 .... AMM2c Bernard Gordon Robinson, USN, Redwood City, CA, VT-11, R4D5 crash

June 8, 1943 .... AOM1c Jack Foster Young, USN, San Diego, CA, VT-11, R4D5 crash

June 8, 1943 .... ARM3c Carl Lee Cobb, USN, Tipton, MO, VT-11, R4D5 crash

June 8, 1943 .... ARM2c Alley Burton Conrad, USN, Silverton, OR, VT-11, R4D5 crash

June 8, 1943 .... ARM2c William Thomas Owens, USNR, Santa Barbara, CA, VT-11, R4D5 crash

June 8, 1943 .... ARM3c Ellwin Albert Teal, USNR, Crookston, MN, VT-11, R4D5 crash

June 16, 1943....... Lt. (jg) George Winthrop Ricker, USNR, Berwick, ME, VF-11, MIA

June 16, 1943....... Lt. (jg) Chandler Gantt Boswell, USNR, New Orleans, LA, VF-11, MIA

June 16, 1943....... Lt. (jg) Teddy Louis Hull, USNR, Winslow, AR, VF-11, MIA

July 9, 1943........ Lt. (jg) Cyrus George Cary, USNR, Cowlitz, WA, VF-11, MIA

July 17, 1943 .... Lt. (jg) Edward Francis Hughes, USNR, Medford, MA, VB-11, MIA

July 17, 1943 .... ARM2c Harold Milton Marrs, USN, Grays Harbor, WA, VB-11, MIA

October 10, 1943. . . . Ens. Virgil David Roland, USNR, Richmond, VA, VF-11, training

October 28, 1943. . . . Ens. Fred Homer Kater, USNR, Macon, IL, VB-11, training

November 1, 1943 . . . Ens. Robert Alexander McKinney, USNR, Saginaw, MI, VT-11, training

November 1, 1943 . . . AOM3c Ward Leroy Evans, USNR Chicago, IL, VT-11, training

February 11, 1944 . . . Ens. William Herbert Graebner, USN, Milwaukee, WI, VB-11, training

February 12, 1944 . . . Lt. (jg) Edward Harold Johnson, USNR, Orlando, FL, VF-11, accident

March 16, 1944. . . . . Ens. George William Papen Jr., USNR, Cambridge, MA, VF-11, training

April 19, 1944 . . . . . . Ens. Thomas B Reed Jr., USNR, Los Angeles, CA, VF-11, training

May 23, 1944 . . . . . . Ens. William Saylor Culver, USNR, Los Angeles, CA, VB-11, training

May 23, 1944 . . . . . . ARM3c John Phillip Hall, USNR, Phoenix, AZ, VB-11, training

June 1, 1944 . . . . Lt. (jg) Thomas Jack Warren, USNR, San Francisco, CA, VB-11, training

June 26, 1944 . . . . . . Lt. (jg) Johnny Wilson Patterson, USNR, Palestine, TX VB-11, training

June 26, 1944 . . . . . . ARM2c Robert Ronald Cox, USNR, Clovis, NM, VB-11, training

July 3, 1944. . . . . Ens. Jack Anderson, USNR, TX, VB-11, training

July 3, 1944. . . . . ARM2c Joyce Eugene Swaim, USNR, Little Rock, AR, VB-11, training

July 12, 1944 . . . . Ens. Thomas William Ooglie, USNR, San Mateo, CA, VB-11, training

July 12, 1944 . . . . ARM1c William Peter Carey, USNR, La Porte, IN, VB-11, training

August 24, 1944 . . . . Cdr. George Thurston McCutchan, USN, Evansville, IN, CAG-11, training
October 10, 1944 . . . Lt. (jg) Kenneth Chancellor Chase, USNR, Dayton, OH, VF-11, MIA
October 12, 1944. . . . Ens. George Edgar Grier Lindesmith, USNR, Los Angeles, CA, VF-11, MIA
October 13, 1944. . . . Ens. Leon Edsel Lee, USNR, Pratt, KS, VF-11, MIA
October 13, 1944. . . . Cdr. Frederick Rutherford Schrader, USN, Lawrence, IL, CAG-11, MIA
October 14, 1944 . . . Lt. Edward Erwin Helgerson, USNR, Minneapolis, MN, VFN-78, MIA
October 14, 1944 . . . Lt. Nelson Woodrow Dayhoff, USNR, Manhattan, KS, VF-11, MIA
October 14, 1944 . . . Ens. Frederick James Campbell Blair, USNR, Seattle, WA, VF-11, MIA
October 14, 1944 . . . Lt. Samuel Elsworth Goldberg, USNR, Oakland, CA, VF-11, MIA
October 14, 1944 . . . Ens. Henry Ptacek, USNR, Omaha, NE, VF-11, MIA
October 15, 1944. . . . Ens. Robert Christian Dance, USNR, Norfolk, VA, VF-11, MIA
October 18, 1944. . . . Ens. George Gordon Anderson, USNR, Eugene, OR, VF-11, MIA
October 18, 1944. . . . Ens. Warren Kenneth De Rolf, USNR, Hammond, IN, VF-11, MIA
October 19, 1944. . . . Lt. (jg) Warren James Sailor, USNR, Gray, TX, VB-11, MIA
October 19, 1944. . . . ARM3c Duane Frederick Brash, USNR, Sargent, ND, VB-11, MIA
October 19, 1944. . . . Lt. William Howard Winner, USNR, San Diego, CA, VT-11, KIA
October 19, 1944. . . . ARM2c Paul James Chleborad, USN, Omaha, NE, VT-11, KIA
October 19, 1944. . . . ARM2c Fred Joseph Baker, USNR, Grand Rapids, MI, VT-11, KIA

October 27, 1944 . . . Ens. Charles Ray Bratcres, USNR, Castle Rock, WA, VF-11, MIA

November 3, 1944. . . Ens. John James McVeigh, USNR, Grand Rapids, MN, VF-11, MIA

November 5, 1944. . . AMM2c Norman Everett Morgan, USNR, Tulsa, OK, VT-11, KIA

November 5, 1944. . . ARM1c Homer Russell Johnson, USNR, Lincoln, NE, VT-11, KIA

November 5, 1944. . . Ens. William Manierre Mann, USNR, Chicago, IL, VF-11, MIA

November 13, 1944 . . Lt. Cdr. Radcliffe Denniston Jr., USN, Wauwatosa, WI, VT-11, KIA

November 13, 1944 . . ARM1c Glenn Allen Faulk, USNR, Lindsay, OK, VT-11, MIA

November 13, 1944 . . AOM2c Clint Thomas Steed Jr., USNR, Tyler, TX, VT-11, MIA

November 13, 1944 . . Ens. Burton Thelin Oberg, Cromwell, CT, VT-11, MIA

November 13, 1944 . . AOM3c Dowd (n) Hamaker, USNR, Grand Junction, CO, VT-11, MIA

November 13, 1944 . . AMM3c Robert Verne Burgess, USNR, Berwick, ME, VT-11, MIA

December 10, 1944 . . AOM2c Wilfred Warren Le Blanc, USNR, Sterling, CO, VT-11, MIA

January 7, 1945 . . . . . Lt. (jg) Richard Glen Aubel, USNR, Los Angeles, CA, VB-11, MIA

January 7, 1945 . . . . . ARM2c Marion Russell Young, USNR, Vermont, IL, VB-11, MIA

January 7, 1945 . . . . . Ens. James Houston Bethel Jr., USNR, Massies Mill, VA, VF-11, MIA

January 7, 1945 . . . . . Lt. (jg) John Peak Sims, USNR, Paducah, TX, VF-11, MIA

January 9, 1945 . . . . . Lt. (jg) Gordon Woolfolk Bell, USNR, Berkeley, CA, VT-11, MIA

January 9, 1945 . . . . . AMM1c Claude Ellsworth Haley, USN, Salida, CO, VT-11, MIA

January 9, 1945 . . . . . ARM2c Laurence Ernest Sawyer, USN, Grand Junction, CO, VT-11, MIA

January 9, 1945 . . . . . ARM2c Roger Balcombe, USNR, Cosmopolis, WA, VT-11, KIA, buried at sea

January 12, 1945 . . . . Lt. (jg) William Maier, USNR, Berkeley, CA, VT-11, MIA

January 12, 1945 . . . . Lt. (jg) Joseph Matthew Hyland, USNR, Jackson Heights, NY, VT-11, MIA

January 12, 1945 . . . . AOM2c Edward Paul Speckner, USNR, Louisville, KY, VT-11, MIA

January 15, 1945. . . . . ARM2c William Malloy Rivers Jr., USNR, Tampa, FL, VB-11, MIA

January 16, 1945 . . . . Ens. Richard Everett Wilson, USNR, Chicago, IL, VF-11, MIA

January 16, 1945 . . . . Lt. (jg) Edwin William McGowan, USNR, Norfolk, MA, VT-11, KIA

January 16, 1945 . . . . AOM1c Charles Henry Cunningham, USNR, Bisbee, AZ, VT-11, MIA

January 16, 1945 . . . . ARM2c Lawrence Cornelius Schiller, USNR, Cameron, TX, VT-11, KIA

APPENDIX C

Poems and Poetry of CVG-11

"Reflections on Fighters" by H. B. Shonk[3]

The Navy has its classy planes, their names on every lip.
The newest Grumman fighter needs a three-mile landing strip.
Those boys in Fighting Squadron Eleven may make America free,
But give me the Douglas Dauntless, pal—for that's the plane for me!

Oh, I'm not one for flips and frills, I never zoom the mat.
You'll never see me showing off and swooping like a gnat.
The English have their victory roll when they have "popped a blighter."
But I don't do that in an SBD, It ain't no blasted fighter!

I watch the boys in F4Fs as they go roaring by,
In baseball caps and earphones, making runs on lesser fry.
They'll return as conquering heroes while the whole damn country shouts.
But they still lose all their money to the Bombers and the Scouts!

I never was a glamour-boy, I never posed for Arrow.
I haven't got a slick physique like Joseph Louis Barrow.
I'm not an ace, I'm not in Life I'm not a daring hero.
And I'd rather run in an SBD than climb to fight a Zero!

Maybe my butt gets sore and stiff from a tough six-hour patrol,
While the fighters sit in the ready-room and gamble away their roll . . .
But it's worth it all when the chips are down and you're roaring into
your dive,
And you're aiming at the biggest one with a thousand pound bee-hive.

Of course, you're not thinking about it then, but just the same it's true:
That they've got to shoot down the F4Fs before they can get to you.
So here's the latest dope, boys—Every Admiral agrees
That all the fighters are good for is to protect the SBDs!

So let them prance and let them boast, and let them hog the sky;
And let the natives dance and cheer as they go flashing by.
Yes, let the fighters have their fling, as they zoom our poor Tent City—
For they're Air Group Eleven's Cannon Fodder—Boy! ain't that a pity!

VT-11 Poem

Crude by modern sensibilities and standards, it was certainly representative of the generation:

Her name was Lulu, she was one of the best,
That night I put her to the test,
She looked so pretty, so sweet, so slim,
The night was dark, the lights were dim,
I was so excited, my heart missed a beat,
For I knew that I was in for a damn good treat.
I'd seen her stripped, I'd seen her bare,
I'd felt her over everywhere.
I got inside her, she screamed for joy,

That was the first night boy-oh-boy.
I got up quickly, as far as I could,
I handled her gently, I knew she was good.
I rolled her over, then on her side.
Then on her back, I also tried.
She was one big thrill, the gift from heaven,
That Grumman Avenger of the Torpedo Squadron Eleven.

VT-11 Gunner's Theme Song

I wished to be a pilot, and you along with me
But, if we all were pilots, where would the Air Force be?
It takes guts to be a gunner, to sit out in the tail
When the Zeros are coming, and the slugs begin to wail
The pilot is just a chauffeur, it's his job to fly the plane
But, it's we who do the fighting, tho' we do not get the fame
If we all must be gunners, then let us make this bet
That we'll be the best damned gunners, that have left this squadron yet!

Acknowledgments

As with all of my previous works, a veritable carrier-full of individuals helped me throughout this process. The actual writing of history is a solitary art form, but the processes of preparing to write and then editing the manuscript take the generosity and willingness of innumerable folks.

There is no way this book would have come to fruition without the help of George Retelas and Tim Hampton. Their generosity of spirit, their willingness to share documents and trade information, their enthusiasm for what I wanted to accomplish—all were boundless. Their emails and past research into the air group were absolutely essential to this book. They are the real Air Group Eleven historians, and their work to preserve the group's history and the history of the USS *Hornet* will survive all of us. George's desire to track down his grandfather's group shipmates resulted in not only the exceptional film *Eleven: The Movie*, but also George's wonderful YouTube channel filled with dozens of videos and hours of interviews with the survivors of the air group. To both George and Tim, I am eternally grateful.

Naval historian Barrett Tillman, "the man who owns naval aviation history," was likewise generous in his time and effort to locate sources for this book, and nothing you have read previously was possible without his extensive work on the history of "Eleven," the aircraft of World War II, and other aspects of naval history too numerous to name here. Thanks to Dr. Lance Blyth, the command historian at North American Aerospace Defense Command and U.S. Northern Command, whose grasp of naval warfare and amphibious operations is second only to his knowledge of mountain warfare, which proved indispensable in helping to outline early Japanese operations. Other distinguished naval historians include Trent Hone and Chuck Steele, both willing to share sources, books, and ideas. To my colleague and friend Dr. Michael Hankins, the Don Mrozek to my Robin Higham, thanks for your phone calls and support of all of my writing efforts.

For other sources, special thanks go to the National Archives and Records Administration, especially anyone who has ever worked on Record Group 38, the McDermott Library at the United States Air Force Academy, and the Naval History and Heritage Command.

I have worked closely for many years with the fine publishing crew at the U.S. Naval Institute, including my editor Padraic (Pat) Carlin, press director Adam Kane, Claire Noble, Ashley Baird, and many, many others. Thanks to my copyeditor Lisa Yambrick and my indexer Galen Schroeder. Naval Institute Press has been in business since 1898 and has the single greatest collection of works on naval history ever published. Besides, this also allows me to state that I published with the same press that first released *The Hunt for Red October*. One ping only, Vasily.

Notes

Preface

1. James D. Hornfischer, "All the Tin Can Sailors Are Gone: What Naval History Loses with the Passing of the World War II Generation," in Thomas J. Cutler, *The Battle of Leyte Gulf at 75: A Retrospective* (Annapolis, MD: Naval Institute Press, 2019), 185. Sadly, we lost a great historian when Hornfischer passed away at the age of fifty-five on June 2, 2021.
2. Tom Brokaw, *The Greatest Generation* (New York: Random House, 1998); Studs Terkel, *"The Good War": An Oral History of World War II* (New York: Pantheon, 1984).
3. Drew Gilpin Faust, *This Republic of Suffering: Death and the American Civil War* (New York: Random House, 2008), xviii; David W. Blight, *Race and Reunion: The* ry," The National WW II Museum, https://www.nationalww2museum .org/war/articles/american-memory-of-world-war-ii.
4. Kaylie McCarthy, "The Ghosts of Past and Present: Analyzing American WWII Memory," The National WW II Museum, https://www.nationalww2museum .org/war/articles/american-memory-of-world-war-ii.

5. Blight, 381; McCarthy; Paul V. Murphy, "'The Good War': Collective Memory and World War II in America," *Grand Valley Review* 25, no. 1 (2022).
6. Jack King, "'Masters of the Air,' Which Finally Has a Trailer, Looks Like Peak Dad TV," *GQ*, November 9, 2023, https://www.gq-magazine.co.uk/culture/article/band-of-brothers-sequel-masters-of-the-air; Charlie Hall, "Tom Hanks' 'Masters of the Air' Looks Like the Dad TV Event of 2024," Polygon.com, November 13, 2023, https://www.polygon.com/23959061/masters-air-trailer-apple-tv-release-date-call-and-tell-your-dad.
7. George Retelas, *Eleven: The Movie*, YouTube, January 11, 2021, https://www.youtube.com/watch?v=YfMhcK9gcqM&t=651s.
8. James J. Mahoney and Brian H. Mahoney, *Reluctant Witness: Memoirs from the Last Year of the European Air War 1944–45* (Victoria, BC: Trafford Publishing, 2001), 13.
9. Mahoney and Mahoney, 13; Gus Van Sant, director, *Good Will Hunting*, Miramax, 1997.
10. Michael S. Shull and David E. Witt, *Doing Their Bit: Wartime American Animated Short Films, 1939–1945* (Jefferson, NC: McFarland and Company, 1987), 129, 135.
11. John Dower, *War without Mercy: Race and Power in the Pacific War* (New York: Pantheon Books, 1987).

Introduction

1. Barrett Tillman, *U.S. Navy Fighter Squadrons in World War II* (North Branch, MN: Specialty Press, 1997), 6; Mark L. Evans and Roy A. Grossnick, *United States Naval Aviation 1910–2010*, vol. II (Washington, DC: Naval History and Heritage Command, 2015), 299–313.
2. Evans and Grossnick, 615–17.
3. Adolf Carlson, *Joint U.S. Army-Navy War Planning on the Eve of the First World War* (Carlisle Barracks, PA: U.S. Army War College Press, 1998), 13–14.
4. Ronald H. Spector, *Eagle Against the Sun: The American War with Japan* (New York: Random House, 1985), 59.
5. Edward S. Miller, *War Plan Orange: The U.S. Strategy to Defeat Japan, 1897–1945* (Annapolis, MD: Naval Institute Press, 1991), xix.
6. Miller, 333.
7. John B. Hattendorf, "The Idea of a 'Fleet in Being' in Historical Perspective," *Naval War College Review* 67, no. 1 (Winter 2014).
8. History remembers the "Zeke" as the Zero, and the names were used interchangeably and sometimes in an overlapping manner in Allied and American reports throughout the war.

9. Mark R. Peattie, *Sunburst: The Rise of Japanese Naval Air Power, 1909–1941* (Annapolis, MD: Naval Institute Press, 2001), 303–4.
10. Peattie, 171–72.

Chapter 1. The Forming of Air Group Eleven

1. National Archives and Records Administration (NARA), Record Group (RG) 38, 134052858, COMCAR REP AIR GR 11—War Diary, 10/10/42 to 11/30/42.
2. Paul Hubert Ramsey, Navy Cross citation, https://valor.militarytimes.com/hero/20092.
3. COMCAR REP AIR GR 11—War Diary, 10/10/42 to 11/30/42.
4. "Charles Rudolph Fenton," Naval History and Heritage Command (NHHC), Modern Biographical Library, https://www.history.navy.mil/research/library/research-guides/modern-biographical-files-ndl/modern-bios-f/fenton-charles-rudolph.html.
5. Barrett Tillman, *Sundowners: VF-11 in World War II* (St. Paul, MN: Phalanx, 1993), 7; Frank Olynyk, *Stars and Bars: A Tribute to the American Fighter Ace 1920–1973* (London: Grun Street Publishing, 1995), 575–76, 583; NHHC, "Winds of War, Winds of Change: The U.S. Naval Academy During the World War II Era," https://www.history.navy.mil/browse-by-topic/heritage/naval-academy/usna-wwii.html.
6. Tillman, *Sundowners*, 7.
7. Barrett Tillman, *Wildcat: The F4F in World War II* (Baltimore: Nautical and Aviation Publishing Company of America, 1983), xi.
8. Gordon Swanborough and Peter M. Bowers, *United States Navy Aircraft since 1911*, 2nd ed. (Annapolis, MD: Naval Institute Press, 1990).
9. As noted, the third letter in an aircraft's nomenclature indicated its manufacturer: *M* for General Motors, *D* for Dauntless, *F* for Grumman.
10. Stephen Hall, "From Beverly to Nagasaki: The 'Dick' Ashworth Story," WickedLocal.com, December 14, 2005, https://web.archive.org/web/20131216173517/http://www.wickedlocal.com/beverly/news/opinions/x21534932.
11. Frederick L. Ashworth Jr., USN, interview by Paul Stillwell, U.S. Naval Institute, April 17, 2000.
12. Ashworth, interview by Stillwell.
13. Ashworth, interview by Stillwell.
14. Ashworth, interview by Stillwell.
15. John Baxter, *Disney During World War II: How the Walt Disney Studio Contributed to Victory in the War* (New York: Disney Editions, 2014), 122–23; NARA, RG 38,

77678183, VT-11—War Diary, 16. The squadron re-approached the Disney Studios in early 1944 to re-license the insignia for use on decalcomanias (to be placed on the squadron's airplanes). The studios agreed but directed the squadron to the Vidachrome Company in Los Angeles to have the pieces produced. Although designed and provided in late 1942, the insignia was not officially recognized as that of the requesting group until 1945. Executive officer Lieutenant L. H. Grau contacted the studios in May 1945 seeking confirmation that the insignia in question was indeed designed solely for Torpedo Squadron Eleven's use, asking the studios to document such information so that it could be reviewed for final approval by the Bureau of Aeronautics, Washington, DC. The studios complied and confirmed the information for the squadron on June 12, 1945.

16. Peter C. Smith, *The Dauntless in Battle: The Douglas SBD Dauntless Dive-Bomber in the Pacific 1941–1945* (Yorkshire, UK: Pen and Sword Aviation, 2019), x–xi.
17. "Weldon L. Hamilton, LCDR, USN," United States Naval Academy Virtual Memorial Hall, https://usnamemorialhall.org/index.php/WELDON_L._HAMILTON,_LCDR,_USN.
18. "Weldon L. Hamilton."
19. "History: First Tour of Bombing Eleven, 10 Oct 1943 to 1 September 1944" (reprinted for the May 1987 reunion), courtesy of George Retelas; Roy A. Grossnick, *Dictionary of American Naval Aviation Squadrons* (Washington, DC: NHHC, 1995), 178.
20. "Bombing Eleven Insignia," *The Hook: Tailhook Association Magazine* (Winter 1983).
21. NARA, Record Group 38, Carrier Replacement Air Group Eleven, "War Diary for the Month of October," December 13, 1942.
22. "The Countess and the Flyboys," *Maui Magazine* (November-December 2012); Harry W. Patton, *The Tiger and I* (unpublished, 2009), 27–30; Hill Goodspeed, "A Wall of Memories: The von Tempsky Wall Gets a New Home at the National Naval Aviation Museum," Naval Aviation Museum Foundation (Fall 2014). A wall etched with the signatures of more than 20,000 aviators who visited the von Tempsky residence during the war now resides at the National Naval Aviation Museum in Pensacola, FL.
23. Patton, 27–30.
24. Carrier Replacement Air Group Eleven, "War Diary for the Month of December," no date.
25. Barrett Tillman, "The Tale of Eleven," *Naval History Magazine* 33, no. 4 (August 2019).

26. Carrier Replacement Air Group Eleven, "War Diary for the Month of February," March 5, 1943.
27. Harry A. Fredrickson, Scouting Squadron Eleven VS-11/VB-21, undated memoir, courtesy of George Retelas.
28. Carrier Replacement Air Group Eleven, "War Diary for the Month of March," April 7, 1943.

Chapter 2. Guadalcanal

1. Samuel Eliot Morison, *History of United States Naval Operations in World War II*, vol. 5, *The Struggle for Guadalcanal, August 1942–February 1943* (Boston: Little, Brown and Co., 1949), 369.
2. Morison, *The Struggle for Guadalcanal*, 369. The USS *Essex* (CV-9) arrived in the Pacific Theater ready for operations in May 1943 not long after CVG-11 began operations out of Guadalcanal.
3. Theodore Taylor, *The Magnificent Mitscher* (Annapolis, MD: Naval Institute Press, 1991), 144–45; E. B. Potter, *Bull Halsey* (Annapolis, MD: Naval Institute Press, 1985), 240.
4. Taylor, 145.
5. Thomas Alexander Hughes, *Admiral Bill Halsey: A Naval Life* (Oxford: Oxford University Press, 2016), 271.
6. Miller, 335.
7. Peattie, 177, 179.
8. Matome Ugaki, *Fading Victory: The Diary of Matome Ugaki*, trans. Masataka Chihaya (Pittsburgh, PA: University of Pittsburgh Press, 1991).
9. Ugaki, 331, 352–55.
10. Tillman, *Sundowners*, 7; "First Tour of Bombing Eleven: 10 Oct 1943 to 1 Sept 1944," courtesy of George Retelas.
11. Torpedo Squadron 11 scans, VT-11, Diaries, April 1943, courtesy of George Retelas.
12. Don Meyer, "Air Group Eleven, Fighting Squadron Eleven, The Sundowners," informal history, August 9, 1943, courtesy of George Retelas.
13. "Dauntless Dick and Daring Ose: Reuniting SBD Dauntless Gunners Dick Miralles and Ose Veesey," George Retelas, YouTube, https://youtu.be/Ln2sOt6JE8g.
14. CV-11 Historical Association, CVG-11, briefing sheets: Munda Point, March 19, 1943; Vila Plantation (Kolombangara Island), March 19, 1943; Rekata Bay, March 19, 1943.
15. CV-11 Historical Association, CVG-11, briefing sheets.

16. Meyer, informal history, 3; "Roll Call trailer, '11': The Movie," https://youtu.be/MDSLfc9voLc; Carisa Cegvske, "World War II Veteran Kermit Enander Fixed the Fighter Planes that Shot Down the Enemy," *The News-Review*, February 28, 2018.
17. Meyer, informal history, 5. There are certainly both socio-economic and racial overtones to the assistant secretary's comments.
18. Harry H. Crosby, *A Wing and a Prayer: The "Bloody 100th" Bomb Group of the U.S. Eighth Air Force in Action in World War II* (New York: Harper Collins, 1993), 103.
19. Meyer, informal history, 5.
20. "Dauntless Dick and Daring Ose."
21. Meyer, informal history, 4–5.
22. "Dauntless Dick and Daring Ose."
23. George Gay, *Sole Survivor: Torpedo Squadron 8, Battle of Midway* (Naples, FL: Midway Publishers, 1980), 205.
24. Meyer, informal history, 5.
25. John W. Fike, USN, VT-11 Memoir, *The Deadly Green* (undated).
26. Hughes.
27. Meyer, informal history, 3; VT-11—War History, 22.
28. Retelas, *Eleven: The Movie.*
29. VT-11—War History, 22.
30. Meyer, informal history, 3.
31. VT-11—War History, 9.
32. Gay.
33. Ashworth, interview by Stillwell.
34. Ashworth, interview by Stillwell.
35. Meyer, informal history, 4.
36. "First Tour of Bombing Eleven," 6.
37. Hughes.
38. Meyer, informal history, 5.
39. Bombing Squadron Eleven, "Summary of VB-11 Operations and at Henderson Field"; "First Tour of Bombing Eleven."
40. William Robert "Bob" Maxwell, USNR, "VF-11 Memoir, 2 May to 18 May 1943" (undated).
41. VF-11 after-action report, May 2, 1943. Vangu Island noted in the report is almost certainly Vangunu Island, and East Island was either Nggatokae or Mbulo Island.

42. Naval Intelligence Report—Lt. (jg) Maxwell, United States Pacific Fleet, South Pacific Force, Intelligence Division Confidential, 8 June 1943 (contained in VF-11 Material).
43. Maxwell.
44. Maxwell.
45. Maxwell.
46. Maxwell.
47. Maxwell.
48. "'Bob' Maxwell: Survivor of Grim Gamble with Death," *Daily Record Herald* (Wausau, WI), June 16, 1943.
49. "Courtesy of George Retalas," VS-11/VB-11, after-action report, May 3, 1943.
50. CV-11 Historical Association.
51. Meyer, informal history.
52. E. Howard Hunt, *Limit of Darkness* (New York: Stein and Day Publishers), 1985. This is the same Howard Hunt who organized the break-in of the Democratic National Committee in the Watergate Hotel on June 18, 1972.
53. Fike. In the narrative, Fike did not give the names of his other crewmembers in the TBF with him.
54. Fike.
55. Fike.
56. Fike.
57. VT-11—War History, 5–6.

Chapter 3. Operation Cartwheel and Bougainville

1. "First Tour of Bombing Eleven," 8. Operations as part of Cartwheel (including Postern, Goodtime, Blissful, and Cherryblossom) continued through the rest of 1943 and 1944, but the Cartwheel operations were over when CVG-11 returned to the Pacific Theater in the later part of 1944.
2. Ronnie Day, *New Georgia: The Second Battle for the Solomons* (Bloomington: Indiana University Press, 2016), 52.
3. "Dauntless Dick and Daring Ose."
4. Richard Miralles, diary, June 5, 1943; "Dauntless Dick and Daring Ose."
5. "Dauntless Dick and Daring Ose."
6. "Dauntless Dick and Daring Ose."
7. NHHC, VB-21, after-action report, June 5, 1943.
8. Intelligence report, VT-11, Cactus, May 18, 1943.

9. Ashworth, interview by Stillwell.
10. Ashworth, interview by Stillwell.
11. Ashworth, interview by Stillwell.
12. Intelligence report, VT-11, Cactus, May 21, 1943; VB-21, U.S. Aircraft Action with Enemy, June 5, 1943.
13. "First Tour of Bombing Eleven," 1.
14. VT-11—War History, 7.
15. Ashworth, interview by Stillwell.
16. Ashworth, interview by Stillwell.
17. VT-11—War History, 7.
18. Retelas, *Eleven: The Movie.*
19. Edward H. Johnson, USN, VF-11 memoir, 7 June to 17 June 1943, Solomon Islands (undated), courtesy of George Retelas.
20. Tillman, "Sundowners," 11.
21. Tillman.
22. Johnson.
23. Johnson.
24. Johnson.
25. Barrett Tillman and Henk van der Lugt, *VF-11/111 "Sundowners" 1942–95* (London: Osprey Publishing, 2010), 6–8. As Tillman noted, the Johnson story had a tragic ending: "He was sent home to recover and rejoined his wife, whereupon he learned that his brother had been killed in Europe. Johnson attended the funeral on the East Coast, then caught a ride back west on a USAAF bomber. The aircraft crashed and Johnson—the U.S. Navy hitchhiker—was the only man killed."
26. Action Report of Fighting Squadron Eleven, June 12, 1943.
27. Vernon E. Graham, USNR, VF-11 memoir, "Ace in a Day," as told to Tom Bailey (undated).
28. Graham; Action Report of Fighting Squadron Eleven, June 12, 1943.
29. Retelas, *Eleven: The Movie*; Olynyk, 304; Graham.
30. Meyer, informal history, 8.
31. Action Report of Fighting Squadron Eleven, June 12, 1943.
32. Graham.
33. Graham.
34. Graham.
35. Tillman, *U.S. Navy Fighter Squadrons in World War II*, 37; Action Report of Fighting Squadron Eleven, June 12, 1943.

36. Mark Stille, *The Solomons 1943–44: The Struggle for New Georgia and Bougainville* (London: Osprey Publishing, 2018).
37. George Retelas, director, "Finding Elio: Meeting the Sailor that Served with My Grandfather in 1943," 2018, https://youtu.be/2FeEJKiTlWg; VF-11, after-action report, June 16, 1943.
38. Harry A. Fredrickson, Scouting Squadron Eleven VS-11/VB-21 Memoir (undated).
39. VF-11, after-action report, June 16, 1943.
40. Barrett Tillman, "Charlie Stimpson's War," *Flight Journal: WWII Aces* (Fall 2011).
41. Taylor, 158; Tillman, "The Tale of Eleven"; VF-11, after-action report.
42. Gay, 223–24.
43. "First Tour of Bombing Eleven," 7; VB-11 after-action report, 1943, "VB-11 VMSB-132," July 17, 1943.
44. VB-11 AAR 1943, "VB-11 VMSB-132"; "First Tour of Bombing Eleven," 9.
45. Strahan.
46. Strahan.
47. Gay, 213.
48. Potter, 241.
49. Miralles diary, July 27–29, 1943.
50. Strahan; Ashworth, interview by Stillwell.
51. Tillman, "The Tale of Eleven"; Tillman, *Sundowners*, 42; Olynyk, 304, 575, 583; "First Tour of Bombing Eleven," 9.
52. Peattie, 181.
53. Tillman, *Sundowners*, 17, 19; B. S. Meyer, "The History of Torpedo Squadron 11 from September 1943–1945"; "First Tour of Bombing Eleven," 9.
54. VB-11—Second Combat Tour.
55. Retelas, *Eleven: The Movie*; Barrett Tillman, *Hellcat: The F6F in World War II* (Annapolis, MD: Naval Institute Press, 1979), xii.
56. Tillman, *Sundowners*, 19.
57. VB-11—Second Combat Tour.
58. Strahan.
59. Meyer.
60. VF-11 official history, 20.
61. VB-11—Second Combat Tour, 7; Meyer.
62. CVG-11 History, biographical sketches, Lt. (jg) Joseph Matthew Hyland; George Retelas, "RADIOMAN FLYER: Taking a WWII Aircrewman back up in a TBM Avenger," https://www.youtube.com/watch?v=vJX_Qz_4M9I.

63. VB-11—Second Combat Tour, 12.
64. VB-11—Second Combat Tour, 12.

Chapter 4. The *Hornet*, Halsey's Run, and Leyte Gulf

1. Colin S. Gray, *Defining and Achieving Decisive Victory* (Carlisle, PA: U.S. Army War College Press, 2002), 3, https://press.armywarcollege.edu/monographs/823.
2. Peattie, 183.
3. Samuel Eliot Morison, *History of United States Naval Operations in World War II*, vol. 7, *Aleutians, Gilberts, and Marshalls, June 1942–April 1944* (Boston: Little, Brown and Co., 1951).
4. Clark G. Reynolds, *The Fast Carriers: The Forging of an Air Navy* (Annapolis, MD: Naval Institute Press, 1968), 63.
5. Gray, 3.
6. NHHC, "History of the USS *Hornet* (CV-12)," https://www.history.navy.mil/research/histories/ship-histories/danfs/h/hornet-viii.html.
7. "History of the USS *Hornet* (CV-12)."
8. Ship's Log, USS *Hornet*, 1944–45.
9. The USS *Hornet* (CV-12) also remains as one of the four *Essex* ships serving as museums today. Alan Raven, *Essex-Class Carriers* (Annapolis, MD: Naval Institute Press, 1988), 23; Ship's Log, USS *Hornet*, 1944–45.
10. VB-11—Second Combat Tour, 12.
11. VB-11—Second Combat Tour, 13; Andrew Faltum, *The Essex Aircraft Carriers* (Baltimore: The Nautical and Aviation Publishing Company of America, 1996), 1.
12. Even in 2024, it would be easy to overlook Ulithi on a map. It is administered by the state of Yap in the Federated States of Micronesia and as of 2000 had a population of less than 1,000 inhabitants on four occupied islands. There is a small regional airport and the "Ulithi Adventure Lodge," a small resort hotel.
13. Retelas, *Eleven: The Movie.*
14. Strahan.
15. Ugaki, 465.
16. Paul C. Warren, "One Day Off the Hornet: A Lifetime of Adventure—Combat Log of an F6F Hellcat Pilot," *Wings* 12, no. 5 (October 1982).
17. Warren.
18. VB-11—Second Combat Tour, 14.
19. Diary of Lt. John W. Ramsey, VF-11, USS *Hornet*, 1944–45.
20. Retelas, *Eleven: The Movie.* The gunnery officer, Lt. (jg) Nicholas Satterlee, was also a pilot with VT-11.

21. Retelas, *Eleven: The Movie.*
22. Ramsey; Milan N. Vego, *The Battle for Leyte, 1944: Allied and Japanese Plans, Preparations, and Execution* (Annapolis, MD: Naval Institute Press, 2006), 157.
23. Vego, 157; CV-12, Action Report, October 2–27, 1944, 3.
24. CV-12, Action Report, October 2–27, 1944, 3; "Commander Frederick R. Schrader," Defense POW/MIA Accounting Agency, https://dpaa-mil.sites.crmforce.mil/dpaaProfile?id=a0Jt000001nzQwCEAU. The POW/MIA Accounting Agency notes on their page that

    > because the crash occurred in enemy-controlled territory, immediate search efforts could not be attempted. On February 14, 1946, American Graves Registration Services (AGRS) personnel recovered a set of unidentified remains from Rinpen Public Graveyard in Takao Province, Formosa, near the seaplane base where CMD Schrader was shot down. The AGRS concluded that the individual must have been a Hellcat pilot involved in the air raids on the area but could not identify him. The remains were later interred as an unknown in the National Memorial Cemetery of the Pacific. In August 2022, research by an independent researcher and the DPAA led to the disinterment of the remains for further study. The laboratory analyses and the totality of the circumstantial evidence available established the remains as those of CMD Schrader.
25. VB-11—Second Combat Tour, 14; CV-12, Action Report, October 2–27, 1944, 3.
26. USS *Hornet*, war diary, October 1944, 8–11; Warren.
27. Warren.
28. The A6M3 Hamp was really just a much improved Zero. Since it looked quite different from the Zeke, the Allies initially called it the "Hap" after the commanding general of the AAF, General "Hap" Arnold. This was later changed to "Hamp" after General Arnold supposedly complained about the honor. Thus, depending on the account one might see "Hamp," "Hap," "Zero," or even "Zeke." Tillman, "Charlie Stimpson's War"; Tillman and van der Lugt.
29. Tillman, "Charlie Stimpson's War"; Tillman and van der Lugt. Blair was flying in F6F-5 BuNo 43137.
30. Ramsey; Tillman, *Sundowners*, 24–25, 43.
31. Ramsey.
32. Ramsey; Richard Overy, *Why the Allies Won* (New York: W. W. Norton and Company, 1995), 301.

33. Shigeru Fukudome, "The Air Battle off Taiwan," in David C. Evans, ed., *The Japanese Navy in World War II: In the Words of Former Japanese Naval Officers* (Annapolis, MD: Naval Institute Press, 1986), 347.
34. Fukudome, 347.
35. Reynolds, 260.
36. Strahan.
37. Strahan.
38. Ugaki, 472–73.
39. VB-11—Second Combat Tour, 15; Ramsey; Tillman, *Sundowners*, 26.
40. Tillman, *Sundowners*, 26.
41. Strahan.
42. Strahan.
43. Strahan.
44. Strahan.
45. Samuel Eliot Morison, *History of United States Naval Operations in World War II*, vol. 12: *Leyte: June 1944–January 1945* (Boston: Little, Brown and Co., 1958), 57–58.
46. Trent Hone, "Halsey's Decision," in Cutler, *The Battle of Leyte Gulf at 75*, 81–82, 95–96; Thomas J. Cutler, *The Battle of Leyte Gulf: 23–26 October 1944* (Annapolis, MD: Naval Institute Press), 115.
47. Morison, *Leyte: June 1944–January 1945*, 60.
48. Morison, *Leyte: June 1944–January 1945*, 134–36.
49. Vego, 196.
50. Cutler, *The Battle of Leyte Gulf*, 138, 260; Tillman, *Sundowners*, 26; Vego, 257.
51. Strahan.
52. Strahan.
53. VB-11—Second Combat Tour, 16.
54. Matthew Cabe, "One Man's Memories: Victorville Veteran Recalls Stories from the Pacific Theater," *Victorville Daily Press*, May 29, 2016.
55. Vergil E. Bloomquist and Robert W. Cocks, panel with George Retelas, January 8, 2016, https://youtu.be/z_B2uP2pNpY.
56. USS *Hornet* Museum, Official Reports, Bombing Squadron Eleven Publicity Release—Lieutenant Cocks.
57. NHHC, "History of the USS *Hornet* (CV-12)," 7, https://www.history.navy.mil/research/histories/ship-histories/danfs/h/hornet-viii.html.
58. Bloomquist and Cocks, interview; Retelas, *Eleven: The Movie.*

59. "Robert Emmett Riera," https://www.findagrave.com/memorial/15870795/robert-emmett-riera; NHHC, "USN 1066165 Rear Admiral Robert E. Riera, USN," https://www.history.navy.mil/our-collections/photography/numerical-list-of-images/nhhc-series/nh-series/USN-1066000/USN-1066165.html.
60. "History of the USS *Hornet* (CV-12)," 7.
61. Reynolds, 254.

Chapter 5. Mindoro

1. Air Force Historical Research Agency, "RENO V Working Draft of Outline Plan for Operations in the Southwest Pacific Area 1944–1945."
2. Air Evaluation Board Group, "Report No. 12: Luzon," May 1, 1946, vol. 1, McDermott Library, U.S. Air Force Academy.
3. "Vice Admiral Gerald F. Bogan, U.S. Navy, Retired," https://www.history.navy.mil/content/dam/nhhc/research/library/research-guides/Commander%20First%20Fleet/bogan-gerald-francis_Redacted.pdf.
4. VB-11—Second Combat Tour, 17; CV-12 war diary, November 5, 1944, 3.
5. CV-12 war diary, November 5, 1944, 3.
6. VB-11—Second Combat Tour, 17.
7. The day's dogfight was really two separate engagements by VF-11 and other squadrons over separate airfields. Both were large battles.
8. Tillman, *Sundowners*, 27–28.
9. Tillman and van der Lugt. Ensign Mann was flying an F6F-5P photo-reconnaissance, and his wingman, Lt. William R. Sisley, was flying an F6F-3. Tillman postulates that if Sisley had been in an F6F-4/5, he might have gotten to the Oscar before it shot Ensign Mann down.
10. Tillman and van der Lugt.
11. VB-11—Second Combat Tour, 17.
12. History of Torpedo Squadron 11 from September 1943–1945.
13. VB-11—Second Combat Tour, 17; Strahan.
14. Ramsey.
15. VB-11—Second Combat Tour, 18–19.
16. Ramsey.
17. VB-11—Second Combat Tour, 19.
18. Retelas, *Eleven: The Movie*; Tillman, "The Tale of Eleven"; NARA, RG 38, VT-11 war diary, 96.
19. Retelas, *Eleven: The Movie.*

20. VT-11 War History, 96.
21. VB-11—Second Combat Tour, 19; Ramsey.
22. VB-11—Second Combat Tour.
23. VB-11—Second Combat Tour.
24. Strahan.
25. VB-11—Second Combat Tour, 20.
26. VB-11—Second Combat Tour, 19.
27. "John Anthony Fidel," NHHC, biographical files, https://www.history.navy.mil/research/library/research-guides/modern-biographical-files-ndl/modern-bios-f/fidel-john-anthony.html.
28. VT-11 War History; CV-12 war diary, December 1944, 4.
29. Edwin M. Wilson, USNR, VB-11 Scrapbook (1945).
30. Jon Guttman, "John Zink: The Roving Ace," *Foundation* 39, no. 1 (Spring 2018). The "Frances" was the Yokosuka P1Y. Ginga was a twin-engine bomber and late replacement for the Betty developed for the Japanese Imperial Navy in World War II. In this instance it was performing duties as a reconnaissance plane.
31. Guttman.
32. Wilson.
33. Wilson.
34. Hughes, *Admiral Bill Halsey*, 382–83.
35. VB-11—Second Combat Tour, 21; Strahan; Retelas, *Eleven: The Movie.*
36. Robert W. J. Cocks, interview by George Retelas, April 4, 2014, May 1, 2014.
37. After-Action Report, USS *Hornet*, "Typhoon of 15–21 December, 1944," January 13, 1945; Greg Bankoff, "From the Art of Practical Sailing to the Electronic Science of Navigation: Typhoons, Seamanship, and U.S. Naval Operations in the Northwest Pacific, 1944–1945," *Journal of Military History* 86, no. 4 (2022): 960.
38. VB-11—Second Combat Tour, 22.

Chapter 6. Hunting Season

1. Samuel Eliot Morison, *History of United States Naval Operations in World War II*, vol. 13, *The Liberation of the Philippines: Luzon, Mindanao, The Visayas, 1944–1945* (Boston: Little, Brown and Company, 1959), 87–88, 315–18.
2. Tillman and van der Lugt, 45.
3. Strahan.
4. CV-12 war diary, January 1945, 4; Ramsey; VB-11—Second Combat Tour, 22.

5. Ramsey.
6. Steven K. Bailey, *Target Hong Kong: A True Story of U.S. Navy Pilots at War* (London: Osprey Publishing, 2024), 112; VT-11 War History, 163; VB-11—Second Combat Tour.
7. Sam Whiting, "Long-Lost World War II Journal Turns into 8-Year Film Project," *San Francisco Chronicle*, May 29, 2016; Retelas, *Eleven: The Movie*.
8. Keith Wheeler, "State Flyer Buried at Sea; Navy Colors at Half Mast," North American Newspaper Alliance, February 10, 1945; USS *Hornet*, Ship's War Diary, January 1945, 13; VT-11 War History, 163.
9. VB-11—Second Combat Tour, 21; Martin L. Mickelsen, "A Mission of Vengeance: Vichy French in Indochina in World War II," *Air Power History* 55, no. 3 (Fall 2008): 32.
10. VT-11—War Diary; Meyer, 6.
11. NHHC, "80-G-469326 Lieutenant Junior Grade H. Blake Moranville, USNR," https://www.history.navy.mil/our-collections/photography/numerical-list-of-images/nhhc-series/nh-series/80-G-469000/80-G-469326.html.
12. H. Blake Moranville, USN, VF-11, *Memoir: My Indochina Odyssey* (undated).
13. Moranville.
14. Mickelsen, 42.
15. Moranville.
16. Moranville later discovered that the individual who rescued him, Comte Coataudon de Kerdu, was the administrator of the district where he had landed. The count was arrested some weeks later during the takeover by the Japanese and held in a Japanese prison camp until the end of the war.
17. Moranville.
18. Moranville noted he was taken to Maison Centrale de Saigon and not to the newer Chí Hòa prison.
19. Moranville. The prison bears a striking resemblance to the French-built Hỏa Lò Prison in the capital city of Hanoi where American prisoners of war were interned during the Vietnam conflict.
20. Moranville.
21. Mickelsen, 42; Moranville.
22. Moranville.
23. Mickelsen, 42.
24. Moranville.
25. Moranville.

26. Mickelsen, 42.
27. Moranville.
28. Moranville. Of the 250 French Foreign Legion column, fewer than 50 survived.
29. Barrett Tillman, "A Sundowner's Adventure," *Journal—American Aviation Historical Society* 20, no. 4 (Winter 1975).
30. Morison, *Liberation of the Philippines*, 173.
31. VB-11—Second Combat Tour, 21.
32. USS *Hornet* Museum, CVG-11 Memorial Honor Roll 1942–1945, https://www.eleventhemovie.com/exhibit. The three crewmembers flew in TBM-1C Avenger Bureau Number 73493.
33. Bailey, 138; Guttman.
34. CV-12 war diary, January 1945. Wilson was in F-44 Bureau Number 70561.
35. Ensign Crehan flew in F6F Bureau Number 71082. Tillman, *Sundowners*, 38.
36. Tillman and van der Lugt; Moranville.
37. CV-12, USS *Hornet*, War Diary, January 1945, 23–25. Wolf was in F6F F-49 (Bureau Number 41517).
38. Tillman and van der Lugt, 51.
39. VF-11 Official History, 19; Paul C. Warren, "One Day Off the Hornet: A Lifetime of Adventure—Combat Log of an F6F Hellcat Pilot," *Wings* 12, no. 5 (October 1982); Tillman, "The Tale of Eleven."
40. Morison, *Liberation of the Philippines*, 173.
41. VB-11—Second Combat Tour, 21.
42. George Retelas, "The Terrier and the Hare: The Heartfelt WWII Story About a Dog and His Pilot," https://www.youtube.com/watch?v=cW4Ue6DHFzw.
43. Bill Marien, Australian war correspondent (1945).

Conclusion

1. Annual Report, USS *Hornet* Sea, Air, and Space Museum, 2014; Tillman and van der Lugt, 54.
2. Peattie, 195.
3. USS *Hornet* Sea, Air, and Space Museum, https://uss-hornet.org/history.
4. CV-12, Ship's Log, 1944–45.
5. American Battlefield Monuments Commission, Manila American Cemetery, https://www.abmc.gov/Manila.
6. Goodspeed; NHHC, National Aviation Museum, Von Tempsky Wall, https://www.history.navy.mil/content/history/museums/nnam/explore/exhibits

/permanent-exhibits/west-wing/von-tempsky-wall.html; citation to Alexa von Tempsky Zabriskie from Admiral J. H. Towers, 1945.

7. Letter to Alexa von Tempsky Zabriskie from Fleet Adm. Chester W. Nimitz, 1945.
8. Charles W. Sweeney, *War's End: An Eyewitness Account of America's Last Atomic Mission* (New York: Avon Books, 1997), 201; Paul Leighton, "Beverly Native's Role in Atomic Bomb Overlooked," *The Salem News*, August 9, 2010, https://www.salemnews.com/news/local_news/beverly-natives-role-in-atomic-bomb-overlooked/article_105840fc-75b8-5859-9557-e2072ee9134c.html; Dennis McClellan, "Frederick Ashworth, 93; Weaponeer on Plane That Dropped 2nd A-Bomb," *Los Angeles Times*, December 11, 2005, https://www.latimes.com/archives/la-xpm-2005-dec-11-me-ashworth11-story.html.
9. https://www.findagrave.com/memorial/166730252/charles-russell-stimpson/photo; Scott Harris, "Death of Charles Stimpson Recalls Naval Air Heroics," *Los Angeles Times*, August 1983.
10. https://www.findagrave.com/memorial/10366282/james-s-swope.
11. https://www.findagrave.com/memorial/13119721/horace-blake-moranville.
12. https://www.findagrave.com/memorial/244179423/vernon-earl-graham.
13. https://www.findagrave.com/memorial/68123630/john-warren-ramsey.
14. https://www.findagrave.com/memorial/52180200/william-l-strahan.
15. Matthew Cabe, "Navy Veteran Robert 'Jack' Cocks Dies at 96," *Daily Press*, May 17, 2017.
16. https://www.findagrave.com/memorial/191356501/william-robert-maxwell.
17. Helen Matson, "Veteran Salute: Vergil E. Bloomquist," *Columbus Dispatch*, April 6, 2011, https://www.dispatch.com/story/lifestyle/2011/04/06/veteran-salute-vergil-e-bloomquist/45415947007/; Barrett Tillman, "Verg's War," *Naval History Magazine* 33, no. 4 (August 2019).
18. "World War II Veteran Kermit Enander Fixed the Fighter Planes that Shot Down the Enemy," *News-Review*, February 28, 2018; https://www.findagrave.com/memorial/191656026/kermit_howrie-enander/photo.

Appendices

1. Roster of Officers, CV-12, December 1944.
2. Meyer; Official Navy History of Fighting Squadron Eleven; Air Group 11 Exhibit at USS *Hornet* Museum, "Roll of Honor," https://www.eleventhemovie.com/exhibit.

3. Shonk was killed while flying in his SBD-3 Bureau Number 06589, in a midair collision on March 25, 1943: "At 0945 Pilot and radioman were killed following a mid-air collision piloted by Lt. (jg) Shonk, and P-40E Kittyhawk 41–25100/12 airplane piloted by Sq/Leader Allen Crighton NZ/1124, RNZAF, 15 Squadron during group tactical exercises. Both planes were observed to crash into the sea from an altitude of 10,000 feet; no attempt to parachute on the part of any of the personnel could be observed, an extensive search failed to reveal any trace of planes or personnel. Both planes sank immediately."

Selected Bibliography

Primary Sources

National Archives and Records Administration, Record Group 38: Records of the Office of the Chief of Naval Operations, Series: World War II War Diaries, Other Operational Records and Histories

Library of Congress Veterans History Project
- Vergil E. Bloomquist Collection (AFC/2001/001/81576), https://www.loc.gov/item/afc2001001.81576/
- Gerald A. Coeur Collection (AFC/2001/001/18624)
- USS *Hornet* Sea, Air, and Space Museum, Alameda, CA, Collections of Air Group Eleven, Courtesy of Tim Hampton and George Retelas

Naval History and Heritage Command (NHHC)
- Modern Biographical Files
- Photography
- Reno V Plan (Philippine operations)
- CINCPOA Op Plans for Leyte and Luzon (https://www.usnwcarchives.org/repositories/2/archival_objects/22526)

CINCPOA Insurgent Joint Staff Studies (Leyte and Luzon)
7th Fleet Op Plans for Mindoro and Luzon
3rd Fleet Op Plans for Mindoro and Luzon
Fast Carrier Task Force Plans
Action reports (VF11, CAG11, USS *Hornet*, TG, TF, Fleet)

U.S. Air Force Academy Library
Air Evaluation Board SWPA, Luzon Campaign (vols. I, II, III)

Bibliography

Bailey, Steven K. *Target Hong Kong: A True Story of U.S. Navy Pilots at War*. London: Osprey Publishing, 2024.

Baxter, John. *Disney During World War II: How the Walt Disney Studio Contributed to Victory in the War*. New York: Disney Editions, 2014.

Bergerud, Eric M. *Fire in the Sky: The Air War in the South Pacific*. Boulder, CO: Westview Press, 2000.

Buell, Thomas. *The Quiet Warrior: A Biography of Admiral Raymond A. Spruance*. Annapolis, MD: Naval Institute Press, 1987.

Clark, J. J. *Carrier Admiral*. New York: David McKay Company, Inc., 1967.

Cleaver, Thomas McKelvey. *Pacific Thunder: The U.S. Navy's Central Pacific Campaign, August 1943–October 1944*. London: Osprey Publishing, 2017.

Collier, Peter, and Nick Del Calzo. *Wings of Valor: Honoring America's Fighter Aces*. Annapolis, MD: Naval Institute Press, 2016.

Cutler, Thomas J. *The Battle of Leyte Gulf: 23–26 October 1944*. Annapolis, MD: Naval Institute Press, 1994.

———. *The Battle of Leyte Gulf at 75: A Retrospective*. Annapolis, MD: Naval Institute Press, 2019.

Day, Ronnie. *New Georgia: The Second Battle for the Solomons*. Bloomington: Indiana University Press, 2016.

Evans, David C., ed. *The Japanese Navy in World War II: In the Words of Former Japanese Naval Officers*. Annapolis, MD: Naval Institute Press, 1986.

Evans, David C., and Mark R. Peattie. *KAIGUN: Strategy, Tactics, and Technology in the Imperial Japanese Navy, 1887–1941*. Annapolis, MD: Naval Institute Press, 1997.

Faltum, Andrew. *The Essex Aircraft Carriers*. Baltimore: Nautical and Aviation Publishing Company of America, 1996.

Fuchida, Mitsuo, and Masatake Okumiya. *Midway: The Battle that Doomed Japan, the Japanese Navy's Story*. Annapolis, MD: Naval Institute Press, 1955, 1992.

Gay, George. *Sole Survivor: Torpedo Squadron Eight, Battle of Midway*. Naples, FL: Midway Publishers, 1980.

Giangreco, D. M. *Hell to Pay: Operation Downfall and the Invasion of Japan, 1945–1947*. Annapolis, MD: Naval Institute Press, 2009.

Heinrichs, Waldo, and Marc Gallichio. *Implacable Foes: War in the Pacific, 1944–1945*. Oxford: Oxford University Press, 2017.

Hone, Trent. *Mastering the Art of Command: Admiral Chester W. Nimitz and Victory in the Pacific*. Annapolis, MD: Naval Institute Press, 2022.

Hornfischer, James D. *The Fleet at Flood Tide: America at Total War in the Pacific, 1944–1945*. New York: Random House, 2016.

Hughes, Thomas Alexander. *Admiral Bill Halsey: A Naval Life*. Oxford: Oxford University Press, 2016.

Hughes, Wayne P., and Robert P. Girrier. *Fleet Tactics and Naval Operations*, 3rd ed. Annapolis, MD: Naval Institute Press, 2018.

Hunt, E. Howard. *Limit of Darkness*. New York: Stein and Day Publishers, 1985.

Lundstrom, John B. *The First Team: Pacific Naval Air Combat from Pearl Harbor to Midway*. Annapolis, MD: Naval Institute Press, 1990.

———. *The First Team and the Guadalcanal Campaign: Naval Fighter Combat from August to November 1942*. Annapolis, MD: Naval Institute Press, 1994.

Mahoney, James J., and Brian H. Mahoney. *Reluctant Witness: Memoirs from the Last Year of the European Air War, 1944–45*. Victoria, BC: Trafford Publishing, 2001.

Miller, Edward S. *War Plan Orange: The U.S. Strategy to Defeat Japan, 1897–1945*. Annapolis, MD: Naval Institute Press, 1991.

Miller, Nathan. *The Naval Air War, 1939–1945*. Baltimore: Nautical and Aviation Publishing Company of America, 1980.

Moore, Stephen L. *Rain of Steel: Mitscher's Task Force 58, Ugaki's Thunder Gods, and the Kamikaze War Off Okinawa*. Annapolis, MD: Naval Institute Press, 2020.

Morison, Samuel Eliot. *History of United States Naval Operations in World War II*. Vol. 5, *The Struggle for Guadalcanal, August 1942–February 1943*. Boston: Little, Brown and Co., 1949.

———. *History of United States Naval Operations in World War II*. Vol. 7, *Aleutians, Gilberts, and Marshalls, June 1942–April 1944*. Boston: Little, Brown and Co., 1951.

———. *History of United States Naval Operations in World War II*. Vol. 12, *Leyte, June 1944–January 1945*. Boston: Little, Brown and Co., 1958.

———. *History of United States Naval Operations in World War II*. Vol. 13, *The Liberation of the Philippines: Luzon, Mindanao, The Visayas, 1944–1945*. Boston: Little, Brown and Co., 1959.

Murphy, Paul V. "'The Good War': Collective Memory and World War II in America." *Grand Valley Review* 25, no. 1, 2002.

Naito, Hatsuho. *Thunder Gods: The Kamikaze Pilots Tell Their Story.* Tokyo: Kodansha International, 1982.

Olynyk, Frank. *Stars and Bars: A Tribute to the American Fighter Ace, 1920–1973.* London: Grun Street Publishing, 1995.

Overy, Richard. *Why the Allies Won.* New York: W. W. Norton and Company, 1995.

Peattie, Mark R. *Sunburst: The Rise of Japanese Naval Air Power, 1909–1941.* Annapolis, MD: Naval Institute Press, 2001.

Potter, E. B. *Bull Halsey.* Annapolis, MD: Naval Institute Press, 1985.

———. *Nimitz.* Annapolis, MD: Naval Institute Press, 1976.

Prados, John. *Islands of Destiny: The Solomons Campaign and the Eclipse of the Rising Sun.* New York: Nal Caliber, 2012.

Raven, Alan. *Essex-Class Carriers.* Annapolis, MD: Naval Institute Press, 1988.

Reardon, Carol. *Launch the Intruders: A Naval Attack Squadron in the Vietnam War, 1972.* Annapolis, MD: Naval Institute Press, 2005.

Retelas, George, director. *Eleven: The Movie.* Lazy Panda Studios, 2014.

Reynolds, Clark G. *The Fast Carriers: The Forging of an Air Navy.* Annapolis, MD: Naval Institute Press, 1968.

Scott, James M. *Rampage: MacArthur, Yamashita, and the Battle of Manila.* New York: W. W. Norton and Company, 2018.

Sheftall, M. G. *Blossoms in the Wind: Human Legacies of the Kamikaze.* New York: Nal Caliber, 1995.

Smith, Douglas V. *Carrier Battles: Command Decision in Harm's Way.* Annapolis, MD: Naval Institute Press, 2006.

Smith, Peter C. *The Dauntless in Battle: The Douglas SBD Dauntless Dive-Bomber in the Pacific, 1941–1945.* Yorkshire, UK: Pen and Sword Aviation, 2019.

Spector, Ronald H. *Eagle Against the Sun: The American War with Japan.* New York: Free Press, 1985.

Stansfeld, Martin. *Japanese Carriers and Victory in the Pacific: The Yamamoto Option.* Yorkshire, UK: Pen and Sword, 2021.

Stern, Rob. *SBD Dauntless in Action.* Carrollton, TX: Squadron/Signal Publications, 1984.

Stille, Mark. *The Solomons 1943–44: The Struggle for New Georgia and Bougainville.* London: Osprey Publishing, 2018.

Swanborough, Gordon, and Peter M. Bowers. *United States Navy Aircraft since 1911,* 2nd ed. Annapolis, MD: Naval Institute Press, 1990.

Sweeney, Charles W. *War's End: An Eyewitness Account of America's Last Atomic Mission.* New York: Avon Books, 1997.

Taylor, Theodore. *The Magnificent Mitscher.* Annapolis, MD: Naval Institute Press, 1991.

Tillman, Barrett. *Hellcat: The F6F in World War II.* Annapolis, MD: Naval Institute Press, 1979.

———. *Sundowners: VF-11 in World War II.* St. Paul, MN: Phalanx, 1993.

———. *U.S. Navy Fighter Squadrons in World War II.* North Branch, MN: Specialty Press, 1997.

———. *Wildcat: The F4F in World War II.* Baltimore: Nautical and Aviation Publishing Company of America, 1983.

Tillman, Barrett and Henk van der Lugt. *VF-11/111 "Sundowners" 1942–95.* London: Osprey Publishing, 2010.

Trimble, William F. *Admiral John S. McCain and the Triumph of Naval Air Power.* Annapolis, MD: Naval Institute Press, 2019.

Ugaki, Matome. *Fading Victory: The Diary of Matome Ugaki.* Trans. Masataka Chihaya. Pittsburgh, PA: University of Pittsburgh Press, 1991.

Vego, Milan N. *The Battle for Leyte, 1944: Allied and Japanese Plans, Preparations, and Execution.* Annapolis, MD: Naval Institute Press, 2006.

Wheeler, Gerald E. *Kinkaid of the Seventh Fleet: A Biography of Admiral Thomas C. Kinkaid, U.S. Navy.* Annapolis, MD: Naval Institute Press, 1996.

Wukovits, John F. *Devotion to Duty: A Biography of Admiral Clifton A. F. Sprague.* Annapolis, MD: Naval Institute Press, 1995.

Yeo, Mike. *Desperate Sunset: Japan's Kamikazes Against Allied Ships, 1944–1945.* London: Osprey Publishing, 2019.

Index

About the Author

BRIAN D. LASLIE is the command historian at the United States Air Force Academy. A historian of airpower studies, Dr. Laslie received his bachelor's degree in history from The Citadel: The Military College of South Carolina in 2001, his master's degree from Auburn University, Montgomery, in 2006, and his doctorate from Kansas State University in 2013. His dissertation focused on the realistic training revolution that took place in the U.S. Air Force after Vietnam and the impact of training exercises on Operations Desert Storm and Allied Force. He is the author of numerous books and chapters on Air Force and airpower history, including *The Air Force Way of War: U.S. Tactics and Training after Vietnam* (selected for the 2016 Chief of Staff of the Air Force's professional reading list and the Royal Air Force's Chief of the Air Staff's reading list in 2017), *Architect of Air Power: General Laurence S. Kuter and the Birth the U.S. Air Force*, *Air Power's Lost Cause: The U.S. Air Wars of Vietnam*, and *Fighting From Above: A Combat History of the U.S. Air Force.*

The Naval Institute Press is the book-publishing arm of the U.S. Naval Institute, a private, nonprofit, membership society for sea service professionals and others who share an interest in naval and maritime affairs. Established in 1873 at the U.S. Naval Academy in Annapolis, Maryland, where its offices remain today, the Naval Institute has members worldwide.

Members of the Naval Institute support the education programs of the society and receive the influential monthly magazine *Proceedings* or the colorful bimonthly magazine *Naval History* and discounts on fine nautical prints and on ship and aircraft photos. They also have access to the transcripts of the Institute's Oral History Program and get discounted admission to any of the Institute-sponsored seminars offered around the country.

The Naval Institute's book-publishing program, begun in 1898 with basic guides to naval practices, has broadened its scope to include books of more general interest. Now the Naval Institute Press publishes about seventy titles each year, ranging from how-to books on boating and navigation to battle histories, biographies, ship and aircraft guides, and novels. Institute members receive significant discounts on the Press' more than eight hundred books in print.

Full-time students are eligible for special half-price membership rates. Life memberships are also available.

For more information about Naval Institute Press books that are currently available, visit www.usni.org/press/books. To learn about joining the U.S. Naval Institute, please write to:

U.S. Naval Institute
291 Wood Road
Annapolis, MD 21402-5034
Telephone: (800) 233-8764
Fax: (410) 571-1703
Web address: www.usni.org